1 and 2 Peter, Jude

New International Biblical Commentary

1 and 2 Peter, Jude

Norman Hillyer

New Testament Editor,
W. Ward Gasque

HENDRICKSON
PUBLISHERS
PEABODY, MASSACHUSETTS 01961-3473

Copyright © 1992 by Hendrickson Publishers, Inc.
P.O. Box 3473
Peabody, Massachusetts 01961–3473
All rights reserved.
Printed in the United States of America

ISBN 0–943575–87–7

Library of Congress Cataloging-in-Publication Data

Hillyer, Norman
    1 and 2 Peter, Jude / Norman Hillyer.
       p.   cm. — (New International biblical commentary; 16)
    Includes bibliographical references and indexes.
    ISBN 0–943575–87–7 (pbk.)
    1. Bible. N.T. Peter—Commentaries. 2. Bible. N.T.
Jude—Commentaries. I. Bible. N.T. Peter. English.
New International. 1992. II. Bible. N.T. Jude.
English. New International. 1992. III. Title. IV. Title:
First and Second Peter, Jude. V. Series.
BS2795.3.H555   1992
227'.92077—dc20   92-24097
                                                CIP

Scripture taken from the HOLY BIBLE, NEW INTERNATIONAL
VERSION. Copyright © 1973, 1978, 1984 International Bible Society.
Used by permission of Zondervan Bible Publishers.

This is for Jean.

Table of Contents

2 Peter

Jude

Foreword
New International Biblical Commentary

Although it does not appear on the standard best-seller lists, the Bible continues to outsell all other books. And in spite of growing secularism in the West, there are no signs that interest in its message is abating. Quite to the contrary, more and more men and women are turning to its pages for insight and guidance in the midst of the ever-increasing complexity of modern life.

This renewed interest in Scripture is found both outside and inside the church. It is found among people in Asia and Africa as well as in Europe and North America; indeed, as one moves outside of the traditionally Christian countries, interest in the Bible seems to quicken. Believers associated with the traditional Catholic and Protestant churches manifest the same eagerness for the Word that is found in the newer evangelical churches and fellowships.

We wish to encourage and, indeed, strengthen this world-wide movement of lay Bible study by offering this new commentary series. Although we hope that pastors and teachers will find these volumes helpful in both understanding and communicating the Word of God, we do not write primarily for them. Our aim is to provide for the benefit of every Bible reader reliable guides to the books of the Bible—representing the best of contemporary scholarship presented in a form that does not require formal theological education to understand.

The conviction of editor and authors alike is that the Bible belongs to the people and not merely to the academy. The message of the Bible is too important to be locked up in erudite and esoteric essays and monographs written only for the eyes of theological specialists. Although exact scholarship has its place in the service of Christ, those who share in the teaching office of the church have a responsibility to make the results of their research accessible to the Christian community at large. Thus, the Bible scholars who join in the presentation of this series write with these broader concerns in view.

A wide range of modern translations is available to the contemporary Bible student. Most of them are very good and much to be preferred—for understanding, if not always for beauty—to the older King James Version (the so-called Authorized Version of the Bible). The Revised Standard Version has become the standard English translation in many seminaries and colleges and represents the best of modern Protestant scholarship. It is also available in a slightly altered "common Bible" edition with the Catholic imprimatur, and the New Revised Standard Version appeared in 1989. In addition, the New American Bible is a fresh translation that represents the best of post–Vatican II Roman Catholic biblical scholarship and is in a more contemporary idiom than that of the RSV.

The New Jerusalem Bible, based on the work of French Catholic scholars but vividly rendered into English by a team of British translators, is perhaps the most literary of the recent translations, while the New English Bible is a monument to modern British Protestant research. The Good News Bible is probably the most accessible translation for the person who has little exposure to the Christian tradition or who speaks and reads English as a second language. Each of these is, in its own way, excellent and will be consulted with profit by the serious student of Scripture. Perhaps most will wish to have several versions to read, both for variety and for clarity of understanding—though it should be pointed out that no one of them is by any means flawless or to be received as the last word on any given point. Otherwise, there would be no need for a commentary series like this one!

We have chosen to use the New International Version as the basis for this series, not because it is necessarily the best translation available but because it is becoming increasingly used by lay Bible students and pastors. It is the product of an international team of "evangelical" Bible scholars who have sought to translate the Hebrew and Greek documents of the original into "clear and natural English . . . idiomatic [and] . . . contemporary but not dated," suitable for "young and old, highly educated and less well educated, ministers and laymen [sic]." As the translators themselves confess in their preface, this version is not perfect. However, it is as good as any of the others mentioned above and more popular than most of them.

Each volume will contain an introductory chapter detailing the background of the book and its author, important themes, and other helpful information. Then, each section of the book will be expounded as a whole, accompanied by a series of notes on items in the text that need further clarification or more detailed explanation. Appended to the end of each volume will be a bibliographical guide for further study.

Our new series is offered with the prayer that it may be an instrument of authentic renewal and advancement in the worldwide Christian community and a means of commending the faith of the people who lived in biblical times and of those who seek to live by the Bible today.

W. WARD GASQUE
Provost
Eastern College
St. Davids, Pennsylvania

Abbreviations

APOT	*Apocrypha and Pseudepigrapha of the Old Testament*, ed. by R. H. Charles, 2 vols., Oxford: Clarendon Press, 1913; repr. 1963
b.	Babylonian Talmud
BAGD	W. Bauer, W. F. Arndt, F. W. Gingrich, and F. Danker, *A Greek-English Lexicon of the New Testament and Other Early Christian Literature*, 2d ed., Chicago: University of Chicago Press, 1979.
Barclay	W. Barclay, *The New Testament: A New Translation*, 2 vols., London: Collins, 1969.
BDB	F. Brown, S. R. Driver, and C. A. Briggs, *A Hebrew and English Lexicon of the Old Testament*, Oxford: Clarendon Press, 1929
Dead Sea Scrolls (Qumran)	
CD	Cairo Damascus Document
1Q	(documents discovered in) Qumran Cave 1
1QH	Hymns of Thanksgiving
1QM	The War of the Sons of Light with the Sons of Darkness
1QpHab	Commentary on Habakkuk
1QS	Rule of the Community
1QSa	Rule of the Congregation
1QSb	Collection of Benedictions
4Q	(documents discovered in) Qumran Cave 4
4Q169	Commentary on Nahum
DSB	Daily Study Bible
ExpT	*Expository Times*
Gk.	Greek
GNB	Good News Bible
Heb.	Hebrew

IBD	*Illustrated Bible Dictionary*, 3 vols., Leicester: InterVarsity Press/Wheaton: Tyndale House Publishers, 1980
ICC	International Critical Commentary
ISBE	*International Standard Bible Encyclopedia*, 4 vols., General Editor, G. W. Bromiley, Grand Rapids: Eerdmans, 1979–88
j.	Jerusalem Talmud
JB	Jerusalem Bible
JBL	*Journal of Biblical Literature*
JTS	*Journal of Theological Studies*
KJV	King James Version (Authorized Version, 1611)
Lat.	Latin
LB	Living Bible
LSJ	H. G. Liddell and R. Scott, *A Greek-English Lexicon*, rev. by H. S. Jones, Oxford: Clarendon Press, 1966
LXX	Septuagint (Greek translation of Old Testament)
m.	Mishnah
MNTC	Moffatt New Testament Commentary
Moffatt	J. Moffatt, *A New Translation of the Bible*, London: Hodder and Stoughton, 1934
MS(S)	manuscript(s)
NAB	New American Bible
NASB	New American Standard Bible
NCB	New Century Bible Commentary
n.d.	no date
NEB	New English Bible
NIDNTT	*New International Dictionary of New Testament Theology*, 4 vols., ed. by C. Brown, Exeter: Paternoster Press/Grand Rapids: Zondervan, rev. ed., 1986
NIV	New International Version
NT	New Testament
NTS	*New Testament Studies*
OT	Old Testament
P^{72}	Bodmer Papyrus of Jude, 1 and 2 Peter (about A.D. 300)

Phillips	J. B. Phillips, *The New Testament in Modern English* (1959)
REB	Revised English Bible (1989)
RSV	Revised Standard Version
RV	Revised Version
SNT	Supplements to *Novum Testamentum*
Str-B	H. L. Strack and P. Billerbeck, *Kommentar zum Neuen Testament aus Talmud und Midrasch*, 6 vols., 1922–38
TBC	Torch Bible Commentary
TDNT	G. Kittel and G. Friedrich, eds., *Theological Dictionary of the New Testament*, trans. G. W. Bromiley, 10 vols., Grand Rapids: Eerdmans
ThC	Thornapple Commentary
TNTC	Tyndale New Testament Commentary
TynB	Tyndale Bulletin
v. (vv.)	verse(s)
WBC	Word Biblical Commentary
WC	Westminster Commentary
ZPEB	*Zondervan Pictorial Encyclopedia of the Bible*

Introduction[†]

Introduction to 1 Peter

The Writer

Although doubts have been expressed about Simon Peter's being the author of the two letters bearing his name, especially 2 Peter, there are no irrefutable reasons for rejecting the claims of the letters themselves to have been written by the apostle (1 Pet. 1:1; 2 Pet. 1:1). From the earliest days, 1 Peter was accepted as the apostle's work. Possibly 2 Peter 3:1 refers to it. Clement of Rome (A.D. 95)[1] appears to know it. But without question Polycarp, baptized about A.D. 69 and once a disciple of the apostle John, quotes 1 Peter as authentic. So does Papias (A.D. 60–130), who also mentions John Mark's close association with Peter (1 Pet. 5:13).

The letter itself reflects Peter's role as an eyewitness of our Lord's life and ministry, and it is also reminiscent of Peter's speeches in the Acts of the Apostles.[2]

Allusions to the Gospels include the following:

1 Pet. 1:10–12	Luke 24:25–27	prophecies fulfilled in Christ
1:16	Matt. 5:48	the divine standard
1:17	Matt. 22:16	God's impartiality
1:18	Mark 10:45	Jesus' death a ransom
1:22	John 15:12	love one another
3:9	Matt. 5:39	no retaliation
3:14; 4:13	Matt. 5:10	blessing in persecution
4:11	Matt. 5:16	Christian witness praises God
5:3	Matt. 20:26	no lording over others
5:7	Matt. 6:25–34	let God carry anxieties

[†]The three letters in this volume are brought together because 1 Peter and 2 Peter are reputed to be by the same author, while 2 Peter and Jude have a good deal of material in common. A list of the abbreviations used in the commentary is found on pp. xiii–xv. See also "For Further Reading" (pp. 271–76); full bibliographical references for works referred to in short-form notes within the commentary are supplied there.

Peter's speeches in Acts are echoed:

1 Pet. 1:3, 21; 3:21	Acts 2:32; 3:15; 4:10	resurrection
1:17	Acts 10:34	God's impartiality
1:20	Acts 2:23; 3:18	Christ's death foreordained
1:20	Acts 2:17	revelation of last days
2:4	Acts 4:11	Christ the capstone (Ps. 118:22)
2:8	Acts 1:16	fate of disobedient foretold
2:24	Acts 5:30; 10:39	the cross a "tree"
3:18	Acts 3:14–15	Christ the righteous killed
3:19	Acts 2:27	triumph over Hades

Objections to the apostolic authorship of 1 Peter have also been raised on the ground that the Greek is beyond Peter's competence. Who knows? Running a fishing consortium (Luke 5:3) in such a cosmopolitan port as Bethsaida[3] meant that Peter would need to be bilingual, even if his accent remained thick (Matt. 26:73). While he was not a graduate of Tarsus University like Paul, thirty and more years of preaching to Greek-speaking audiences would have honed his grasp of the language[4]—no doubt with the help of friends such as Silas, who may indeed have had a hand in the Greek style of the letter (see commentary on 5:12). If 1 Peter had been pseudepigraphic, a forger would surely have suggested the apostle's long-time colleague *Mark* as Peter's amanuensis, yet he is mentioned in the very next verse with no hint of being involved in the writing.

Historical objections to traditional authorship have also been put forward. The letter is addressed to persecuted Christians (1:6; 2:12, 15; 3:14, 16; 4:4, 12; 5:8–9), and in particular refers to their suffering for the name of Christ (4:14, 16). But the claim that this must mean an official government policy against Christians and thus points to a late date for the letter goes beyond the evidence.[5] In any case, persecution for "the name" was suffered by believers from the first (Acts 4:17; 5:28, 40; 9:16). The ancient world took it for granted that religion (that is, paganism) permeated the whole of society. So for Christians to refuse to take part in pagan practices (4:4) meant their being ostracized. In particular, many trades and professions involved paganism, and that made employment for Christians doubly difficult. Such everyday problems facing believers living among uncomprehending and scandalized pagan neighbors are ample explanation of the references to suffering in the letter. Persecution was localized and spasmodic, even if unpleasant at best. That aside, Peter's exhortation to good citizenship (2:13–14) is enough to reject suggestions of official Roman policy against Christians at this date. On the contrary, it implies that Peter was writing his letter before the emperor Nero had changed from the public's darling on his accession in A.D. 54 to the monster he became following the outbreak on 19 July 64 of the great fire of Rome, which he later tried to blame on the Christians.[6]

Date

Assuming traditional authorship for 1 Peter, the most likely date for its writing appears to be about A.D. 63, immediately before the troubles in Rome flared up under Nero. If the Neronic terror had already struck, the comment in 3:13 that no harm came to good citizens is incredible. Scholars who argue that 1 Peter was written well after the apostle's death (which may have taken place during the mass violence of July 65),[7] infer that the letter's own claim to be Peter's work is false. Usually those who take this position go on to say that in the ancient world the practice of using a famous name as a pseudonym to support a view being put forward was widespread, well understood, and so harmless.[8] But the early church did not take that line over Christian writings: an Asian elder was deposed for publishing an innocent romance, *The Acts of Paul and Thecla*. The church emphasized apostolicity as a test for canonicity and rejected much literature put out under well-known names—including a rash of "Petrine" material, such as the *Gospel of Peter*, the *Acts of Peter*, and the *Apocalypse of Peter*.

The Readers

The letter is addressed to Christians north of the Taurus mountains in present-day Turkey. The order in which the five Roman provinces are named (Pontus, Galatia, Cappadocia, Asia, Bithynia; 1 Pet. 1:1) may well indicate the route[9] taken by the one carrying the letter; this was probably Silas (5:12). The messenger may have disembarked at Amisus (Sinope, while larger, was a port only, with no inland roads through the impassable mountains behind it), called at the more important Christian centers (no doubt leaving behind a copy of the letter), and ended up at

Nicomedia or Chalcedon. Then he would have sailed back to
Rome, from which Peter is apparently writing (see commentary
on 5:13).

The readers Peter had in mind seem to have been a mixed
group, though mainly Gentile Christians, for he refers to their
pre-conversion days in terms of ignorance of the true God (1:14),
their earlier way of life (1:18), previous spiritual darkness (2:9),
and pagan vices (4:3–4). The readership included slaves (2:18),
and although masters are not mentioned, the reference to the
duties of citizens implies people who, unlike slaves, enjoyed civil
rights (2:13–17).

No church in the early days was exclusively Gentile, and
indeed, preaching the gospel invariably began among Jews, for
whom messianic prophecy offered an immediate point of contact. Peter's considerable use of OT language, including explicit
quotations, seems to imply that there were Jewish Christians
among his readers, although OT terminology probably tells us
more about the writer's own background than about the sort of
people he was addressing.

Purpose

The writer's emphasis throughout 1 Peter is on hope, in
the vigorous and positive NT sense of that term (1:3, 13, 21; 3:15),
as believers scattered throughout a wide area of Asia Minor (1:1)
face suffering and persecution on account of their Christian faith.
As a consequence of their new spiritual life in Christ (1:3, 23),
believers belong to God, and as such they can count on his power
and grace to overcome their present trials and tribulations (1:5;
4:14). Ahead of them is a divinely prepared inheritance, beyond
this transient world and out of the reach of enemies (1:4), a life of
joy and light in the glorious presence of Christ (1:7; 5:10).

Although it seems that some readers may not have been
Christians for very long (2:2), Peter encourages all believers with
the reminder that God's gracious choice of them was made before they realized it, and it rests on divine foreknowledge (1:2).
They are now God's own people, called out of spiritual darkness
into his wonderful light (2:9). They can trust God absolutely
(4:19; 5:10), whatever testing situations this present life may
bring (2:20; 3:16–17; 4:4, 14, 16). Meanwhile, Christians must
develop their faith (2:2) and stand firm in it (5:9, 12). They must
be prepared to witness to a pagan world by giving a calm expla-

nation of their belief (3:15), by accepting suffering in the same spirit as their Master (2:21), and by maintaining the quality of their everyday lives (2:15; 3:1, 16). Troubles are never welcome, but for Christians God causes them to serve his purpose of strengthening and purifying their faith (2:20), since that is of supreme spiritual value (1:7).

Persecutions

Throughout the letter, the subject of persecution is never far away, whether it be potential, imminent, or incipient (1:6; 2:12, 19–20; 3:13–17; 4:12, 14; 5:8–10). The attacks are blamed not on Jews (although they may have been involved), but on pagans who are baffled and angry by the believers' "peculiar" manner of life in opting out of so much of everyday practices. As a consequence, they slander Christians as wrong-doers (2:12; 3:16) and abuse them as renegades (4:3–4). But the persecutions are apparently localized and spasmodic. They do not indicate official action at this date, for believers are urged to be patient under provocation by uncomprehending neighbors (2:12, 15–17; 3:16–17; 4:14, 16) and to be model citizens with regard to the state (2:13–14; 4:15).

Literary Form

A glance at the Additional Notes reveals that passing reference is often made to the Greek vocabulary. Of the 578 different Greek words employed in the letter, no fewer than 62 occur in the NT only in 1 Peter, more than 11 percent, and this in the course of a mere 105 verses. That piece of arithmetic alone has caused some scholars to doubt traditional authorship. But we do not know Peter's own capabilities with the language at this late stage of his life; neither can we estimate how much of the terminology may be due to any assistance he may have had from colleagues (5:12).

Suggestions have been made that the doxology at 4:11 and the apparently more urgent references to persecution after that point indicate that a later editor joined two documents to form a single epistle. But rather than signaling the close of a letter, the doxology is more likely to be due to the writer's thoughts at this point, prompting an outburst of praise. We find the same with Paul (Rom. 11:36; Gal. 1:5; Eph. 3:21; 1 Tim. 1:17). Other scholars have seen traces of early Christian hymns or of homiletical material behind the text.[10]

In view of the emphasis in 1 Peter on Christian initiation (1:3, 23; 2:2), proposals have been made that the document as we have it was originally a baptismal liturgy,[11] without the rubrics and modified for the purpose of a letter. The bishop's actions in the liturgy are said to be indicated by the repeated "now" (1:6, 8, 12, 22; 2:3, 7, 10, 25; 3:21; 4:6), with the actual baptism taking place between 3:21 (the only specific reference to the sacrament) and 3:22. But the hypothesis has been severely criticized, for it is incredible that

> a liturgy-homily, shorn of its rubrics . . . but with its changing tenses and broken sequences all retained, could have been hastily dressed up and sent off (without a word of explanation) to Christians who had not witnessed the original setting.[12]

Be that as it may, one factor throws considerable doubt on any proposals that discount the original unity of the letter. There is not the least textual support in extant MSS for hypotheses of this nature.

First Peter is as good an argument as there is against the claim sometimes heard that "Christians can do without the Old Testament; the New Testament is sufficient." The whole letter is soaked with OT references and language and cannot be understood in any full sense without consulting the Hebrew Scriptures. People, themes, and events mentioned include OT prophets and their messianic messages (1:10–12), "stone" imagery (2:4–8), the people of God (2:9–10), Sarah and Abraham (3:6), Noah and the Flood (3:20).

The significance of the OT exodus from Egypt is never far away from the background of Peter's thought. See, for example,

1:1, 17; 2:11	pilgrim life
1:4	inheritance (promised land)
1:14–15; 2:9–10, 16; 3:15; 4:2	change of master[13]
1:18	redemption (cf. 3:20)
2:5	new priesthood
2:10	"not a people"
2:16	servants (slaves); newly acquired freedom
4:9	grumbling in the wilderness
5:6	mighty hand of God

Echoes of the Feast of Tabernacles are also to be heard in the language used in 1 Peter.[14]

The theme of suffering constantly recurs, but in 1:1–9 (and only here in this letter) there are an impressive number of parallels with the testing of Abraham's faith over the sacrifice of his beloved only son Isaac. (Judaism made much of this "Binding of Isaac" or *Akedah*.) Read the story in Genesis 22:1–18 against the opening nine verses of 1 Peter:

1 Pet. 1:1	apostle (i.e., "one sent"); elect (cf. "beloved,"Gen. 22:2)
2	obedience (Gen. 22:18)
2	sacrificial blood (Gen. 22:2)
3	living hope (Gen. 22:5)
3	resurrection (Gen. 22:13; cf. Heb. 11:19)
4	inheritance assured (Gen. 22:18)
5	kept through faith (Gen. 22:12)
6	trials (Gen. 22:1)
7	faith proved through fire (Gen. 22:7)
8	God unseen, yet loved (Gen. 22:8; cf. Isa. 41:8)
9	receiving goal of faith, salvation (Gen. 22:17–18)

Peter, in common with all the other NT writers, normally uses the Septuagint (LXX) when quoting or alluding to the OT. Direct quotations in 1 Peter are:

1 Pet. 1:16	Lev. 11:44
1:24–25	Isa. 40:6–8
2:6	Isa. 28:16
2:7	Ps. 118:22
2:8	Isa. 8:14
2:22	Isa. 53:9
3:10–12	Ps. 34:12–16
3:14	Isa. 8:12
4:8	Prov. 10:12
4:18	Prov. 11:31
5:5	Prov. 3:34
5:7	Ps. 55:22

Much of Peter's text is couched in OT language, an outstanding example being 2:22–25, which includes one straight quotation in 2:22 (Isa. 53:9), with the rest of the passage permeated with the thought of that same chapter in Isaiah, especially Isaiah 53:5, 7, 12.

Other allusions to the OT include:

1 Pet 1:7	Job 23:10; Mal. 3:3
1:17	Ps. 89:26; Jer. 3:19; Mal. 1:6
1:18	Isa. 52:3
1:19	Exod. 12:5
2:3	Ps. 34:8

2:4	Ps. 118:22
2:9	Exod. 19:5–6
2:10	Hos. 1:6, 9; 2:1, 23
2:11	Ps. 39:12
2:17	Prov. 24:21
3:6	Gen. 18:12
3:20	Gen. 7:7, 17
3:22	Ps. 8:4–6; 110:1
4:14	Isa. 11:2
4:17	Jer. 25:29; Ezek. 9:6
4:18	Prov. 11:31
4:19	Ps. 31:5
5:7	Ps. 37:5

Relation to Other NT Books

Parallels with Paul. Whether 1 Peter is accepted as being written by the apostle or deemed to be a later writing, it would be surprising not to find examples of similar vocabulary and thought in the letters of Paul. Here are a few striking parallels:[15]

1 Pet. 1:1	God's elect	Titus 1:1
1:2	chosen by God's foreknowledge	Rom. 8:29
1:2	sprinkling by Jesus' blood	Rom. 3:25
1:3	doxology	2 Cor. 1:3; Eph. 1:3
1:5	shielded by God's power	Phil. 4:7
1:14	do not conform	Rom. 12:2
	(*syschēmatizesthai*; used in NT only here)	
1:18	redeemed	Titus 2:14
	(*lytrousthai*: Paul's only use of verb)	
2:4	chosen by God	Rom. 8:33; Col. 1:27
2:9	God's special people	Titus 2:14
2:11	reject sinful passions	Titus 2:12
3:16	in Christ	passim

The above is only a selection of ideas or terms in 1 Peter to be noted in Paul's letters. Such agreements do not imply literary dependence either way, but they do offer evidence that the thought of 1 Peter is in line with that of the apostolic period.

Parallels with James. Again we have an impressive list of similarities:

1 Pet. 1:1	Diaspora ("scattered")	James 1:1
1:6	all kinds of trials	1:2
1:7	proof of faith	1:3
1:17	divine impartiality	2:1
1:23	rebirth through word	1:18
1:24	Isa. 40:6–8	1:10–11
2:1	get rid of immorality	1:21

4:8	love covers sins	5:20
5:5	Prov. 3:34	4:6
5:6	humble yourselves under God	4:10
5:8–9	resist devil	4:7

The closeness of thought suggests that the body of teaching the two writers used was traditional in the Christian circles of their day. But as to date, this takes us little further, since scholarly opinion for the writing of the letter of James has ranged from A.D. 40 to 130, depending on the identity of the name of the author in James 1:1. The majority of modern scholars, however, support an earlier rather than a later date.

In sum, although a majority of German commentators in particular reject 1 Peter's claim to be an apostolic work, there are more English-speaking scholars in favor of the letter's authenticity than there are against it.[16] But the division of opinion does serve to reflect the number and complexity of problems modern scholarship sees in the letter, and which have been discussed in this introduction. While certainty one way or the other about the letter's authenticity cannot be reached, the burden of demonstration lies with those who consider the letter to be pseudonymous.

It is worth remarking that, unlike the case of some other NT writings, the early church fathers were in overwhelming agreement about the genuineness of 1 Peter. Uncertainties on this score have arisen in relatively recent times.[17]

Introduction to 2 Peter

Writer

The letter purports to be by Simon (or Symeon[18]) Peter, a servant and apostle of Jesus Christ (1:1). He alludes to the prediction of his own death (1:14–15; cf. John 21:18) and claims to have been an eyewitness of the transfiguration of Jesus (1:16–18; cf. Matt. 17:1–8; Mark 9:2–8; Luke 9:28–36).

Many modern scholars dismiss these personal references as being deliberately included by a later author to give an air of verisimilitude to a letter he wanted to pass off as apostolic. But the presumption that in ancient times *personal letters* were frequently published under assumed names (pseudepigraphy) has been shown to be greatly exaggerated.[19] Furthermore, the early church was very alert to the need to check the authenticity of writings purporting to be apostolic. Even when a writer was solidly orthodox, and with the best of intentions was trying only to promote the good name of a figure like Paul by means of an innocent romantic tale, he was deposed for forgery.[20] The motives for pseudepigraphy were usually far less worthy. Writers were more often intent on spreading some heresy and sought to claim apostolic authority as a cover. There is no suggestion in 2 Peter of heretical teaching being put forward. Apart from anything else, if 2 Peter is pseudepigraphic and the reference in 2 Peter 3:1 to an earlier letter[21] is intended to mean 1 Peter, then why did the writer make virtually no use of the content of that first letter? The two epistles have little in common as far as subject matter is concerned.

The writer refers to Paul as one who to the readers is, by repute if not in person, "our dear brother" (3:15), and he puts the authority of Paul's epistles on a par with the OT Scriptures (3:16; cf. 1:21; 1 Pet. 1:11–12). By implication, the author of 2 Peter is claiming similar authority for his own present writing.

Although 2 Peter was by no means as widely known or recognized in the early days of the church as 1 Peter, it may have been quoted as authentic by the end of the first century, in 1 Clement, usually dated about A.D. 95, although that document may be dated earlier,[22] before the destruction of the Jerusalem temple in A.D. 70. Even a century later, Origen (185–253) implies that some still had doubts about its authenticity, although he himself speaks of Peter blowing "on the twin trumpets of his own epistles" *(Homily on Joshua* 7.1). While Eusebius (265–340) classified 2 Peter among the "questioned" NT books (but not among the "spurious" writings), he says that by his day the majority of Christians accepted it as being by the apostle. It is significant that the great fourth-century Councils of Hippo, Laodicea, and Carthage all accepted 2 Peter as canonical. They must have had solid grounds for doing so, for at the same time they rejected the letter of Barnabas and the writings of Clement of Rome (1 Clement), both of which had for years been included in the church lectionaries alongside the canonical Scriptures.

The much wider agreement concerning the authenticity of 1 Peter raises the question as to whether the same writer could have been the author of 2 Peter, for the two letters are in contrast at a number of points. For one thing, their use of the OT is markedly different. First Peter enlists clear quotations and obvious allusions, whereas 2 Peter employs no direct quotations and few allusions. The literary style of one letter is unlike that of the other, although (apart from the different subject matter and occasion for writing) this could be due to whatever part Silas may have played in the writing of the first letter (1 Pet. 5:12); no hint of an amanuensis is given in 2 Peter, although one may have been used—it was common practice. Apart from anything else, we have no means of telling what facility in writing Greek the apostle Peter may have had at this stage of his life after many years of preaching in that language.

Such evidence as we have is insufficient to decide for or against accepting 2 Peter as apostolic, although the letter's own claim cannot be said to be disproved; consequently its claim must be given full weight. Any reasons for the early hesitation about the letter's authenticity are never spelled out. No charges of heresy were made, and the superior spiritual quality of 2 Peter, when compared with second-century "Petrine" literature (*Gospel of Peter, Preaching of Peter, Acts of Peter, Apocalypse of Peter*) is only too obvious, even on a casual reading. It may simply be that, in the earlier days of the Christian church, 2 Peter was not widely known, due perhaps to its limited initial circulation. Then, by the time copies of 2 Peter were being more widely distributed, the rash of pseudepigraphic Petrine works available could easily have aroused suspicions that here was another document of the same brand.

Readers

Unlike the case of 1 Peter, this letter is addressed not to groups of Christians in specified areas (1 Pet. 1:1) but much more vaguely to those who share with the writer a like faith in Jesus Christ (2 Pet. 1:1). Yet, although the readers of 2 Peter are not named, the writer clearly has a particular company of believers in view. If 2 Peter 3:1 ("this is now my second letter") relates to 1 Peter, then of course the same recipients are in mind for both epistles. But 2 Peter 1:16 reveals that the writer is known to his readers as a result of a preaching mission, whereas 1 Peter lacks indications of the apostle's personal work among the people addressed, even if he knows a good deal about their situation. Perhaps the most that can be said is that the writer of 2 Peter is not penning a circular letter to believers in general, but warning a specific though unnamed community against insidious plots by infiltrators out to disrupt their Christian faith (2:1).

Date

Deciding when 2 Peter was written will depend on the view taken of authorship. If the letter is by Peter, it may be dated in the early sixties, that is, shortly before Peter's execution under Nero. The apostle's expected violent death is touched upon (1:14). Yet the writer makes no attempt to expand on the theme of martyrdom, which surely would have been likely if the letter were pseudepigraphic and written in the second century, for by then Christian literature was making much of martyrdom. Some consider that the reference in 3:4 points to a later date, for "ever since our fathers died" presumably means the first Christian leaders. Yet the additional comment that "everything goes on as it has been since the beginning of creation" more naturally indicates that the writer has in mind OT figures (see commentary). But even if 3:4 is taken to refer to the first Christians who had died, by the early sixties a whole generation *had* passed. As early as 1 Thessalonians 4:17 and 1 Corinthians 15:6, 52, the problem of believers who had died without Christ's returning was being faced. Although the form in which the scoffers' question is framed may suggest a time when expectation of the imminent return of Christ was still high—in other words, a date before the death of Peter—perhaps not too much store either way can be placed on the interpretation of 3:4.

The eschatology of 2 Peter is certainly primitive, even by comparison with some other parts of the NT.[23] The early church fathers do not express concern about the delay in the Parousia, but such an anxiety did mark the apostolic age. The destruction of the world by fire (3:12) has sometimes been adduced as evidence of a late date, since this is the only reference to the event in the NT. But the theme is already present in the Dead Sea Scrolls (1QH 3.29–35).

From the rash of pseudepigraphic writings ascribed to the apostle Peter (*Acts of Peter, Apocalypse of Peter, Gospel of Peter, Preaching of Peter*), it is likely that 2 Peter 1:15 ("I will make every effort to see that after my departure you will always be able to remember these things") was a text authors seized upon to add plausibility to their work. In turn, this suggests that 2 Peter itself must have been widely accepted as authentic at an early date, despite any later uncertainties that crept in.

Purpose

The object of Peter's onslaught are libertines, men promising a so-called freedom which, in practice, amounts to moral license; it leads not to true liberty but to sensual slavery (2 Pet. 2:19; cf. Gal. 5:13; 1 Pet. 2:16). Peter's opponents are also guilty of denying the lordship of Christ (2:1)—they are their own masters. Moreover they reject belief in the second coming (3:4), a subject that these men have evidently been dismissing as "cleverly invented stories" promulgated by the apostles (1:16; cf. 1 Tim. 1:4; 4:7; 2 Tim. 4:4; Titus 1:14). The consequence of denying the Parousia entailed a rejection of the reality of any final judgment, but in this the writer grimly declares that such men are going to find themselves fatally mistaken (2:3, 9–10). In their efforts to deceive others, they are deceiving themselves (2:12–14).

Literary Relations

Between 2 Peter and Jude. A great deal of the material in Jude appears in a somewhat similar form in 2 Peter:

2 Peter		Jude
2:1	false teachers denying Christ's lordship	4
2:4	fallen angels imprisoned in darkness	6
2:6	Sodom and Gomorrah burned	7
2:10	slanderers of celestial beings	8
2:11	angels maintain restraint	9
2:12	blasphemers like brute beasts	10
2:15	they follow Balaam's way	11
2:17	storm clouds	12
2:17	blackest darkness	13
2:18	boast, lust, entice	16
3:2	foretold by apostles	17
3:3	scoffers in last days	18

The frequency with which such parallels appear *in the same order* plainly points to some connection between the two documents that is probably not oral but literary. This can be explained in one of three ways: Jude has used 2 Peter; 2 Peter has used Jude; or both have used a common source. Most scholars accept the second solution, for it is hard to suggest any reason for publishing Jude after 2 Peter, if the former is more or less just an abstract of the latter.

Yet the third explanation, that both writers have employed a common written source, seems more probable, for while the same topics are touched upon in the same sequence, the differences in treatment are palpable (see commentary). Jude, as will be noted in the Introduction to that book (p. 16), makes great use of *threesomes*, unlike 2 Peter. To take one instance, Jude denounces the godless infiltrators as men who are copying the conduct of the three examples of Cain, Balaam, and Korah (Jude 11), whom he names without expanding on their misdemeanors. Jude evidently assumes that his readers know the OT background well enough to appreciate the point. By contrast, the parallel reference in 2 Peter 2:15 is limited to the single example of Balaam, but with much more about what he did. This scarcely suggests direct borrowing by one writer from the other, but it does fit the proposal that both authors individually adapted a common source.

There may also be some significance in the fact that Peter arranges his material (regarding judgments on the godless) in chronological order, whereas Jude does not. Compare the following:[24]

	2 Peter	Jude
1.	—	Israel in wilderness
2.	fallen angels	fallen angels
3.	Noah and Flood	—
4.	Cities of Plain (and Lot)	Cities of Plain (Lot not mentioned)
5.	—	Cain
6.	Balaam	Balaam
7.	—	Korah

Between 2 Peter and 1 Peter. Most scholars are of the opinion that the author of 1 Peter could not have written 2 Peter and consider that ideas in the second epistle that can be traced in the first argue *against* the authenticity of 2 Peter. The assumption is that such common ideas indicate borrowing. Others would claim that the similarities are to be expected if one author is behind both letters. Both conclusions, of course, depend upon one's presuppositions.

Doctrinal differences between the two letters have been put forward as evidence for a different author. Most of the major themes in 1 Peter (the cross, resurrection, ascension, baptism, prayer) do not occur in 2 Peter. The Parousia appears in both letters, and indeed 2 Peter majors on this topic.

But any contrasts in subject-matter may well be due to the different situations addressed by the two letters—which reveal a considerable change in atmosphere. There is a calmer and more deliberate manner evident in the composition of 1 Peter, whereas 2 Peter was plainly composed with much greater urgency.

For all the contrasts noticed in these two letters, the differences can be exaggerated. There are an impressive number of similarities in vocabulary and ideas that could indicate that the same mind is behind their composition:

2 Peter	1 Peter
1:1 "precious"	1:19
1:2 lit. "grace and peace be multiplied"	1:2
1:3 God's "goodness" (*aretē*)	2:9 God's "praises" (*aretas*)
1:4 doctrine of new birth	1:23
1:5 "add" (*epichorēgēsate*)	4:11 "provide" (*chorēgei*)
1:7 "brotherly kindness" (*philadelphi*a)	1:22 "love for your brothers" (*philadelphi*a)
	3:8 "love as brothers" (*philadelphoi*)
1:10 doctrine of election	1:2; 2:2
1:16 "eyewitnesses" (Gk. noun *epoptai*)	2:12 "see" (Gk. verb *epopteuontes*)
1:16 second coming	1:7, 13; 4:13; 5:4
1:19–20 stress on prophecy	1:10–12
2:1 divine purchase	1:18
2:2 "shameful ways" (*aselgeiai*)	4:3 "living in debauchery" (*aselgeiai*)
2:4 angels in prison	3:19
2:5 Noah	3:20
2:10–22 immorality and judgment	4:2–4
2:19 freedom	2:16
3:6 Flood	3:20
3:10 end of the world	4:7
3:14 "spotless, blameless" (*aspiloi, amōmētoi*)	1:19 "without blemish or defect" (*amōmos, aspilos*)
3:14–18 exhortation to Christian living	4:7–11
3:18 doxology (last clause)	4:11

As in the case of the first letter, scholars who reject apostolic authorship for 2 Peter have to produce persuasive evidence for pseudonymity. The hesitations about 2 Peter that were voiced in the early church were based not on suggestions of unorthodox doctrine, the usual objection to pseudonymous works, but on other factors, the nature of which can be but conjectured. While the many differences in tone, style, and content between 1 Peter and 2 Peter can be identified, no factor unquestionably excludes Petrine authorship, and perhaps this is as far as one can go.

Introduction to Jude

Author

The writer of the letter of Jude identifies himself as "a brother of James" (Jude 1). But which James? It is a common enough name (Jacob is the corresponding Hebrew version). Assuming that this James is one of those mentioned in the NT, we have a number of choices:

1. James the son of Zebedee: he was one of the Twelve (Matt. 10:2).

2. James the son of Alphaeus: he also was one of the Twelve (Matt. 10:3) and is usually identified with

3. James the younger, son of Mary (Mark 15:40).

4. James the father of the apostle Judas (not Iscariot) (Luke 6:16; Acts 1:13; in Matt. 10:3 and Mark 3:18 he is called Thaddaeus).

5. James the author of the NT letter by that name (James 1:1), probably to be identified with

6. James a brother of Jesus (Matt. 13:55).

Only two of these possibilities directly link a Jude with a James. One of these, the fourth James, can also be excluded since the literal translation of Luke 6:16, "Judas of James," would normally mean "Judas *son* of James," not "brother."

So the most likely candidate to be the brother of Jude the letter-writer is the last on the list, the James who was also a brother of Jesus.

Readers

Jude addresses his readers in the most general fashion as those who are divinely "called," "loved," and "kept" (v. 1), terms that could apply to believers from a Jewish or from a Gentile background. But at least it can be said that Jude has in mind a definite group of Christians (vv. 3–5, 17–18, 20). He knows about the particular perils they are suddenly facing from certain false teachers, libertines, who have managed to infiltrate their fellowship. The reference in verses 17–18 to Jude's friends having previously heard some apostles firsthand, together with the general atmosphere of the letter, has prompted several scholars to guess that the letter may have been sent to Antioch in Syria. But it can be little more than a guess. The heresy attacked by Jude surfaced in many of the churches, notably at Corinth, where Paul's doctrine of free grace was perverted into a license for some to behave as they chose, especially in matters of morality.

Date

The antinomian heresy attacked by Jude, which is similar to that in 2 Peter, was widespread in the early days of the church,[25] though it was particularly prevalent during the second century. Similarly, the references to the Parousia (vv. 1, 14, 21, 24) reflect the expectations of the first century, not the second. But verse 18 is decisive, "they said to you," implying that most of the original converts were still living when Jude wrote.

The unadorned way in which brother James is mentioned (v. 1) would be consistent with his still being alive when Jude wrote. Had James already been martyred (that happened in A.D. 62), it has been plausibly suggested[26] that the writer might well have added "good," "blessed," or, more likely, James' frequent nickname "just."

In short, there is nothing in the letter that demands a date beyond the lifetime of Jude the brother (*adelphos*) of Jesus (v. 1). In view of Jude's use of apocryphal works[27] and in view of the brevity of his letter, it is not surprising that its first mention by name as canonical is not until the Muratorian Canon (ca. A.D. 175), though there are probable allusions in earlier writings.[28]

Purpose

Jude had intended to write a leisurely general exhortation about "the salvation we share" (v. 3). But then news broke of the peril threatening the faith of his Christian readers because of the arrival of "certain men" (v. 4), out to spread their pernicious heresy of sexual license dressed up as Christian liberty. Although such a corrupting doctrine was widespread, it is worth mentioning its promotion by the Nicolaitans among the churches of Asia Minor, for the reference to Balaam in the book of Revelation (2:14), in 2 Peter (2:15), and in Jude (v. 11) may indicate a common link.[29]

Jude's letter reveals that the heresy involved license for immorality (v. 4), sexual immorality (v. 7), perversion (vv. 7–8), sensuality (vv. 10, 19) self-aggrandizement (v. 16), and scoffing at spiritual matters (v. 18)—all of which were threatening the stability and purity of the Christian fellowship (v. 12).

Upon learning what was going on, Jude at once abandons his original intention in order to send his friends a powerful exhortation to stand firm in the pure faith they had originally received (v. 3). He exposes and denounces the intruders in colorful terms and spells out their inevitable doom, which had been prophesied long ago. Finally, Jude assures his readers in a splendid doxology (v. 24) of the power of the God of glory to keep his loyal people both now and hereafter.

Literary Relations

Between Jude and 2 Peter. The puzzle over the many parallels in subject-matter between Jude and 2 Peter has been discussed in the Introduction to 2 Peter (see pp. 13–15). The answer probably lies in the use by Jude and Peter of a third document which denounced false teaching, then widespread in the early church, with each writer probably independently adapting the material for the purpose of his own letter. The variation in vocabulary is considerable, with but a single clause (in Jude 13 and 2 Pet. 2:17) being virtually identical. An examination of the parallel passages reveals that of the 256 words in Jude's version and 297 in 2 Peter's, only 78 are common to both letters. This means that some 70 percent of the vocabulary is different.[30] The suggestion, therefore, that Jude *copied* from 2 Peter, or vice versa, and made such a large number of vocabulary changes in the process, seems unlikely. There were no copyright laws in those days to encourage such fastidious attention to details of this sort.

Apocryphal Works. Jude freely uses several Jewish apocryphal writings; this may have prompted later hesitations about the canonicity of his letter. The main apocryphal passages Jude quotes are from 1 Enoch (dated ca. 170 B.C., with parts added later) and the *Assumption of Moses* (dated ca. 4 B.C.–A.D. 30).[31] These works were highly popular among both Christians and Jews during the first century, but Jude's use of them is not to be taken as an endorsement of their inspiration. His citations are such as a present-day preacher might make from a well-known novel to illustrate a biblical point.[32]

Literary Style

Triple Expressions. The writer reveals a fondness for using threesomes (conspicuously absent from the corresponding verses in 2 Peter), as these examples demonstrate:

Jude	1	called, loved, kept (readers)
	2	mercy, peace, love (prayer)
	3, 17, 20	"dear friends" (readers)
	4	godless, antinomian, deniers of Christ (infiltrators)
	5–7	Israel, angels, Sodom and Gomorrah (OT examples)
	8	self-polluting, rebels, slanderers ("these dreamers")
	11	Cain, Balaam, Korah (OT examples)
	12	blemishes, brazen, selfish
	19	disrupters, sensuous, unspiritual

The widespread view that the letter of Jude is merely a shorter version of 2 Peter is superficial. The two writers treat the material quite differently. But their common subject matter is probably responsible for the relative neglect of Jude among Christians. Yet the letter's warnings of the certainty of divine judgment against evil practices, while unfashionable at the present time, are nonetheless applicable to every age.

Notes

---

1. The traditionally accepted date of 1 Clement. But some argue cogently for a date prior to the destruction of the Jerusalem temple in A.D. 70. See Robinson, *Redating*, pp. 327–35.

2. See Selwyn, pp. 28–36.

3. Bethsaida in Galilee was the home of Peter (John 1:44). It was a cosmopolitan port where Greek would have been spoken. Peter himself bore both Hebrew and Hellenistic names: Symeon (in the Greek of Acts 15:14; 2 Pet. 1:1) and Simon (Matt. 4:18), the latter being not a transliteration of Symeon but a genuine Greek name. Andrew and Philip, from the same district (John 1:44; 12:21), both had Greek names.

4. The historian Josephus (A.D. 37–after 100) is a good example of a Jewish writer, given the mind and the motive, who had a facility in Greek.

5. See Additional Note on 4:16.

6. Tacitus, *Annals* 15.44.

7. According to Eusebius (*Eccl. Hist.* 2.25.2–5), Linus succeeded Peter as Bishop of Rome in A.D. 66; this supports the suggested date for Peter's death in the previous summer. See Robinson, *Redating*, p. 149.

8. Despite the usual assumption among scholars, there is scant evidence of *letters* in ancient religious literature being written under assumed well-known names (pseudepigraphy) in order to gain acceptance. See "Epistolary Pseudepigraphy," in Guthrie, *New Testament Introduction*, pp. 1011–28.

9. C. J. Hemer, "The Address of 1 Peter," *ExpT* 89 (1977–78), pp. 239–43, who went to Turkey to see for himself what was a likely route for the messenger to take.

10. An account of these hypotheses can be seen in Guthrie's volume (note 8 above), pp. 788–93.

11. Originating with R. Perdelwitz, *Die Mysterienreligionen und das Problem des ersten Petrusbriefes* (Giessen: A. Töpelmann, 1911), and carried forward by, among others, F. L. Cross, *1 Peter: A Paschal Liturgy* (London: Mowbray, 1954).

12. C. F. D. Moule, "The Nature and Purpose of 1 Peter," *NTS* 3 (1956–57), p. 4.

13. Daube, *Exodus Pattern*, pp. 42–46.

14. See Hillyer, "First Peter and the Feast of Tabernacles," pp. 39–70.

15. There are convenient lists, for example, in Bigg, pp. 16–21; Kelly, p. 11; and Plumptre, pp. 68–70.

16. Among commentaries in English, those by Bigg, Clowney, Cranfield, Grudem, Marshall, Michaels (on balance), Selwyn, Stibbs/Walls, and Wand decide in favor of apostolic authorship; against are Beare and Best, while Kelly remains on the fence.

17. A persuasive rebuttal of modern objections is in Stibbs/Wall, pp. 15–68.

18. Both Simon and Symeon are used about equally in the Greek MSS of 2 Pet. 1:1. The name Symeon is applied to Peter elsewhere in the NT only in Acts 15:14. A later writer seeking to carry off his letter as Petrine is unlikely to have chosen such a rare name for the apostle.

19. See Guthrie, *New Testament Introduction*, pp. 820–24, 1011–28.

20. The writer of *The Acts of Paul and Thecla*, noted by Tertullian (*On Baptism* 17).

21. It seems more probable that 2 Pet. 3:1 refers to a previous letter which has not survived (cf. 1 Cor. 5:9).

22. Robinson, *Redating*, pp. 327–35.

23. Green, *2 Peter Reconsidered*, pp. 18–23.

24. Bigg, p. 221.

25. Acts 20:30; Rom. 6:1; 1 Cor. 5:11; 6:12; Gal. 5:13; 1 Pet. 2:16; 2 Pet. 2:14.

26. Robinson, *Redating*, p. 197.

27. 1 Enoch (Jude 6, 12–16); *Assumption of Moses* (Jude 9, 16).

28. Didache 2.7 (Jude 22); Polycarp, *To the Philippians* 3.2 (Jude 3, 20); Shepherd of Hermas, *Similitudes* 5.7.2 (Jude 8); *Martyrdom of Polycarp*, inscription (Jude 2); 20.2 (Jude 25).

29. The term Nicolaitan is probably a Graecized form of the Hebrew name Balaam, the policy of the Nicolaitans being likened to the OT figure who corrupted Israel (Num. 31:16). See *ISBE*, vol. 3, pp. 533–34.

30. Guthrie, *New Testament Introduction*, p. 925.

31. See commentary and Additional Notes on Jude 6, 9, 14, 15.

32. Even Paul is prepared to make use of the work of a heathen poet (Acts 17:28; 1 Cor. 15:32, 33; Titus 1:12).

1 Peter

§1 Greetings to Readers (1 Pet. 1:1–2)

1:1 / The writer introduces himself in a brief and modest manner. The Gospels all agree on the prominence of **Peter**, a born leader, impulsive, yet burning with love and enthusiasm. It was to him that Jesus said both the toughest and the choicest things. Whatever Peter's faults, a cold heart was not one of them. His warm pastoral concern for others glows in his letters.

Peter succinctly states his credentials by describing himself simply as **an apostle**, an accredited messenger, **of Jesus Christ**. It is never to teachers, or to prophets, or even to evangelists that the definitive phrase **of Jesus Christ** is applied in the New Testament, but only to apostles. The paramount office of apostle bestows a unique authority upon Peter to address his readers in the name and on behalf of the Lord Jesus Christ, and so the letter he is about to compose is to be received as a divinely authoritative word. **Christ** is the inspiration and the theme of Peter's message. The Greek term *Christos* appears no less than twenty-one times in the 105 verses of this short epistle.

Peter describes his readers in three ways. First, he calls them **God's elect**, his chosen ones; NIV has added **God's**, not in the Greek, to expound the significance of the term **elect** (*eklektois*), which was an ancient title for Israel (1 Chron. 16:13; Ps. 105:6). In the OT, it expressed the Jews' conviction that God had marked them out as his special people—because of his love, not because they had merited it (Deut. 4:37; Hos. 11:1). Now, in line with other NT writers, Peter speaks of Christians as the heirs of the divine privileges, bestowed out of divine love; but they are also the heirs of divinely imposed responsibilities. By quoting Isaiah 43:21 at 1 Peter 2:9, Peter will stress the motive behind God's choice: it was "to declare his praises."

Second, Peter calls his readers **strangers in the world**, a single word in the Greek: *parepidēmois*. The term always refers to temporary residents as aliens in a foreign place. Although dated, the translation "sojourners" comes nearer the sense than the NIV's **strangers**, not very apt for those who may have lived all their lives in one place, or the RSV's rendering "exiles," which has inappropriate overtones of compulsion.

The third expression Peter uses to define his readers is that they are **scattered throughout** (*diasporas*) certain named areas of the Roman Empire. The "Dispersion" (*diaspora*) was a technical term used to describe Jews "scattered" throughout Gentile nations, "dispersed" from their ancient earthly homeland, Israel (John 7:35). Here, as in James 1:1, *diaspora* is used to depict *Christian* believers "scattered" among other peoples, Jewish and Gentile. Their true homeland is not to be found anywhere on earth but in heaven. They are journeying to this home as they make their way through the present transitory life as spiritual pilgrims (1 Pet. 1:17; 2:11; cf. Eph. 2:19; Phil. 3:20; Heb. 11:13; 13:14).

Each of the three Greek terms adds something to the description of Peter's Christian readers: *eklektos* denotes their theological relationship to God; *parepidēmos* underlines the transient nature of this earthly pilgrimage; *diaspora* speaks both of the underlying unity of believers, wherever their geographical setting happens to be, and of their position as heirs of the Old Testament promises (cf. 1 Pet. 2:1–9).

Peter's readers are spread over a vast area, north of the Taurus mountains, mostly in modern Asiatic Turkey. The order in which the places are listed, **Pontus, Galatia, Cappadocia, Asia** (not the continent, but the Roman province of that name), **and Bithynia**, probably indicates the route taken by the letter carrier. The messenger, who may have been Silas (5:12), would need only to call on a few Christian communities in each province, leaving a copy of the letter to be duplicated by local believers and shared with others nearby.

1:2 / NIV adds the words **who have been chosen** to make it clear that the rest of the verse follows on from "God's elect" (or "chosen") in verse 1, and involves the function of each of the three Persons of the Trinity: the Father purposes; the Spirit sanctifies; the Son brings believers into a right relationship with himself.

The divine choice of believers is **according to the foreknowledge of God the Father**. This includes far more than a divine capacity to foretell the future. It implies God's intention all along, and his ability to bring his desired end to pass (Acts 2:23; Rom. 8:29).

This divine purpose is fulfilled **through the sanctifying work of the Spirit**. It is he who sets in motion and will ultimately complete (Phil. 1:6) the process of making believers what God has in mind for them to become, a holy people set apart for himself.

The consequence of the Father's choice and of the Spirit's sanctifying work is expressed in the believer's act of **obedience to Jesus Christ** in accepting him as Lord of their lives. This new relationship to him is brought about through **sprinkling by his blood**. The expression alludes to the making of the divine covenant in Exodus 24:3–8, in which the blood of the sacrifice was sprinkled on the people after they had promised to obey the Lord.

Thus, on the human side, **obedience** expresses one's response to the gospel's proclamation of Christ's saving act. On the divine side, the **blood** of Jesus Christ, that is, his sacrificial death, results in a new covenant being ratified between God and his people.

Although the status of believers is that of pilgrims—or as the opening verse has put it, **strangers** with regard to this world—Peter brings his readers comfort with the reminder that all is known to God and has been taken care of in his perfect plan of salvation. He chose them in the first place, and his power will finally bring about the consummation of the divine plan, whatever the particular circumstances of a believer's life in this world.

The form of the greeting, **grace and peace** (*charis kai eirēnē*), is frequent in NT letters. It is often said that it brings together for the first time the usual Greek greeting, **grace** (*charis*) and the Hebrew greeting **peace** (*šālōm*)—even if the two terms are not mentioned in what we might regard as "chronological" order. But the likelihood is that the phrase **grace and peace** echoes early Christian worship and derives from the daily Jewish liturgy in the temple, with its priestly blessing of Numbers 6:25–26, "The Lord . . . be *gracious* to you; . . . and give you *peace*."

Grace and peace define in a nutshell the extent of the mighty benefits of Christ's saving acts: **grace**, the free and undeserved divine gift to the believer in bringing to pass a right relationship with God involving love, mercy, forgiveness, and power; and **peace**, the soul's inward rich enjoyment of that divine bounty.

Peter's prayer is that God's grace and peace may be bestowed upon his readers **in abundance**, lit. "may be multiplied," that is, be appreciated and enjoyed increasingly by each individual. The "multiplication" of peace implies a quality of personal inward peace that is independent of worldly circumstances, because it is God-given, God-inspired, God-created (cf. the abundance of *seeds*), not some outward peace imposed by human authority, which is frequently to be more accurately described as a stifling of social or political unrest.

Additional Notes   §1

1:1 / **Peter** (*petros*, rock, stone; in Aramaic, Cephas; John 1:42) is the nickname given by Jesus to Simon (Matt. 16:18). The theme of rock/stone is spiritualized in 1 Pet. 2:4–8. On the significance of the name-change Simon/Cephas/Peter, see Cullmann, *Peter*, pp. 17–21.

An apostle of Jesus Christ: the office authorized apostles to express God's own words, whether oral or written (Acts 5:3–4; Rom. 2:16; 1 Cor. 1:17; 2:13; 2 Cor. 13:3; Gal. 1:8–9; 1 Thess. 2:13; 4:8, 15; 2 Thess. 3:6; 2 Pet. 3:2; 1 John 4:6). Such divinely inspired utterances were recognized as Scripture since they took their place in the NT (1 Cor. 14:37; 1 Thess. 5:27; 2 Thess. 3:14; 2 Pet. 3:16; Rev. 22:18–19).

By **elect** (*eklektos*) Peter here designates the widely scattered Christian churches as the new Israel of God. In 2:4, *eklektos* ("chosen") contrasts God's action with the rejection of Christ by unbelievers. In 5:13, the compound term *syneklektē* ("chosen together") refers to the church at Rome. See *TDNT*, vol. 4, pp. 181–92; Turner, pp. 127–30; *NIDNTT*, vol. 1, pp. 536–41.

Strangers translates *parepidēmoi*, sojourners. The Greek term occurs twice in the LXX (Gen. 23:4; Ps. 39:12) and again in 1 Pet. 2:11, where it is coupled with a similar word *paroikia*, used in 1:17. See *TDNT*, vol. 2, pp. 64–65; *NIDNTT*, vol. 1, p. 690; vol. 2, pp. 788–90.

Scattered throughout (*diaspora*): The corresponding verb, *diaspeirein*, combines *dia*, through, and *speirein*, to scatter as seed. The term implies an action suffered for a purpose: seed dies, resurrects, and multiplies for the benefit of the owner of the field (the world, Matt. 13:38). In the LXX, *diaspora* occurs twelve times (first in Deut. 28:25) and always in the technical sense of the Jews scattered among the Gentiles; cf. 2 Baruch 1:4 (the Syriac *Apocalypse of Baruch*, a Pharisaic work dated soon after A.D. 70): "I will scatter this people among the Gentiles, that they may do good to the Gentiles." See *TDNT*, vol. 2, pp. 98–104; *ISBE*, vol. 1, pp. 962–68; Turner, pp. 113–14; *NIDNTT*, vol. 1, pp. 685–86; vol. 2, pp. 33–35.

The way Peter describes his readers as **God's elect, strangers in the world, scattered** is expounded upon well by an anonymous second-century writer:

> "The difference between Christians and the rest of mankind is not a matter of nationality, or of language, or of customs. They pass their time in whatever township, Greek or foreign, each one's lot has determined, conforming to ordinary local usage in their clothing, diet, and other habits. Nevertheless, the organization of their community does exhibit some features that are remarkable. For instance, they live in the lands of their birth, but more like temporary residents. They take their full part as citizens, yet submit to disabilities as if they were aliens. Any foreign country is homeland to them, and any motherland is foreign territory. Their days are passed upon earth, but their citizenship is in heaven" (*Letter to Diognetus* 5).

There were Jews from **Pontus**, **Cappadocia**, and **Asia** among the pilgrims in Jerusalem on the day of Pentecost (Acts 2:9), who may well have carried the gospel message home and established the first Christian communities in their districts. Aquila (Acts 18:2) came from **Pontus**.

Three of the areas (**Galatia, Cappadocia, Asia**) are Roman provinces. The other two names Peter mentions form a single province, Bithynia-Pontus, set up by the Romans in 64 B.C. The reason for the separation of the double name in Peter's list, with **Pontus** first and **Bithynia** last, suggests that the order of the five districts indicates the route taken by Peter's messenger. The messenger may well have landed at Amisus, modern Samsun, the only port in **Pontus** which also offers a feasible route inland (much of the coastline is impenetrably mountainous). From there he could travel into **Galatia** via Amasia, and into **Cappadocia** via Caesarea, then west along the great trade route through Iconium and Pisidian Antioch (again in **Galatia**), to Laodicea in the Roman province of **Asia**, and end at the major Christian centers of **Bithynia** (Nicea, Nicomedia) before embarking for Rome, either at Chalcedon or Byzantium on the Bosphorus. See C. H. Hemer, "The Address of 1 Peter," *ExpT* 89 (8, 1977–78), pp. 239–43, for a detailed discussion of the messenger's possible route by one who went there to see for himself.

1:2 / God's **foreknowledge** (*prognōsis*) in his choice of believers is a prominent theme in the NT (Rom. 8:29–30; 11:2; Eph. 1:4–6, 11–14; 2 Thess. 2:13), even though this particular Greek word occurs again only once more. In Acts 2:23 God's foreknowledge is explicitly coupled with his determinate counsel; cf. Jer. 1:5, "Before I formed you in the womb I knew you."

The doctrine of providence expressed in Peter's wording is well illustrated in Judith 9:5–6 LXX: "What you designed has come to pass. The things you ordained come forward and say, 'We are here.' All your ways are prepared beforehand: foreknowledge (*prognōsis*) determines your judgments."

The sanctifying work of the Spirit is a phrase which appears again in 2 Thess. 2:13. The individual cannot engage in self-sanctification: that is a divine work. But the process does require the believer's practical cooperation in daily conduct (1 Pet. 1:15–16). In the Dead Sea Scrolls, the Spirit appears as a cleansing purifying power (1QS 3.7–9; 4.20; 1QH 16.12).

The Greek translated **for obedience to Jesus Christ and sprinkling by his blood** (*eis hypakoēn kai rhantismon haimatos Iēsou Christou*) poses grammatical problems. Literally it means "for obedience and for sprinkling of the blood of Jesus Christ." To link *hypakoēn* with Jesus Christ (**for obedience to Jesus Christ**), as in NIV and most modern translations, involves taking the genitive "of Jesus Christ" as both objective (with **obedience**) and subjective (with **blood**). But the translators are probably right in not expecting a letter-writer to be a pedant!

The idea of **sprinkling** can have several references. It can imply the transfer to the elect of the merits of the atoning and cleansing virtue of Christ's death (Num. 19:9; Heb. 9:13–22) and also of consecration to priestly service, including access to God (Exod. 29:21; Lev. 8:30; Heb. 10:19–22; 1 Pet. 2:4, 9).

Grace (*charis*) **and peace:** The letter in 2 Macc. 1:1–2 LXX couples the corresponding verb *charein* with **peace**, so the association of the two notions in that order was not unknown before Christian times. The Aaronic blessing of Num. 6:25–26 (see commentary) was daily repeated in the temple. See Edersheim, *The Temple, Its Ministry and Services*, p. 141. It was also integral to Qumran worship (1QS 2.2; 1QSb 3.4).

Peace be yours: "When we consider the rich possibilities of . . . *šālōm* [peace] in the Old Testament, we are struck by the negative fact that there is no specific text in which it denotes the specifically spiritual attitude of inward peace" (G. von Rad, *TDNT*, vol. 2, p. 406).

Peace . . . in abundance (*plēthyntheiē*: lit. may it be multiplied.) The phrase occurs in Dan. 4:1; 6:25 LXX; also in Jude 2. Peter's prayer here is echoed by his similar thought at the close of his second letter, where he urges his readers to "grow in the grace and knowledge of our Lord and Savior Jesus Christ" (2 Pet. 3:18). He longs for his readers to enter more and more fully into the richness of their inheritance in Christ. The verb *plēthyntheiē* is in the optative mood, infrequent in the NT, and conveys not merely a wish but effective impartation—as in Mark 11:14 ("May no one ever eat fruit from you again!"), where the optative in this instance expresses nothing less than a curse.

The thought of "peace abounding" is messianic, as in Ps. 37:11 ("The meek shall inherit the land and shall delight themselves in the abundance of peace"); Ps. 72:7 ("In his days shall the righteous flourish and abundance of peace"); *Targum of Jonathan* on Isa. 9:6 (" . . . the Messiah, whose peace shall be multiplied upon us in his days"). But by NT times the messianic note had been muffled by formalism. The contemporary letters of Rabbi Gamaliel, Paul's early teacher, all begin "May your peace get much increase," even if he is merely announcing the time of tithes. See E. Nestle, "1 Pet. 1.2," *ExpT* 10 (1898–99), pp. 188–89.

1:3 / Peter at once launches into **praise** of God for planning so magnificent a salvation. The Israelites of old praised God as the creator of the world (2 Chron. 2:12) and as their redeemer from Egyptian slavery (Deut. 4:20). Peter develops the characteristic Jewish approach by adopting an explicitly Christian stance. He praises God as the **Father of** his unique Son, **our Lord Jesus Christ**, and as the One who raised this Jesus from the dead. As a Christian, Peter blesses God for the *new* creation, as expressed in the **new birth** of believers, and for divine provision for them of "an inheritance" of a promised land "in heaven," safe beyond the slavery of sin or the frenzy of foes.

The experiences of **new birth** and of **a living hope** are beyond human procurement. They are God's gracious gift and are bestowed solely on account of **his great mercy**, for there is no way in which they can ever be deserved or earned. They come to us through **the resurrection of Jesus Christ from the dead**, that is, as the direct consequence of his total triumph over the worst that the powers of evil can achieve; namely, death itself.

The concept of **new birth** is based on the teaching of Jesus (John 3:3–8). It speaks of the gift of spiritual life on a plane previously unknown in an individual's experience. It can no more be acquired by self-effort than a babe can bring about its own physical birth.

The first result of this new birth, and the first characteristic of the new pilgrim life of the believer, is **hope** (anchor for the soul, firm and secure: Heb. 6:19). Hope is **living** (cf. 1:23; 2:4–5), not merely because it is active (Heb. 4:12), or is simply an improved version of the Jewish hope (Heb. 7:19). Nor are we to misunderstand the translation "have been born anew to a living hope" (RSV) to mean "hope has been restored." Peter is referring to something of a different order: a sure and confident outlook which has a divine, not a human, source. That new quality of

hope is generated in the believer by the new spiritual life brought
about by the new birth. Peter is writing to encourage readers who
face an uncertain future threatened by persecution of one degree
or another. This **living hope** highlights the fact that the present
life is by no means the limit of the believer's expectation. As the
word is used in everyday parlance, "hope" can prove a delusion
(Job 7:6; Eph. 2:12; cf. Col. 1:5). The **living hope** in the newborn
Christian has a vigor, a patient endurance, and an assurance
beyond any human power: such hope can no more fail than the
living God who bestows it. Peter elaborates the nature and the
content of **living hope** in the following two verses.

1:4 / A "new birth" carries with it the implication of entrance into a new family (Rom. 8:17; Gal. 4:7) and eligibility for
an inheritance. Because for believers that inheritance is of divine
provision, it partakes of divine qualities. It **can never perish, spoil
or fade**: it cannot be subject, as a worldly inheritance must be, to
the ravages of corruption, pollution, or time. The terms under-
score that Peter is writing to encourage his readers as they face
up to an uncertain and threatening future.

Furthermore, the Christian **inheritance** is safely beyond
the clutches of earthly enemies and of evil spiritual powers, for it
is **kept in heaven**, in safe custody, on behalf of believers, ready
for the day when they are able to claim it.

1:5 / Whatever vicissitudes believers may have to face in
this world (and Peter's readers were only too well aware that
severe trials were looming), they can find encouragement in the
reminder that they are not being left to fend for themselves. Even
now they are being **shielded by God's power**, that is, by one who
is all-knowing about the future and all-sufficient to support those
who belong to him in anything they may have to meet. Provided
they firmly believe this as a matter of **faith**, they can rest assured
that God will not fail them in their hour of need.

The divine shield (Gen. 15:1) will continue to be the believer's assurance right to the end, **until the coming of the salvation
that is ready to be revealed in the last time.** The reference to
salvation is not to be confined to that of the individual, but
relates to the fulfillment of the whole divine program for all
creation. The end is imminent, **ready to be revealed**. That reas-
surance will carry threatened believers through their present
anxieties.

1:6 / The prospect of the coming glorious consummation of salvation is one in which believers have every right to **greatly rejoice**. Peter uses the Greek *agalliasthai*, a verb not found in secular writings until the fourth century A.D. In the Greek OT (LXX), the word has strong eschatological overtones: a joy "out of this world," to use modern jargon with much greater precision. Peter will employ *agalliasthai* again in 1:8 ("inexpressible and glorious joy") and in 4:13 ("overjoyed" at the revelation of Christ's glory at his second coming). The rejoicing, as expressed by the verb in the NT, is always a jubilant and thankful exultation for some divine action. It was the early Christians' vivid awareness of the reality of God in their lives that caused them to rejoice in this profound sense, and it carried them through all manner of privation and persecution in a world that looked askance at their "strange" religion. Peter reassures his readers that their joy in Christ is what matters, even though they **may have had to suffer grief in all kinds of trials** during their earthly pilgrimage on account of their faith (John 16:33; 1 John 3:13).

The expression **all kinds**, referring to trials facing believers, here translates the Greek *poikilois*, which literally means "many colored." Peter uses the word again in 4:10 to describe God's grace. The only two occurrences of the Greek word in this letter nicely balance. Christians may have to face all kinds of troubles. But in whatever "color" troubles appear, God's grace will always "match" them and prove perfectly sufficient. Nevertheless, Peter's wording implies that the trials that Christians have to meet will sort out those who are full of faith from others whose profession is less than wholehearted. Writer and readers were living at a time when pagans maligned Christians as criminals (2:12), and this would be the source of many petty local persecutions, even when there was no organized persecution by the civil authorities.

1:7 / The purpose of trials for the believer is said to involve **faith**. The reference is not to saving faith, which looks back to the moment of an individual's conversion, but to the sterling quality of *loyalty* to Christ in everyday living, especially at a time of trial (as again in 4:12 and 5:9).

Although **gold** is among the most precious of metals on earth, it can by its nature belong only to this passing world. People may consider it well worth their while going to great lengths to cleanse it from impurities, yet the treasures of the spirit are of far greater true value, and indeed eternal in quality (Ps. 19:10; 119:27; Prov. 3:11). As gold is nevertheless subjected to **fire** in the purifying process, so too the Christian's faith must be refined. "Faith is not known to be what it is, unless it is tested by suffering" (Plumptre, p. 95).

The triumphant proving of faith through trials will redound in **praise, glory and honor** at the second coming, **when Jesus Christ is revealed** in all his majesty. The thought here is not primarily that Jesus will be glorified by his followers' loyalty, however true that is. It is the believers themselves who will receive **praise, glory and honor** (Rom. 2:7, 10; 1 Cor. 4:5), for such will be the expression of his "well done, good and faithful servant" (Matt. 25:21).

1:8 / Unlike Peter himself, his readers, for reasons of time and geography, never saw Jesus in the flesh, and now that he has ascended back into heaven they will not have an opportunity in this life of setting eyes on him. The next life will be another story (1 John 3:2). Yet the inability to see him in this world has not prevented them from becoming believers, for faith does not depend upon sight (2 Cor. 5:7). And more: committing their lives to Christ as Savior has not been restricted to an unemotional transaction. As a consequence of their conversion, they found, and are continuing to find, love for the unseen Christ growing within them. His presence in their lives is real, even if unseen. And more even than that: they are being blessed in a special way. Peter knew the reason. He was present when the risen Christ told Thomas, "Blessed are those who have not seen and yet have believed" (John 20:29). So Peter's readers in every generation are eligible for such a blessing—which he interprets as **inexpressible and glorious joy**.

That joy is **inexpressible**, beyond human description, for in truth it does not belong to this world-order, and it is certainly not of human origin. It is a divine gift (Ps. 16:11; John 15:9–11; 16:24; Rom. 15:13; Gal. 5:22) and a direct consequence of a living relationship with the Lord (1 Cor. 2:9). As such, it is a witness to others (Luke 15:4–10) of divine care and loving activity in the believer's life.

1:9 / That joy, Peter declares, is based on the assurance that **you are receiving the goal**, the end purpose, **of your faith**, of your unswerving trust in Jesus Christ: none other than the final and complete **salvation of your souls**. That **salvation** began at conversion (1:3), continues through the process of sanctification, of growth in the grace and knowledge of the Lord (2:2; 2 Pet. 3:18), and it will ultimately find its perfect fulfillment in the presence of the glorified Christ (1 Pet. 1:7).

If it seems curious that Peter should speak in such glowing terms of his readers exulting in joy at a time when they faced trials and tribulation, the comment of Archbishop Leighton (1611–1684) still shines meaningfully through the centuries: "Even in the midst of heaviness itself, such is this joy that it can maintain itself in the midst of sorrows; this oil of gladness still swims above, and cannot be drowned by all the floods of affliction; yea, it is most often sweet in the greatest distress" (Leighton, vol. 2, p. 70). Union with Christ (1:3, 10–12, 21) is the ever-present basis for unconditional consolation: the believer's soul in Christ's care is utterly safe, whatever the earthly trials and assaults.

Additional Notes   §2

1:3 / Praise be to . . . God: By **praise** here and in 5:11, Peter is following Jewish practice: "He that begins the reading from the Law, and he that completes it, say a benediction, the one at the beginning and the other at the end" (m. *Meg.* 4.1). The benediction is typical of early Tannaitic piety: it blesses God for qualities and deeds attributed to him in Scripture (as in Ps. 66:20; 2 Macc. 15:34). See Daube, *New Testament and Rabbinic Judaism*, p. 93.

The doxology was characteristic of Jewish prayer. It became focused in the Eighteen Benedictions, which were recited three times daily in the synagogue. But the Christian doxology is richer in its concepts of God and of the afterlife, as can be seen by comparing Peter's paean of praise with the meager wording of the Second Benediction: "Blessed art thou, O Lord, that quickenest the dead."

The same opening eleven Greek words of this verse occur coincidentally in 2 Cor. 1:3 and Eph. 1:3; but literary dependence either way is unlikely. The wording was doubtless already established in Christian worship; cf. similar expressions in Rom. 15:6; 2 Cor. 11:31; Eph. 1:17.

On *eulogētos* (**praise**, blessed), see Turner, pp. 48–49.

This is the only verse in which Peter uses the full title **our Lord Jesus Christ**, but it is appropriate. All that follows in his letter is due to the divinely provided relationship, which Peter shares (hence **our**): the believer confesses the Son as **Lord**, i.e., as divine, for the Greek term *kyrios* corresponds to the Hebrew Yahweh; the Savior's earthly name **Jesus** speaks of his life, ministry, death, resurrection, and ascension; and his messianic status, denoted in the term **Christ**, has implications for the life to come.

His great mercy . . . living hope: cf. the parallel thought in Eph. 2:4–5, "God, who is rich in mercy, made us alive with Christ."

New birth is NIV rendering of the Greek participle *anagennēsas*, having been born anew (the verb occurs again in 1:23, but not elsewhere in the NT). In later times the verb was commonly used of Christian baptism (Justin, *Apology* 1.51; *Clementine Homilies* 11.26), but it doubtlessly derived from this verse in 1 Peter.

The concept of **new birth** (also in 1:23; 2:2) and related ideas, such as the believer's new creation, are found in John 1:12–13; 2 Cor. 5:17; Gal. 6:15; Eph. 2:10; Col. 3:10; Titus 3:5; James 1:18; 1 John 2:29; 3:9; 4:7; 5:1, 4, 18). The notion of rebirth was familiar from the mystery religions, where curiously the resultant "eternal life" was taken to last only twenty years. In Judaism, a proselyte was "like a child newly born" (b. *Yebam.* 48b); but this referred to the convert's legal status. See C. K. Barrett, *The Gospel According to St John* (London: SPCK, 1955), p. 172. Peter is referring to something of a different order: spiritual life on a new plane through direct divine action on a soul.

The **resurrection of Jesus Christ from the dead** was recognized as fundamental in Christian preaching from the very first (Acts 2:31; 3:15; 4:2, 33; 10:40).

Hope is a main theme of the whole letter: see also 1:13, 21; 3:5, 15. Hope is not directed to realizing a picture of the future as projected by a human being, but it is the believer's trust in God, a trust that turns away from self and the world and waits patiently and expectantly on God. See Turner, pp. 213–15; *TDNT*, vol. 2, pp. 517–33; *NIDNTT*, vol. 2, pp. 238–46; vol. 3, pp. 968–70.

1:4 / The Jews understood the idea of **inheritance** in material terms, such as the promised land of milk and honey, Canaan (Lev. 20:24; Deut. 15:4). But even before the shock of the exile made them spiritualize this interpretation, their inheritance was sometimes thought of as God himself (Deut. 10:9; Ps. 73:26). In the NT the Christian's inheritance is variously interpreted as eternal life (Mark 10:17; Titus 3:7), glory with Christ (Rom. 8:17), immortality (1 Cor. 15:50), or the new Jerusalem (Rev. 21:2, 7). Peter himself later identifies it with "the gracious gift of life" and "a blessing" (see commentary on 3:7, 9).

Never perish, spoil or fade translates three adjectives: *aphthartos, amiantos, amarantos*, all three prefixed by *alpha*-privative (Gk. *a-* = Eng. *un-*). The first, *aphthartos*, derives from the verb *phtheirein*, often used of the ravaging of land by hostile armies. The second, *amiantos*, is from *miainein*, to pollute, especially by godless action. The third, *amarantos*, unfading (from *marainein*, to dry up, wither) gives us *amaranth*, the "unfading flower." The Christian inheritance is in a sphere that, unlike the promised land of the OT, will never be laid waste by war, nor defiled by idolatry and sin, nor blasted by pest or drought.

Kept (*tetērēmenēn*) is a perfect participle, the tense bringing out the fact that the inheritance already exists and is kept safe under guard for those who are even now being "shielded by God's power" (v. 5). The Syriac *Apocalypse of Baruch* 52:6 (a Pharisaic work compiled soon after the fall of Jerusalem in A.D. 70) contains the admonition: "Rejoice in the suffering which you now suffer, and prepare your souls for the reward which is laid up for you."

1:5 / **Shielded** is a military term. The verb is used in the NT of the city guard (2 Cor. 11:32) and metaphorically describes those confined under the Mosaic law (Gal. 3:23); it can also be used of God's peace guarding the hearts of believers (Phil. 4:7).

Salvation (*sōtēria*) recurs in 1:9, 10; 2:2; the related verb (*sōzein*, to save, heal, make whole) in 3:21; 4:18; and the compound *diasōzein* (to save through) in 3:20. In the NT salvation is viewed as past, present, and future. The past salvation "saved," Eph. 2:5; 1 Pet. 3:20) looks back to the moment when a Christian first believed in the Lord Jesus Christ as Savior and received forgiveness of sins. The present salvation ("being saved," 1 Cor. 1:18) concerns the subsequent daily growth in grace (1 Pet. 2:2; 2 Pet. 3:18). The future salvation looks ahead to the ultimate fulfillment of God's plan for the whole of his creation (Rom. 8:21–24; 1 Pet. 1:5). See Turner, pp. 390–98; *TDNT*, vol. 7, pp. 965–1024; *NIDNTT*, vol. 3, pp. 177–221.

1:6 / **You greatly rejoice** (*agalliasthe*): Judaism glimpsed this when the rabbis spoke of "ecstatic joy" at the drawing of water during the Feast of Tabernacles, in which, meaningfully for Christians, the ceremony was related to the outpouring of the Holy Spirit, a rabbinic deduction from Isa. 12:3, 6 (j. *Sukka* 55). See Hillyer, "First Peter and the Feast of Tabernacles," *TynB* 21 (1970), pp. 39–70. One use of the Greek verb *agalliasthai* with significance for 1 Peter, where eschatology is never far away, occurs in Ps. 118:24 LXX: "This is the day the Lord has made. Let us *rejoice* and be glad in it." Another verse in the same Psalm (v. 22) is echoed in 1 Pet. 2:4, 7.

Suffer grief . . . trials: The rabbis viewed suffering as redemptive: "Man should rejoice at chastisements more than at prosperity, for chastisements bring forgiveness for his transgressions" (*Sifre Deut.* 32 on Deut. 6:5). But Peter's Christian insight is that grief and trials are the expected lot of believers in the world (John 16:33; 1 John 3:13), but *redemption* is due to the action of God in Christ (1 Pet. 1:3).

May have had to suffer: NIV's **may** loosely covers two Greek words (*ei deon*, lit. "if it is necessary"), meaning "since it has to be." The future is in God's hands, not in ours.

1:7 / **That your faith . . . may be proved genuine** (*hina to dokimion hymōn tēs pisteōs*): lit. "that the proving of your faith." The sense of *to dokimion* is generally that by means of which something is tried, or in which it is tested ("crucible," Prov. 27:21 LXX). Romans 5:2–5 has a similar thought, while James 1:2–3 is a verbal parallel. But James emphasizes "the *testing* of your faith," while Peter here speaks of the "sterling quality of your faith." "The *genuineness* of your love" (2 Cor. 8:8) is an exact parallel.

Faith in rabbinic writings usually means loyalty to the Mosaic law, as also in the Dead Sea Scrolls: "All who enter the order of the community shall enter into a covenant in the presence of God to act *according to all that he has commanded*, and not to withdraw from following him through any fear or terror or trial" —where, incidentally, "trial" is lit. "furnace" or "refiner's fire" (1QS 1.16–17).

Of greater worth than gold: The comparison was a commonplace in the ancient world: "Justice is more precious than many pieces of gold" (Plato, *Republic* 1.336E).

Which perishes is, more fully, "whose nature is to perish." The contrast is between perishable precious metal (cf. 1:18) and the imperishable spiritual wealth of faith. But they are alike in this: both are tested by fire, literal in one case, metaphorical in the other.

The metaphor of precious metals **refined by fire** is frequent in Scripture: Ps. 66:10; Prov. 17:3; 27:21; Isa. 1:25; Jer. 9:7; Zech. 13:9; Mal. 3:3; 1 Cor. 3:15; so too e.g., Didache 16:5. Peter's vocabulary often suggests a close acquaintance with the Wisdom of Solomon, as here: "As gold in the furnace, he proved them" (Wisd. of Sol. 3:6).

Glory: The Greek noun *doxa* and the corresponding verb *doxazein* occur with greater frequency in 1 Peter (1:7, 8, 11, 21, 24; 2:12; 4:11, 13, 14, 16; 5:1, 4, 10) than in any other NT book. Is this because of Peter's unforgettable experience with his Lord on the Mount of Transfiguration? See Selwyn, pp. 253–58.

1:8 / **Though you have not seen** (*idontes*) **him**: Some MSS have *eidontes* (known), but the change probably arose from the common pronunciation confusion of *i* with *ei*.

Inexpressible (*aneklalētos*) occurs in the Bible only here, and rarely elsewhere: "not capable of human description or calculation."

Glorious translates the participle *dedoxasmenē*, glorified, radiant with glory from above.

1:9 / **Receiving** (*komizomenoi*): carrying off safely for oneself. In the NT the verb *komizein* has the sense of "receiving what is due" (e.g., Matt. 25:27; 2 Cor. 5:10; Eph. 6:8). Peter will use the term again in 5:4 and in 2 Pet. 2:13.

Goal: The Greek *telos* means full-orbed mature end, destiny, and is related to *teleios*, perfect, which points to the richness of its meaning. See *TDNT*, vol. 8, pp. 49–57; *NIDNTT*, vol. 2, pp. 59–66; vol. 3, pp. 752–59.

Souls: "The original idea is that of the soul as a gift from God in a pure and holy condition, to be preserved against all contamination by the 'evil inclination', which makes war against it" (P. Carrington, *The Primitive Christian Catechism*. Cambridge: Cambridge University Press, 1940, p. 27).

§3 Salvation Was Prophesied (1 Pet. 1:10–12)

1:10 / Christians are greatly favored, for they already enjoy a foretaste of this great **salvation**—something that the inspired **prophets** of the OT were able only to glimpse. The same can be said of "angels," for despite their exalted status in the spiritual world, even they do not know the range and detail of the divine plan, and they "long to look into" it more deeply.

In this passage, Peter incidentally lets us see how grand a panoramic sweep he himself has learned to take of God's work. In a few words, he brings together in a remarkable fashion the OT and the NT, that is, the old and the new divine covenants, by declaring that it was the Spirit of Christ himself who was inspiring those early OT prophets to speak both of the coming "sufferings of Christ" (Messiah) "and of the glories that would follow." Peter is thus stressing that the whole Christian faith has OT roots. The great OT prophets could see only tantalizing hints of the extent of God's program for his people, but the apostles—and now also Peter's Christian readers—are privileged to be living at the time when they can see how it is all being realized. The OT prophets may indeed have **searched intently and with the greatest care**, but the apostles *know* from firsthand experience the magnificence of God's salvation plan. The authority of Jesus himself is behind this bold claim, for Peter had heard Christ's declaration: "Many prophets and righteous men longed to see what you see but did not see it, and to hear what you hear but did not hear it" (Matt. 13:17; cf. John 8:56; Heb. 11:13).

1:11 / The prophets of old were keenly aware that what had been revealed in part to them was of the utmost importance in God's ultimate arrangements for his people. So they anxiously strove to find out more from the Scriptures. In particular, they wanted to know **the time and circumstances**, or rather (as probably the Greek here is intended to mean), which person and what time were indicated: who would be Messiah? when would he appear? The revelations that the prophets did receive and pass on **predicted the sufferings of Christ and the glories that would follow.**

Once Peter had tried to thwart Jesus from fulfilling the role of the Suffering Servant. But now he has come to realize that this is the clue to the proper understanding of Jesus' ministry as Messiah. It is significant that when Peter speaks of the sufferings of his Lord, he never uses the name *Jesus* in this connection, but the title *Christ* (1:11, 19; 2:21; 3:18; 4:1, 13, 14; 5:1), and *Christ* is, of course, simply the Greek form of the Hebrew *Messiah*. What struck Peter, with his Jewish background, was that Messiah of all people should have to suffer. Now he recognized that it was the preexistent **Spirit of Christ** himself (so also in 1:20) who had been prompting the OT writers in their prophecies about the experiences of Messiah when he did come.

1:12 / But **it was revealed** to the prophets of old that what God had made known to them concerning Messiah referred to a later generation, not to their own. That later generation has turned out to be that of Peter's readers. So the ministry of those ancient prophets, however much of it applied to their contemporaries, has its fulfillment in Peter's day. The prophets, Peter tells his readers, **were not serving themselves** in the deepest sense, **but you**, when they spoke about God's program.

What the early prophets foretold has now been taken up by Christian missionaries who, from their vantage point of knowing about the earthly ministry of Jesus the Messiah, were able to demonstrate the fuller implications of the old message when they **preached the gospel to you.** Furthermore, their preaching was inspired by the same **Holy Spirit** who moved the OT prophets. This is the Spirit **sent from heaven,** as the Day of Pentecost made dramatically plain, thus divinely authenticating the Christian preachers' message (Acts 2:16, "this is what").

The Christian generations are momentous times, for in them the consummation of God's long-prophesied plan for his people is being fulfilled, and the whole universe is caught up in the denouement. No wonder Peter can add: **Even angels long to look into these things.** For all their privileges in the spiritual world, even to that of being commissioned to reveal some of God's secrets to human beings (Ezek. 40:3; Zech. 1:9; Luke 1:13,

26; Rev. 21:9, 15), even angels are not privy to all the details of God's salvation plan. Naturally enough, like the OT prophets in their situation, the angels long to know more, for it is clear to them that the subject is of supreme importance in the divine scheme of things.

Additional Notes   §3

1:10 / **Prophets**: Selwyn (pp. 262–67) argues that this means *Christian* prophets (Eph. 3:5; 4:11), but he has not persuaded most commentators. Peter often speaks of **the prophets** of the OT as messengers who testified of Christ (Messiah): Acts 2:16, 25, 30, 34; 3:13, 18, 21, 25; 4:11, 25; 10:43.

The fulfillment of OT expectations is mentioned many times in the NT: Matt. 5:17; Luke 24:25–27, 44–47; John 5:39, 45–47; Acts 17:2–3; 1 Cor. 15:3–4; Heb. 1:1; 11:32; James 5:10; 2 Pet. 1:21; Rev. 10:7.

Although Peter makes no use of the terms *mystery* and *interpretation*, his comments find remarkable parallels in the Dead Sea Scrolls. According to the Covenanters at Qumran, the OT prophets recorded the *mysteries* of God, while the later Teacher of Righteousness and his disciples understood their *interpretation*. "God commanded Habakkuk to write the things that were coming upon the last generation. But the fulfillment of the epoch he did not make known to him. And as for the words *so he may run who reads it*, their interpretation concerns the Teacher of Righteousness, to whom God made known all the mysteries of the words of his servants the prophets" (1QpHab 7.1–5). See F. F. Bruce, *Biblical Exegesis in the Qumran Texts* (London: Tyndale Press, 1960), p. 76.

Who spoke of the grace that was to come to you: There are frequent hints that OT prophets realized that they were speaking of a future time when referring to divine intervention (Num. 24:17; Deut. 18:5; Hab. 2:1–3; cf. 1 Enoch 1:2, "I understood what I saw, and it is not for this generation but for a remote one in the future.").

Searched intently and with the greatest care translates the Greek *exezētēsan kai exēraunēsan*. The rendering "made earnest quest and query" seeks to bring out the word-play (paronomasia), a notable feature of the Greek of 1 Peter (Beare, p. 90).

1:11 / **Trying to find out** translates one word, *eraunōntes*, a verb elsewhere used of searching the Scriptures (John 5:39; 7:52).

The time and circumstances: The Greek *eis tina ē poion kairon* poses problems, for *tina* (accusative of *tis*) can mean "who?" or "what?" and *poion* can be "what kind of?" or simply "what?" The remaining words *ē* (or) and *kairon* (time, season) are straightforward. Although *tis* occurs well over

500 times in the NT, it is *never* used to ask "what time?" In all four instances in the NT where *poios* is coupled with a word for time, the meaning of *poios* is always "what?" or "which one?" not "what kind of?" ("which day?" Matt. 24:42; "which hour?" Matt. 24:43; Luke 12:39; Rev. 3:3). So the translation for this verse "what person or time" (as in RSV, NASB) is to be preferred to NIV's **the time and circumstances**, or KJV's "what, or what manner of time." The OT prophets would certainly be keen to know the *identity* of the coming Messiah as well as the time of his appearance.

The phrase **the Spirit of Christ** applied to the work of prophecy in the OT points to Christ's preexistence; this is again brought out in 1:20 (cf. Rom. 1:4; 1 Cor. 10:4; Col. 1:15–17).

The sufferings of Christ: lit. destined for (*eis*) Christ: from the OT prophets' viewpoint in time, those sufferings were still in the future. Peter probably has in mind passages such as Ps. 22:1, 7–8, 18; 34:20; 69:21; Isa. 50:6; 52:14—53:12; Zech. 12:10; 13:7.

The glories that would follow: Messiah's glory is referred to in e.g., Ps. 2:6–12; 16:10; 45:7; 110:1 (the most quoted OT verse in the NT); Isa. 9:6; 40:3–5, 9–11; 42:1–4; 61:1–3; Jer. 33:14–15; Ezek. 34:23–31; Dan. 7:18, 27; Hos. 2:23; Joel 2:28–32; Zeph. 3:14–20. The plural **glories** is rare in religious Greek (only in Exod. 15:11; 33:5; Hos. 9:11; 1 Macc. 14:9; Wisd. of Sol. 18:24). Peter himself may have had in mind for the plural **glories** events such as Christ's transfiguration, resurrection, ascension, heavenly session, and return in majesty. Peter several times speaks of glory following suffering (4:13; 5:1, 6, 10).

1:12 / **It was revealed to them**: perhaps referring to such passages as Num. 24:17 ("I see him, but not now; I behold him, but not near. A star will come out of Jacob; a scepter will rise out of Israel"); or Hab. 2:2–3 ("Then the Lord replied: 'Write down the revelation and make it plain on tablets so that a herald may run with it. For the revelation awaits an appointed time; it speaks of the end and will not prove false.' ") See also Gen. 49:1, 10; Deut. 18:15.

In the NT the verb *apokalyptein* (to reveal) always refers to a divine disclosure and never to some human communication.

Serving (*diēkonoun*, "went on ministering"): The imperfect tense suggests that the witness of the OT prophets was significant beyond their own time (Acts 3:24). Peter thus indicates yet another link uniting the two Testaments. The verb *diakonein* is used in the NT for ministry in all its forms.

That have now (*nyn*) **been told you** does not make it clear whether or not the Christian message first reached Peter's readers from lips other than his own. Peter uses two words for "now": *nyn* ("but now, by contrast") draws attention to a changed situation (as also in 2:10, 25; 3:21). The other term, *arti* ("at the present time"), occurs in 1:6, 8.

Preached the gospel … by the Holy Spirit: The early church trusted the Spirit to inspire and to authenticate the preaching of the gospel (Acts 1:8; 5:32; 1 Cor. 2:4; 1 Thess. 1:5; Heb. 2:4).

Even angels: Contrary to popular belief, the Bible suggests that angels are neither all-knowing (Mark 13:32; Eph. 3:10) nor altogether superior to believers (1 Cor. 6:3; Heb. 1:14; 2:16).

Long: *Epithymein* is used of intense desire, for good or ill. The present tense implies that even now the angels are eagerly interested in the unfolding of God's salvation plan, and then still do not know all that there is to know about it.

To look into (*parakypsai*): lit. to bow the head sideways (in order to look at something more carefully). The word is used first of Peter and then of Mary bending down to peer intently into the empty tomb on Easter morning (Luke 24:12; John 20:5, 11).

§4 The Believers' Response in Conduct (1 Pet. 1:13–16)

1:13 / Do the readers now appreciate the magnificence of God's far-reaching salvation plan in which they have been caught up? Then their response has to be a wholehearted commitment to their new life in Christ. They are to **prepare** their **minds for action**, that is, they must put away any distractions which would hinder their growth in grace and their being available to carry forward God's work of salvation in whatever way he may indicate.

The Greek is literally "gird up the loins of your mind" (as KJV), a vivid metaphor of the Eastern worker prepared for action, having hitched up his flowing robe so as not to be impeded. The people of Israel had been told to celebrate the Passover in this fashion, to show that they were ready to go forward (Exod. 12:11). This event may well be at the back of Peter's mind, for exodus symbolism underlies the whole of this section (vv. 13–21). There is a promised land ahead!

The preparation of mind that applies to the Christian believer does not mean engaging in some narrow or specialized intellectual activity (no academic degrees are required for progress in the Christian life). Peter is referring to a Christ-centered attitude of mind that shapes and directs personal conduct. To this end, believers are to **be self-controlled** (lit. to be sober), by which Peter here means more than the avoidance of drunkenness (rebuked in 4:3). The disciplined behavior to which Christians are called entails having a steady, balanced attitude, not one given to intoxication by some passing enthusiasm or novel fad. Discipline in the Christian life is just as essential as in any other walk of life where success depends upon a determined single-minded commitment.

Besides admonishing his readers of the need for single-mindedness and discipline in their daily lives, Peter tells them how to view the future. **Set your hope fully on the grace to be given you when Jesus Christ is revealed**. One particular plus of the Christian life is hope—in the rich and solid sense of that term in the NT—which Peter has in effect been expounding throughout verses 3–12. Because of Jesus Christ, believers have every reason to look forward to the future with total confidence. They may well have to face trials and tribulations—as Peter's readers certainly were at the time—but they can enjoy the complete assurance that in God's hands life has a wonderful purpose. Nothing can deflect God from fulfilling his plans, and that knowledge makes any effort and training involved in discipleship amply worthwhile.

When Jesus Christ is revealed in glory at his second coming, God's plan of salvation will be fully realized, making it abundantly clear that **the grace** being continuously brought to the believer day by day has proved utterly sufficient at every stage of the individual Christian's development (2 Cor. 12:9).

1:14 / Believers are to be **as obedient children**, that is, according to the Semitic idiom behind the Greek, they are to have the characteristics of obedience ingrained, so to speak, in their very being. Obedience to God is to be the motivation behind every action, in the small and everyday matters of life as well as in the great issues—for who knows when some affair, small to our way of thinking, is going to turn out to mean a major change of direction in God's scheme of things. Great doors on little hinges swing.

Peter constantly reiterates the fundamental importance of the Christian duty of obedience. At this point in his letter, the writer relates obedience to the change in attitude which the turn-around of conversion brings. **Do not conform** (Rom. 12:2) **to the evil desires you had when you lived in ignorance**. In their pre-conversion days, when they **lived in ignorance** of God and of his laws, their whole manner of life was governed by their sensual nature, unyielded to God. Now they are no longer to allow this former unspiritual influence to dominate their day-to-day actions. The way Peter words this demand implies two things: first, that under the new lordship of Christ it is possible to live wholly for God; but, second, at present his readers, or at least some of them, are in danger of slipping back into their old ways, and that amounts to leaving God out of account. Peter's language echoes the exodus situation, when the people of God were told to repudiate any pagan lifestyle, whether Egyptian (behind them) or Canaanite (ahead of them), and to obey their Lord's summons to a life of holiness (Lev. 18:2–4).

1:15 / **But . . . as he who has called you is holy, so be holy in all you do.** The character of believers is to be radically different from what it was in their pre-conversion days, for the new spiritual life bestowed upon them as a consequence of their new birth (1:3) is of God—and he is the Holy One. The new people of God have been called not to follow some abstract list of rules of conduct, but to something far more fundamental. They are to express God's nature in all their activities and relationships (cf. 2:21; 4:1), for it is through the witness of Christian lives of moral integrity that God will make himself known to unbelievers in general.

1:16 / Peter's injunction is not of his own creating. He is drawing attention to the teaching of Scripture, which plainly lays down the command **"Be holy, because I am holy."** This is a straight quotation from Leviticus 11:44–45 (the words are repeated in the two verses, which in itself underlines their importance in God's mind), and in that OT context we are told that God's demand for holiness in his people is based upon the fact that it is he who has redeemed them. God's historic rescue of his people from slavery at the exodus foreshadowed his spiritual deliverance of them from sin. In both events, life for those redeemed was to be intrinsically different in future.

Additional Notes   §4

1:13 / **Be self-controlled** (*nēphontes*): "roll up your spiritual sleeves." The verb *nēphein*, to be sober, calm, circumspect, is used twice more in this letter (4:7, "be clear-minded in prayer"; 5:8, "be on the alert for the devil").

Grace to be given: The NIV rendering could suggest a special moment of grace at the second coming, but the Greek verb *pheromenēn* is a present participle, implying the continuous flow of grace that bears (the verb *pherein* means "to carry") the believer's spiritual progress day by day, a process culminating at the revelation of the returning glorified Christ.

1:14 / **Obedient children**: lit. "children of obedience," a common Semitism which points to a particular characteristic; e.g. 2 Sam. 7:10, "children of wickedness" (KJV) = "wicked people" (NIV). The Semitism appears elsewhere in the NT (as in Luke 16:8; John 12:36; Eph. 2:2–3; 1 Thess. 5:5), for while Greek is the language of the NT, most of the writers come from a background of Judaism. In this short letter Peter frequently stresses the vital importance of obedience to God (1:2, 14, 22; 2:13, 18; 3:1, 5, 6; 4:17; 5:5).

Do not conform (*mē syschēmatizomenoi*): The negative *mē* with a present participle (as here) frequently functions in the NT as an imperative (1 Pet. 2:18; 3:1, 7–9; 4:8–10; Rom. 12:9–19; Eph. 4:2; 5:19–21; Col. 3:16; Heb. 13:5), reproducing the rabbinic Hebrew practice of employing participles to express rules of conduct. See D. Daube, "Participles and Imperatives in 1 Peter," in Selwyn, pp. 463–88.

Evil desires (*epithymia*, longing, in good or bad sense): a favorite word with Peter (2:11; 4:2, 3; 2 Pet. 1:4; 2:10, 18; 3:3), but always with its negative meaning. The expression can characterize Gentile behavior (Rom. 1:24; Eph. 2:3; 4:22; 1 Thess. 4:5) and corresponds to the rabbinical "evil inclination." See E. F. F. Bishop, *Apostles of Palestine: The Local Background of the New Testament Church* (London: Lutterworth Press, 1958), p. 162.

Ignorance in Jewish terminology meant more than a lack of knowledge. It characterized those who did not know the true God. The choice of word may imply that many of Peter's readers were from a pagan background (cf. 1:18; 2:10, 25; 4:3), but on at least one occasion he brought the same charge against Jews (Acts 3:17).

1:15 / **As he who called you is holy** (*ton kalesanta hymas hagion*): The verb *kalein*, to call, is used several more times by Peter (2:9, 21; 3:9; 5:10; 2 Pet. 1:3), all stemming from God's original summons to be a pilgrim (1:1; see also commentary on 2:9). The phrase here can be rendered "as it is the Holy One [a frequent divine title in the OT] who called you." Basically, the meaning of "holy" is "separate," but with the emphasis positively on separation *to* God and his service rather than negatively *from* sin and the world. The NT often calls Christians "saints" (lit. "holy ones"), and in 1 Pet. 2:9 the company of believers is described as "a holy nation."

In all you do (*en pasē anastrophē genēthēte*): Peter's frequent use of *anastrophē*, manner of life, life-style (also 1:18; 3:1, 2, 16; 2 Pet. 2:7; 3:11), or the corresponding verb (1 Pet. 1:17; 2 Pet. 2:18), emphasizes the importance of the Christian's everyday conduct in the world. On *anastrephō* and *anastrophē*, see *NIDNTT*, vol. 3, pp. 933–35; *TDNT*, vol. 7, pp. 715–17.

1:16 / **It is written**: The formula often introduces a direct quotation, this time from Lev. 11:44 or 45 (or Lev. 19:2; the same words recur, and Lev. 20:7 also is close). Apart from more or less clear allusions to passages in the OT, there are eight other direct quotations, in 1:24–25; 2:6, 7, 8, 22; 3:10–12; 4:18; 5:5. Peter takes up proof-texts from Scripture to validate his teaching, to demonstrate that he is not expressing his own ideas but passing on divine teaching.

§5　Remember the Cost of Your Salvation (1 Pet. 1:17–21)

1:17 / Following the example of their Master, who addressed his Father as *Abba* (Mark 14:36), Christians have learned to **call on** God as **a Father** (Rom. 8:19; Gal. 4:6). But such an approach commits anyone claiming that family relationship to expect fatherly discipline. In a Jewish family, the father's word was law, and this is the aspect of the intimate title of **Father** that Peter brings out. After all, God as God is in the position of supreme authority, and as such is the one **who judges** (Heb. 12:5). Yet he will do this **impartially**, without favoritism in the family, and, as only God could, with the full knowledge and understanding of all the facts. He makes no distinction, whether on grounds of religion (Rom. 2:10–11), nationality (Acts 10:34–35), status (Gal. 2:6; Eph. 6:9; Col. 3:25), or wealth (James 2:1–4).

But as far as Christians are concerned, there is one major difference. As believers, they have accepted that the Lord Jesus Christ died for their sins. He bore the penalty. So, for Christians, the judgment of sin is past. It has been dealt with on Calvary. Nevertheless, Christians still have to face what Paul describes as the judgment seat of Christ (2 Cor. 5:10). There, the question to be decided concerns not sin but what men and women have made of their lives since they became Christians. The Father **judges each** individual's **work**. The significance of the singular **work** is that God judges each believer according to the whole scope and character of the life lived, whether it was inspired by the fundamental principle of faith, or by self-interest (Matt. 25:31–46).

In the light of their special relationship with God, it follows that believers are to live **as strangers here** in the present world (for their true home is in heaven), and **in reverent fear**, since their prime responsibility is to their heavenly Father. This is not the fear of cowardice or slavery, nor a self-concerned fear of death or punishment, but the proper esteem of an obedient and happy child secure in a close and warm relationship with a much admired Father (Rom. 8:15).

1:18 / The cost of establishing such a relationship with God has been anything but cheap. Nor can it ever be calculated in terms of **perishable things such as silver or gold,** for they belong only to this material world and have nothing to do with eternal values. Peter's reference to silver and gold as **perishable** in comparison with the blood of a sacrifice is remarkable, since in the literal sense the opposite is true. But the very boldness of the unexpected expression brings out the eternal character of the sacrifice of the Lord Jesus Christ.

The redemption wrought by Christ was not the result of a business transaction involving the exchange of money. Nor is it necessary to debate, as did some of the early church fathers, to whom payment was made. That question does not arise, for we have here simply a commercial metaphor—which is still in use: "The victim sold his life dearly."

The effect of Christ's redemptive work is to deliver men and women from their past, which Peter describes as an **empty way of life,** and one that has been inherited, **handed down . . . from your forefathers**. The latter five words represent one word in the Greek, *patroparadotos,* and Peter seems to be the first Christian writer to use it. The term refers to a traditional religious way of life. When we bear in mind how very highly the ancient world esteemed *patroparadotos,* enduring and revered family religious traditions, the dramatic weight of Peter's reference to **empty** (*mataios*) **way of life** is brought home, for the significance of *mataios* is "vain and useless idolatry." The shackles of long-established religious traditions lie shattered, not because Christianity is a rival competitor but as a direct result of the liberation brought about by Jesus. Men and women can rejoice in a totally new life in Christ.

1:19 / The price of redemption is nothing less than **the precious blood of Christ,** that is, his sacrificial death upon the cross. That death fulfilled the meaning of the Passover sacrifice, which demanded **a lamb without blemish or defect**. The sacrifice of an animal, however perfect physically, could never in practice have taken away the sin of human beings. The two, animal and human, are not in the same class of creation. Furthermore, sin is a matter not of physique but of morality. Only another human being, and one who was perfect in every way, could match the need of the human race. But animal sacrifice could at least offer a picture of what was required, and this was the purpose of the OT ritual —until in the fullness of time, God sent his Son into the world (Gal. 4:4–5).

As if to make the association crystal clear, the NT not only likens the Son of God to **a lamb without blemish or defect**, the required standard of the Passover animal (Exod. 12:5), but also reveals that Jesus has the *title* of Lamb (John 1:29, 36; and 28 times in the book of Revelation). Paul unequivocally identifies Christ as "our Passover" (1 Cor. 5:7). Only the blood of the spotless Son of God could ever be sufficient to deal with the problem of sin (Heb. 9:11–14; Rev. 5:9) and thus pay the price of redemption.

1:20 / The divine preparation of the perfect sacrifice had already been made **before the creation of the world**: it was no afterthought hastily produced in order to remedy a human situation that had gone unexpectedly wrong. The Son of God **was chosen before** the world came into being, and the course of his earthly life was foreordained (Acts 4:28). Even Jesus' violent death on the cross was no unfortunate accident but part and parcel of God's controlling purpose. Peter's generation is privileged to be living **in these last times**, at the momentous stage in the unfolding of God's salvation plan that has culminated in the coming of God's Messiah. He **was revealed**, Peter tells his readers, **for your sake**. The purpose of Christ's coming into the world was to benefit their lives individually and eternally.

1:21 / Those benefits of personal salvation have been bestowed upon believers solely on account of what God has done in Christ in raising him **from the dead** and giving him glory. The resurrection of Jesus Christ is referred to thirty times in the NT as God's decisive work, frequently in Peter's speeches in Acts. The event of the resurrection is fundamental to the whole of Christian belief and life.

Additional Notes §5

1:17 / **You call on** (*epikaleisthe*): The verb originally meant "to name" (Acts 10:18), but it usually has the sense of "to appeal to supreme authority" (Acts 7:59; 25:11). Peter is apparently alluding to the use of the Lord's Prayer (Matt. 6:9).

Father: The scarcity of examples in Jewish literature (the Dead Sea Scrolls offer a rare instance in 1QH 9.35) suggests that Judaism in NT times was as reluctant as the OT to speak of God as an individual's Father (cf. Isa. 63:16; Jer. 3:19; Mal. 1:6). The Eastern understanding of the title "father" is well brought out in Jesus' assurance to the disciples: "Do not be afraid, little flock, for your Father has been pleased to give you the kingdom" (Luke 12:32). The comment appears, to Western minds, to confuse three different word-pictures: shepherd/sheep, father/children, king/subjects. But "father" in the East involved all three aspects of provision, intimacy, and authority.

Impartially: Peter's term *aprosōpolēmtōs* (lit. "not receiving the face") occurs only here in the NT, although the thought (which recalls 1 Sam. 16:7) often appears elsewhere: Matt. 22:16; Luke 20:21; Acts 10:34; Rom. 2:11; Gal. 2:6; Eph. 6:9; Col. 3:25; James 2:1–4, 9. The concept goes back to Deut. 10:17. See Turner, pp. 366–67.

Live your lives, *anastraphēte*, the verb corresponding to the noun *anastrophē*, manner of life, conduct. See Additional Note on 1:15.

Strangers (*paroikias*) reminds the readers of their call to the pilgrim life (1:1). They are neither to become too embroiled with worldly affairs, nor to lose sight of their true vocation. The allied term *paroikos* appears in 2:11, and both link up with the synonym *parepidēmos* in 1:1 (see Additional Note on 1:1).

Reverent fear is not the negative fear that cannot coexist with perfect love (1 John 4:18), but the wholesome attitude of adoring gratitude for One who has undisputed first place in the disciple's life.

1:18 / **Redeemed** (*elytrōthēte*, ransomed): see L. Morris, *The Apostolic Preaching of the Cross* (London: Tyndale Press, 3rd ed., 1965), pp. 9–59; V. Taylor, *Jesus and His Sacrifice* (London: Macmillan, 1937), pp. 99–105; *TDNT*, vol. 4, pp. 328–56; *NIDNTT*, vol. 3, pp. 177–221; Turner, pp. 105–7. The Greek verb corresponds to the Hebrew *gā'al*, "to recover and restore a person or object to its original legitimate position" (payment is not essential to the concept). The "Recoverer of Israel" is a divine title invoked in the seventh of the Eighteen Benedictions of Judaism. See Daube, *Exodus Pattern*, pp. 27–29.

Silver or gold: Another echo of the exodus story, but a contrast. Unlike the exodus from Egypt, the redemption wrought by Jesus did not involve worldly valuables (see Exod. 3:22; Ps. 105:37). A further redemption, beyond the exodus period, is already in the prophetical mind, for

Isa. 52:3 declares "You were sold for nothing, and *without money* you will be redeemed."

Handed down . . . from your forefathers is one word in the Greek, *patroparadotos*, and is applied in particular to traditional pagan religious practices. See W. C. van Unnik, "The Critique of Paganism in 1 Peter 1:18," in *Neotestamentica et Semitica*, ed. E. E. Ellis and M. Wilcox (Edinburgh: T. & T. Clark, 1969), pp. 129–42.

1:19 / The precious blood of Christ, a lamb . . . : The two concepts of the Suffering Servant and the Lamb are also brought together in 2:21–25, where the Servant-Lamb is identified with the Shepherd of Israel (so too in Rev. 7:17). In Isa. 49:10 the Servant is distinguished from the Shepherd, who is God himself. On **blood** as a means of redemption, see Eph. 1:7; Heb. 9:12, 22; Rev. 1:5; 5:9; A. M. Stibbs, *The Meaning of the Word "Blood" in Scripture* (London: InterVarsity Press, 1947); *TDNT*, vol. 1, pp. 172–76; *NIDNTT*, vol. 1, pp. 220–26.

Precious (*timios*; also used in 2 Pet. 1:4) recalls the related verb *timan* (twice in 2:17), and the noun *timē* (1:7; 2:7; 3:7; 2 Pet. 1:17), all of which have the twofold meaning of costly (in value) and highly esteemed, held in honor. The English word *precious* derives from the Latin *pretium*, price.

Lamb: On the NT background of sacrificial lambs in Judaism, see Edersheim, *Life and Times*, vol. 1, pp. 342–45.

Without blemish (*amōmos*) **or defect** (*aspilos*): Freedom of physical flaw of any kind (*amōmos*) was the requirement for acceptable sacrificial lambs in general (Lev. 22:19–25), although Peter's reference is to the particular lamb of the Passover (Exod. 12:5). The term *aspilos* implies freedom from sin, i.e., without, so to speak, *inner* blemish. The two words, which appear again in 2 Pet. 3:14, could be roughly translated together as "perfect outside and inside." On *aspilos*, see Turner, p. 483.

1:20 / Chosen (*proegnōsmenos*, foreknown; see Turner, pp. 178–79) **before the creation** (*katabolē*, foundation, lit. laying down) **of the world:** "Seven things were already in being before creation, among which is King Messiah, of whom the Psalmist [Ps. 72:17] said, 'Thy name is for ever' " (*Midrash Proverbs* 67:3). Peter without hesitation applies this messianic teaching in Judaism directly to Jesus.

Was revealed: lit. made visible, i.e., at the incarnation. The expression implies the preexistence of Christ (John 1:1; 17:24; Phil. 2:6–8; Col. 1:18; cf. 1 Pet. 1:11).

1:21 / God . . . raised him from the dead and glorified him finds an echo in rabbinic thought: "He quickens the dead, and he gave a share of his glory to Elijah so that he also revived the dead" (*Numbers Rabbah* 15.13).

Faith and hope are closely associated because true faith includes a confident waiting on God and on what he has in store for the future.

1:22 / The readers, **by obeying the truth** as revealed in Jesus, have accepted the Redeemer's work of salvation as personal for each of them as individuals. By that obedience, Peter tells them, **you have purified yourselves**. The use of a perfect participle in the Greek here for **purified** implies a past action with its effects extending into the future. The believers' acceptance of Christ as Savior has the consequence that Jesus' holy life is now within them. Furthermore, this new spiritual life is constantly prompting believers to grow in grace and in the knowledge of the Lord (2 Pet. 3:18), that is, to grow more Christlike in moral purity. This they achieve by continuing to obey God's word in their day-to-day conduct (Rom. 6:16). That very process of purification, and so of increasingly becoming Christlike, means that their relationship to fellow believers benefits too: **so that you have sincere love for your brothers**. Without this purification, which flows from the new birth (v. 23), believers could not show genuine Christian love for other believers.

Although Peter does not spell out the point here, for his readers to **love one another deeply, from the heart**, would be an immense source of mutual encouragement to stand together in the face of persecution.

1:23–25 / The expression and development of Christian love are possible because believers **have been born again, not of** (*ek*, denoting source) **perishable seed**, as in human procreation to mortal life, **but of imperishable**, for the seed in the latter case is divine and therefore eternal. Christians are those who now live in a new world, on another plane. They have become members of a family that does not die.

In his earlier reference to the new birth (1:3), Peter described it as the gift of God (John 1:13; 3:3), a gift released to believing human beings through the resurrection of Jesus Christ.

Here Peter speaks of the new birth being brought about **through** (*dia*, agent) **the living and enduring word of God**, whether oral as in preaching, or written as in Scripture. Furthermore, when Peter goes on to support his statement with a quotation from the OT, he cites Isaiah 40:6–8 (LXX) with a slight but pointed modification: **but the word of the *Lord* stands forever**, instead of Isaiah's "word of our *God*," thus applying the prophet's words to the Lord Jesus Christ. The application is yet further underlined by the conclusive statement: **And this is the word that was preached to you**. As the creative divine word was proclaimed by the Christian preachers who first brought the gospel to Peter's readers, so that word generated spiritual life in the men and women who accepted it. The word preached was **living and enduring**, since it not only spoke of the ever-living Christ, but also conveyed his **living and enduring** life to believing hearers.

Additional Notes   §6

1:22 / **You have purified yourselves**: Some commentators suggest that the reference is to the converts' profession of faith in baptism, a sacrament which they see as the background to the whole letter. But baptism is explicitly mentioned only once (3:21), where it relates to deliverance from the Flood. The Greek verb (*hagnizein*) is used in the OT for ritual cleansing (as in Exod. 19:10; Num. 31:23) and in the NT for moral purification (James 4:8; 1 John 3:3). The word **yourselves** here translates *psychē*, usually rendered "soul," inward spiritual nature.

The truth: When Jesus, who is the truth (John 14:6), prays for his disciples to be sanctified, he equates truth with God's word (John 17:17, 19). Peter makes a similar association in the next two verses. The Qumran community also taught the purifying nature of truth (1QS 3.6; 4.20).

Sincere (*anypokriton*) **love for your brothers**, love for fellow believers (male and female) that is open and without guile. In this sense, *anypokritos* is a freshly coined word and means the "unaffectedness" of Christian love (Rom. 12:9; 2 Cor. 6:6). See Turner, p. 479. Judaism at its best sensed the necessity for such **sincere love**: "The giving of alms is not enough. The gift to the poor must be made privately with nobody present. It must further be attended by a warmth of feeling and understanding sympathy; and it is in proportion to the kindness and love that flow from an act of charity that it draws its ethical and moral force" (b. *Sukkah* 49b). "I adjure you by the God of heaven to do truth each one to his neighbor, and to entertain love each for his brother" (T. Reuben 6:9).

Deeply is perhaps too passive a translation of *ektenōs*, which means "fervently"; from *ekteinein*, to stretch out (cf. 4:8). In Acts 12:5, prayer for Peter in prison is made with urgency (*ektenōs*).

1:23 / **Born again** (the same verb as in 1:3) **through the living and enduring word of God**: Reference to the creative power of the divine word frequently recurs in Scripture (e.g., Gen. 1:3; John 1:1–3; Phil. 2:16; 1 Thess. 2:13).

1:24 / **All men are like grass**: The contrast between the frailty and transience of all human life (**men** translates *sarx*, flesh), the product of perishable seed, and the eternal nature of the divine is underscored by a quotation from Isa. 40:6–8 LXX. This chapter in Isaiah was much used in early NT preaching (Matt. 3:3; Mark 1:3; Luke 1:68; 2:25, 30–31; 3:4–6; John 1:23; 10:11; 11:40; Acts 17:29; 28:28; Rom. 11:34; 1 Cor. 2:16; James 1:10–11; Rev. 1:5; 18:6; 22:12). See C. H. Dodd, *According to the Scriptures* (London: Nisbet, 1952), p. 84.

1:25 / **Word** is *rhēma* in this verse (twice), though *logos* is used in v. 23, but no distinction seems to be intended. See *TDNT*, vol. 4, pp. 69–136; *NIDNTT*, vol. 3, pp. 74–89, 325–37, 1078–123.

That was preached (*euangelizomenai*, to preach good news) echoes the "good tidings" of Isa. 40:9 LXX, where the same Greek word is used.

§7 *New Life Must Grow (1 Pet. 2:1–3)*

2:1 / As a realist, Peter is well aware of the human condition. So he speaks bluntly. The believer's new life in Christ has no place for any sort of misconduct, such as **all malice and all deceit, hypocrisy, envy, and slander of every kind.** (Peter's vehement threefold **all** (*pas*) is muffled when NIV translates the third *pas* differently as **every kind.**) It is a pretty comprehensive list of the ills to which the human heart is host. Believers are commanded, **Rid yourselves** of them all. The Greek, brought out in most other translations, is literally *put off*, discard, like so much old, soiled and unwanted clothing. To obey this order requires the active will of the individual concerned, for growth in the new life is a cooperative work between divine grace and the believer's determination. Neither will prove effective without the other.

The expressions of evil that Peter lists are all such as militate against Christian fellowship, the "brotherly love" (*philadelphia*) he has been stressing (1:22). One essential for spiritual development is a clear-cut break from attitudes and actions which belong to the unregenerate past; these tend to harm others. The new Christian bearing toward fellow believers is the outgoing, positive, and constructive one summarized as "brotherly love."

2:2 / In place of the destructive attitudes that must be banished by the true believer, Peter charges his readers with positive action. **Like newborn babies**, for that in the spiritual sense is what they are, having newly come to faith in Christ, they are to **crave pure spiritual milk** to foster their spiritual growth—as eagerly as newborn infants desire physical nourishment.

What Peter means by **pure spiritual milk** can be deduced from the context, which of course is not to be limited by our chapter and verse divisions, a relatively modern device. The "therefore" of 2:1 looks back to the end of chapter 1, where after a reference to "purification" (1:22) the subject is the living word of God (1:23–25). Peter and his readers would be familiar with the biblical notion that the spiritual food provided by the Scriptures (Deut. 8:3; Matt. 4:4) is pure (Ps. 12:6; 119:140; Prov. 30:5), and they appropriately likened it to milk for its life-promoting quality (Ps. 119:50, 93; Acts 20:32), especially at an early stage (1 Cor. 3:1–3; Heb. 5:12–14). In any event, the **milk** could well be taken as an allusion (yet again) to the exodus scenario and the believer's entry into the promised land, "flowing with milk and honey," the first food for those embarking upon the new spiritual life as pilgrims.

For the believer to advance no further than an initial commitment to Christ will in the end result at best in a spiritual monstrosity, just as it does on the physical level in the case of an infant that fails to develop in body. At worst, a failure to grow spiritually spells death to faith and a triumph for the powers of evil.

Growth is a sign of vigorous health. Physical growth is naturally limited by age. Spiritual growth **in salvation** goes on forever, in this world and in the next, for there can be no limit to the development of the soul in the fullness of what God intends by "salvation."

2:3 / **Now that you have tasted that the Lord is good** is virtually a straight quotation from Psalm 34:8, a psalm much in Peter's mind (see 3:10–12). The citation is highly appropriate to crown his comments, for **good** translates the Greek *chrēstos*, a play on the title Christ (*Christos*). In common with other NT writers, Peter interprets **Lord** in OT texts as referring to Jesus Christ, and in v. 4 he makes this explicit. Furthermore, the meaning of *chrēstos* is richer than "kindness" (Luke 6:35; Rom. 2:4; Eph. 4:32). An "easy gentle relationship" (Matt. 11:30) paraphrases the sense intended here. How can new believers, who have now experienced the tenderness of divine love when they came into contact with Jesus Christ for the first time, ever want to slide back into their old way of life? But it will be only too easy to do so unless they continue to grow in the faith and the knowledge of their Lord (2 Pet. 3:18). Such development will not follow automatically. They must play their part by taking in spiritual food.

It will not have taken the early church long to see an even deeper meaning in the choice of vocabulary, for *chrēstos* is the regular word also for wholesome and pleasant food (Luke 5:39). An allusion to the Lord's Supper would soon have occurred to them (John 6:35). But feeding on Christ the living Word through the inspired written Scriptures is doubtless what Peter has primarily in mind.

Additional Notes   §7

2:1 / **Rid yourselves,** *apotithēmi*: lit. to put off from oneself as a garment (Acts 7:58), or metaphorically in the ethical sense (Rom. 13:12; Eph. 4:22, 25; Col. 3:8; Heb. 12:1; James 1:21). The Greek verb used by Peter is in the aorist tense, pointing to a deliberate single action, a clean cut with the past. The *fourth*-century evidence (Cyril of Jerusalem) for the practice of changing clothes during the service of baptism as a sign of the new life can hardly be in view given the dating of Peter's letter, despite the suggestions of some commentators.

Malice (*kakia*, malignity) may be intended to head the list of specific examples ("such as deceit, hypocrisy"). This would bring the thought close to the charge of "hatred of the human race" which was regularly levied against Christians at the time of the Neronic persecutions (Tacitus, *Annals* 15.44). Peter's letter was probably written about this date.

Deceit (*dolos*): in thought, and then in word and action; guile, in order to gain advantage over another by unfair means.

Hypocrisy (*hypokrisis*): acting a part, concealing a real motive; saying one thing and meaning another (Matt. 15:7–8).

Envy (*phthonos*): ever the source of trouble in religious companies (Mark 10:41; Luke 22:24).

Slander (*katalalia*), from *kata* (down) and *lalein* (to chatter): disparagement, malicious gossip ("to talk down someone").

2:2 / **Like newborn babies:** The use of such a term would make a special impression on readers with a Jewish background. The tenderness of the Jewish family bond is reflected in the colorful expressions used to describe each stage of child-life. Apart from general Hebrew terms like *ben* (son of) and *bath* (daughter of), the Jews used at least eight other words to depict various stages of growth, such as newly born (Isa. 9:6), suckling (Isa. 53:2), weaned (at the end of two years; Gen. 21:8), sexually mature (Isa. 7:14), ripe to choose (Isa. 62:5). See Edersheim, *Sketches of Jewish Social Life*, pp. 103–21.

A man was made a proselyte to Judaism by a threefold process: by circumcision, by immersion in water, and by the presentation of an offering in the temple. In 1 Peter, these three elements are again seen: "Rid yourselves of all malice . . . like newborn babes" would correspond to circumcision, a symbolic ridding oneself of a physical token that might be taken to represent impurity and evil; the water of baptism is mentioned in 3:21; a temple offering in 2:5. See Moule, *Worship in the New*

Testament, p. 52. Peter's thought here is rather that suggested by 1 Cor. 14:20, "In regard to evil (*kakia*, malice, as in 1 Pet. 2:1) be infants, but in your thinking be adults."

Pure (*adolos*, the only occurrence of the word in the NT): unadulterated; the reverse form of *dolos*, translated *deceit* in v. 1, and so also perhaps a play on words.

For **spiritual** (*logikos*), see Turner, p. 497; *NIDNTT*, vol. 3, pp. 1081, 1105, 1118–19; *TDNT*, vol. 4, pp. 142–43.

For **milk** (*gala*), see Turner, pp. 289–90; *NIDNTT*, vol. 2, pp. 268–69, 277; *TDNT*, vol. 1, pp. 645–47. Milk is included in the eschatological symbolism of food in Joel 3:18; cf. Isa. 55:1.

2:3 / **Good** (*chrēstos*, kind, gracious) easily lends itself to a pun on *Christos*, Christ, since the two words were popularly pronounced in a similar way—since today in modern Greek. There is an apt parallel to Peter's words in a late first-century collection of Jewish-Christian hymns celebrating the union of Christ with the Christian: "A cup of milk was presented to me, and I drank it in the sweet graciousness of the Lord" (*Odes of Solomon* 19:1). The English word "good" is too general a term —as it is also rendered in John 10:11, where "I am the *good* Shepherd" translates *kalos*, more fittingly rendered "attractive." On *chrēstos*, see Turner, p. 247.

The words **you have tasted that the Lord is good** are from Ps. 34:8. This psalm in its Septuagint form is much quoted in the NT, and in the early church it was evidently a favorite source for proof-texts concerning Christ and his life and work. In the following verse (2:4), the words "as you come to him" allude to Ps. 34:5; Ps. 34:12–16 is cited by Peter in 3:10–12. The verb *loutroun*, to redeem, pay ransom (Ps. 34:22) occurs in 1 Pet. 1:18 and is a key term in NT thought; cf. also awesome fear of the Lord (Ps. 34:7, 9, 11; 1 Pet. 1:17; 2:17); lions lack, but not the godly (Ps. 34:10; 1 Pet. 4:11); afflictions of the righteous (Ps. 34:19; 1 Pet. 1:6); praise of God through believers (Ps. 34:1; 1 Pet. 4:11). In the rest of the NT, Ps. 34:8 is reflected in Heb. 6:4–5; Ps. 34:10 in Luke 1:53; 6:24–25; Ps. 34:13 in James 1:26; Ps. 34:15 in John 9:31; Ps. 34:19 in 2 Cor. 1:5; 2 Tim. 3:11; Ps. 34:20 in John 19:36.

§8   *The Stone—Living and Deadly (1 Pet. 2:4–8)*

Peter now turns from exhorting his readers to conduct that befits their life within the believing community to inviting them to consider the nature of that community which Christ has brought into existence.

2:4 / The shift to **stone** from the figure of "milk" (v. 2) is unexpected and seemingly without reason. But for a Jewish reader there is a natural succession of ideas in this passage—not milk : stone, but the Hebraic one of babes : house. A helpful illustration is in Genesis 16:2. Sarai gives her maidservant Hagar to Abram in the hope that "I shall obtain children by her" (RSV). The Hebrew is literally "that I may be built through her." To obtain children is to become a house (as in "house of David"); to become a house is to be built. So Peter's juxtaposition of the themes of birth and building is genuinely Hebraic, and the subsequent reference to "living stones" (v. 5) a perfectly natural one in Jewish thought.

The wording of Psalm 34 may still be in Peter's mind when he continues, **As you come** (*proserchomai*) **to him**, for Psalm 34:5 (in the LXX, which NT writers normally use) reads "Come (*proserchomai*) to him and be enlightened," the last term also being echoed by Peter in verse 9, "his wonderful light." That aside, the Greek verb is highly appropriate, for it is the one used of approaching God in worship or in priestly service (Heb. 4:16; 7:25; 10:1, etc.), to which subject Peter is about to refer (v. 5).

The living Stone—rejected by men but chosen by God introduces the theme of these verses: the "stone," as relating to Christ, and to those who accept him, and to those who reject him.

All three Synoptic Gospels record that Jesus applied Psalm 118:22 to himself: "The stone the builders rejected has become the capstone" (Matt. 21:42; Mark 12:10; Luke 20:17). Peter quotes the Psalmist's words in Acts 4:11, as well as here and in verse 7. A second christological application of the stone theme is based on the foundational cornerstone of Isaiah 28:16, cited by Peter in verse 6; it recurs in Paul (1 Cor. 3:11; Eph. 2:20; cf. Rom. 10:11). A third application is made on the basis of Isaiah 8:14, quoted by Peter in verse 8 (and also found in Paul, in Rom. 9:33), and concerns those who reject God's choice and so find that the **Stone** is to them one that "causes men to stumble and a rock that makes them fall."

To term Christ a **stone** that is **living**, and to go on to use similar language of his followers (v. 5), is a startling paradox, for a stone is anything but alive. Yet the symbolism is perfectly understandable in the light of Christ's resurrection and the life-giving power that flows from it (1:3). Christ was **rejected by men**, a reaction foretold long ago (Ps. 118:22); however, the last word was not a human verdict but in accordance with the divine will and purpose. Christ the living **Stone** was **chosen by God and precious to him**, again as foretold (Isa. 28:16). Whatever the appearance to the contrary at a particular time, the clear implication for Christians facing an antagonistic world is that their God is calmly and surely in complete control of every situation. He has foreseen it all and prepared for it. Ultimately his perfect will is going to prevail, and that good and loving will is the believers' confidence for a future that also includes God's purpose for them.

2:5 / You also are **like living stones**, and so possess a family likeness to Jesus Christ, a likeness that was brought into being by rebirth into the divine family through the power of Christ's resurrection (1:3). These **living stones** are not left uselessly scattered about, forgotten. God has a grand design for them. This is none other than their **being built into a spiritual house**. Two coincidental stages are in view here. Each believer is **being built** up personally in the faith, as individual spiritual growth takes place. At the same time, each believer is being fashioned to fit into a predetermined and unique place in the overall divine blueprint. Thus each is **being built** into and made part of God's house.

Although Peter is making use of OT "stone" symbolism, was he prompted by recollecting some words of the Baptist? John had bluntly warned the Pharisees and Sadducees that salvation was not a matter of having the right family tree: "I tell you that out of these *stones* God can raise up children for Abraham" (Matt. 3:9).

The **house** is to be no ordinary dwelling but a temple, for it exists for the sole purpose of worshiping God. In it **a holy priesthood** is to be constantly **offering spiritual sacrifices acceptable to God through Jesus Christ**. Peter implies a pointed contrast with the Israel of the ot. They had a house of God, the temple in Jerusalem, but that was built of dead stones. We Christians, Peter is saying, are a **spiritual house** of God, built with **living stones**. The Israelites approached God through a special priesthood, composed only of Levites. Now all Christians, claims Peter, are that **holy priesthood**. Levites offered up material sacrifices; Christian sacrifices are purely **spiritual sacrifices**. Peter is taking over the language of Exodus 19:6 ("You will be for me a kingdom of priests and a holy nation"), and he will make the allusion clear in verse 9.

Peter's call for **spiritual sacrifices** was by no means novel. The subject is mentioned in the ot. The letter to the Hebrews is devoted to the argument that the perfect and conclusive sacrifice of Jesus Christ has rendered the ot sacrificial system obsolete. There are still **sacrifices** for Christians to make, but they are **spiritual** in nature. Examples are mentioned by other nt writers, such as the sacrifice of praise (Heb. 13:15), prayer (Rev. 5:8), self-consecration (Rom. 12:1; Phil. 2:17), benevolence (Rom. 15:27; Heb. 13:16), and giving (2 Cor. 9:12; Phil. 4:18). Such sacrifices are **acceptable to God**, not on account of any merit in the one who offers them, but because they are made **through Jesus Christ**, that is, on the grounds of his perfect sacrifice and in response to the prompting of his Spirit, i.e., "in his name."

2:6 / Peter buttresses his argument with a series of ot quotations from Isaiah 28:16 (v. 6), Psalm 118:22 (v. 7), and Isaiah 8:14 (v. 8), all of which were widely used in the early church as part of the "rejected stone" typology. Paul, for example, also mentions the two Isaiah passages (Rom. 9:32–33; 1 Cor. 3:11), though not Psalm 118:22.

Peter applies Isaiah's prophecy concerning the **cornerstone** to Christ. It is noteworthy that a cornerstone controls the design of the building and holds the structure together. In the nt, the symbol of the foundation stone is used both of Christ (1 Cor. 3:11) and of the apostles and prophets (Eph. 2:20). But only Christ combines the functions of both foundation stone and cornerstone, the former pointing to the total dependence of the church of believers upon Christ, and the latter to the interrelationship and unity of believers with one another through their Lord.

2:7 / **Now to you who believe, this stone is precious**. Christians by faith have their eyes opened to recognize the true worth and significance of the stone symbolism, for it indicates the fundamental and vital place of Jesus Christ in their lives. Without his sacrifice and resurrection there would be no spiritual life for them now, and no future beyond the present world. All is completely dependent upon who Jesus is and upon what he has done.

To believers, therefore, **this stone is precious** (*timē*, worthy of honor). However true this may be, the NIV paraphrase is surprising (even if it does follow KJV, RSV, and even Phillips). Commentators rightly complain that this is not what the Greek means! The Greek says nothing about "this stone" here, but runs *hymin oun hē timē tois pisteuousin*, literally "to you believers [is] the honor." This balances the thought of the *dishonor* that Peter indicates in this passage is the lot of unbelievers. Why should translators shy away from suggesting that the people of God are to be honored? Believers have been bought with the price (*timē*, 1 Cor. 6:20) of the precious (*timios*) blood of Christ (1 Pet. 1:19). They are his and are due to share both in the family inheritance (1:4) and in the divine family likeness. To be sure, the honor is due not to any individual's status, worthiness, or achievements, but it is solely the consequence of being made a member of God's family through Jesus Christ. That is the glorious prospect of **you who believe**.

But to those who do not believe, the outlook, if they continue on that slope of unbelief, is perilous in the extreme. To such, the stone, and what it represents in the person of Jesus Christ, will result in their inevitable doom.

At the climax of his ministry, Jesus applied this verse cited by Peter (Ps. 118:22) to himself when he faced the hostility of the scribes and Pharisees (Matt. 21:42; Mark 12:10–11; Luke 20:17). No doubt mindful of his Lord's use of the psalmist's words, Peter repeated them in Jerusalem in addressing the Sanhedrin, the Jewish supreme court, after the healing of the crippled beggar (Acts 4:11). In the Jerusalem setting, the **builders** rejecting the stone were none other than the Jewish religious leaders. They had not simply failed to recognize the Lord's Messiah standing in their midst, but they had by their words and actions disowned him. Yet by so doing they passed judgment upon themselves. *They* stood rejected in God's sight.

2:8 / Such condemnation is the doom of all of any clime or age who follow the Jewish rulers' example and **disobey the message** of the gospel. For them, Christ proves to be, in the words of Isaiah 8:14, **a stone that causes men to stumble and a rock that makes them fall**, a fate **which is also what they were destined for.** The last clause has caused difficulties, since it appears to suggest that God has foreordained some people, whatever their own desires might be, to be unbelievers, and that as such they are already predestined to be condemned. That thought, needless to say, fits ill with the NT perception of a God of love (John 3:16), or for that matter with the OT concept of God as perfectly just (Gen. 18:25). Peter's meaning is that stumbling to disaster is the inevitable consequence of persistently refusing to obey Christ. If any man or woman repudiates the one who is, after all, the Lord of *life*, and persists in such a rebellious attitude, the destination must be the opposite of life, that is, *death*. It is their choice, not some out-of-character forward-planning by God, which determines their end.

Additional Notes   §8

2:4 / The apparent disparate succession of "milk" (v. 2) by **stone** tempted one scholar to speculate that the passage is meant to be read against the background of Ephesus. The image of Artemis in the great temple there was evidently a meteorite (Acts 19:35). But the goddess, whose cult was widespread throughout Asia Minor (Acts 19:27), and so doubtless well known to Peter's readers, was regularly represented as a queenly figure with multiple breasts, capable of nourishing all her devotees with her milk. Instead of a dead stone image, Peter is saying, Christians come to a living Christ, who feeds them with "pure spiritual milk" (v. 2; Beare, p. 75). Attractive though it appears, Beare's suggested foray into exotic fields is unnecessary (see commentary).

When Peter refers to his readers as "drawing near" (**As you come** translates a present participle, *proserchomenoi*), the expression again points to their being recent converts, since it is strikingly similar to the frequent technical term *qrb* in the Dead Sea Scrolls, used for "drawing near (i.e., entering) the community" (1QS 6.16, 19, 22, etc.).

The **living Stone** could have possible connections with the name Peter ("Rock"). Confession of faith made Peter a rock, or part of the Rock (the name is given with explicit reference to a foundation stone). But Peter is also capable of being a stumbling stone (Matt. 16:23), and of stumbling himself (Luke 22:32; cf. Luke 2:34). See C. F. D. Moule, "Some Reflections on the 'Stone-Testimonia' in Relation to the Name Peter," *NTS* 2 (1955–56), pp. 56–59. See also N. Hillyer, "Rock-Stone Imagery in 1 Peter," *TynB* 22 (1971), pp. 58–81, for OT and rabbinical background.

Rejected . . . chosen . . . precious: the vocabulary echoes that in Peter's OT quotations, Ps. 118:22 and Isa. 28:16. For **chosen**, see commentary on 1:1. **Precious** (*entimos*) is used of the centurion's slave (Luke 7:2), and by Paul of Epaphroditus (Phil. 2:29). Of related terms, *timē* occurs in 1 Pet. 1:7; 2:7; 3:7; *timios* in 1:19; and *timan* in 2:17. The theme is clearly prominent in Peter's thinking.

The soil of Palestine did not harbor any precious stones: they had to be *purchased*. Did such a thought cross the mind of early Christian preachers as they pondered Peter's letter?

2:5 / Spiritual house: The concept of the believing community as a *building* is common: the *house* of Israel (Ruth 4:11; Matt. 10:6); the Lord's *house* (Num. 12:7); *built* together to become a *dwelling* for God (Eph. 2:22); God's *house* (Heb. 3:6). In Rev. 21:3, the new Jerusalem, the beloved community, constitutes God's dwelling. The concept appears also in the Dead Sea Scrolls. The council of the Qumran community is called "a holy house for Israel, a most holy assembly for Aaron . . . a house of perfection and truth for Israel" (1QS 8.5). The related verb *oikodomein* (1 Pet. 2:5, 7) is frequent as a term meaning "to edify, build up" the people of God (Amos 9:11 LXX; Acts 9:31; Rom. 15:2; 1 Cor. 8:1). The spiritualizing of the concept of building has no bearing on the date of 1 Peter, whether it was written before or after the Jerusalem temple was destroyed in A.D. 70. Paul makes no explicit reference to that temple either, but he still employs the imagery (1 Cor. 3:16; 2 Cor. 6:16).

A holy priesthood echoes Exod. 19:6. There the entire nation of Israel is addressed. But as a consequence of the golden calf idolatry (Exod. 32:8), the priesthood was restricted to the tribe of Levi as a reward for its loyalty (Exod. 32:26). Under the new covenant introduced by Jesus Christ, the priesthood is once again the privilege of all believers.

Offering: the verb *anapherein* (lit. to carry up) is commonly used in the LXX for the offering of sacrifice, as in Gen. 22:2, 13, of the sacrifice of Isaac (James 2:21); see also Heb. 7:27; 9:28; 13:15; 1 Pet. 2:24.

Spiritual sacrifices were by no means unknown in the OT (Ps. 50:13, 14, 23; 51:17; 141:2; Isa. 1:11–17; Hos. 6:6; Mic. 6:6–8). At Qumran, since the community was cut off from the temple sacrifices made at Jerusalem, spiritual sacrifices were prominent: "An offering of lips is accounted a fragrant offering of righteousness, and perfection of way as an acceptable freewill oblation" (1QS 9.4–6). The Samaritans also offered spiritual sacrifices, for their temple on Mount Gerizim had been destroyed in the late second century B.C.: "We offer sacrifices before the Lord on the altar of prayers . . . we sanctify ourselves and praise and proclaim."

See J. Macdonald, *The Theology of the Samaritans* (London: SCM Press, 1964), p. 274.

Acceptable to God: Rom. 15:16; Phil. 4:18; 1 Tim. 2:3; Heb. 12:28; 13:15–16.

2:6 / The succession of three citations from the OT is reminiscent of the Talmudic practice of chain quotation (called *ḥāraz*, "stringing together like pearls"), originating in the synagogue. There the preacher quoted from the Pentateuch and then strung on comparable passages from the Prophets and from the Writings (Hagiographa), linked with a simple "and" but without further indication of source—as in v. 8 here. Although Peter and the other NT writers do not follow the synagogue order, their motive is similar: it is not to imply that the word of the Law needed confirmation, but to demonstrate how Scripture emphasizes the lesson by reiteration. See Edersheim, *Life & Times*, vol. 1, p. 449; Ellis, *Paul's Use of the Old Testament*, pp. 49–51; G. F. Moore, *Judaism* (Cambridge, Mass.: Harvard University Press, 1927), vol. 1, pp. 239–40.

For in Scripture it says translates *dioti periechei en graphē*, lit. "because it contains in a writing," an unusual expression. The phrase *en graphē* may not mean "in a passage of Scripture," for which other NT writers usually employ the definite article, *en tē graphē* or (plural) *en tais graphais*. But *en graphē* does occur in the LXX (e.g., 2 Chron. 2:11) with the meaning "in writing." So Peter may not be quoting directly from the Bible. Lists of proof-texts on various themes were formed in the early days of the church for the benefit of preachers. That Peter is using such a document here is supported by the fact that in Rom. 9:33 Paul also has Peter's two Isaiah quotations (Isa. 28:16; 8:14), yet both apostles cite *an identical Greek text which is not that of the* LXX. The possibility that one writer quoted from the other is ruled out because Paul wrote Romans many years before 1 Peter was written (so he could not have borrowed from Peter), and for Peter to have used Romans involves the unlikely assumption that he first disentangled Paul's quotations and then added parts of Isa. 28:16 that Paul omitted, and yet not from the LXX (or from the Hebrew, for that matter). See Selwyn, pp. 163, 268–77; Dodd, *According to the Scriptures*, pp. 35, 41–43; Ellis, *Paul's Use of the Old Testament*, pp.86–91.

The **cornerstone** quotation, from Isa. 28:16, is alluded to by Paul again in 1 Cor. 3:11 and Eph. 2:20.

By the time of Justin Martyr (A.D. 100–165), "Stone" is virtually a title for Christ.

A chosen (*eklektos*) **and precious cornerstone**: Peter's citation of Isa. 28:16 does not quite follow the OT, which according to NIV reads "See, I lay a stone in Zion, a *tested* stone, a precious cornerstone for a sure foundation." The word translated *tested* is Heb. *bōḥan*, which is not passive but active, "testing" (so BDB, p. 103, who then promptly translate it as a passive, "tested"!). If Peter's *eklektos*, chosen, corresponds to the Heb. *bōḥan*, it may be that *eklektos* should read *ekklētos*, meaning "selected to judge or arbitrate on a point" (LSJ), which would express the "testing" meaning of the Hebrew—and better match Peter's other Isaiah quotation in v. 8.

At Qumran, Isa. 28:16 is applied to the council of the community (1QS 8.7–8), not to an individual. The Targum, by contrast, applied Isa. 28:16 messianically (Edersheim, *Life & Times*, vol. 2, p. 725).

Zion, strictly speaking, is a hill of Jerusalem, south of the temple and north of the Siloam quarter. In the Bible it usually is identified with the city as a whole, viewed as a religious center that often symbolizes the heavenly city (Heb. 12:22; Rev. 14:1). Peter's use of **Zion** at this point is doubly appropriate, since v. 5 has sketched the eschatological temple of worship being built from the "living stones," which are believers.

2:7 / Psalm 118, quoted here, is the last of the Hallel Psalms (Pss. 113–118), sung at the festivals of Passover, Pentecost, Tabernacles, and Dedication, and as such it is one of the most familiar and loved praise hymns in Jewish worship. "Hallel" derives from the Hebrew root *hll*, to praise, whence *Hallelujah*, "praise the Lord!"

Precious (*timē*): value (Matt. 27:9), honor (Rom. 12:10), or respect (1 Pet. 3:7). Here "honor" may be the most appropriate translation for *timē* for believers (see commentary).

Builders: The Jewish scribes laid claim to the term for themselves, according to *Targum Ps.* 118:22.

Rejected: "Israel . . . produced from their own midst their leaders, kings, priests, prophets, and princes: as it says, Out of them shall come forth the cornerstone (Jer. 2:26–27; cf. Zech. 10:4). This refers to King David, for it says, The stone which the builders rejected is become the chief cornerstone (Ps. 118:22)" (*Midrash Rabbah* 37.1 on Exod. 28:1)—which was understood to refer to David, the humble shepherd who was overlooked by his brothers yet exalted to the throne.

Capstone is the NIV translation of *kephalēn gōnias*, "extremity of the corner." The stone referred to is not necessarily at the *top*; "capstone" tends to miss the thought of a cornerstone (v. 6), a stone on the ground over which someone can trip (v. 8).

2:8 / **A stone that causes men to stumble** (*proskomma*) **and a rock that makes them fall** (*skandalon*) is from Isa. 8:14. The verse is applied to the Messiah in the Babylonian Talmud (*Sanh.* 38a). The Greek words *proskomma* and *skandalon* are virtually synonyms (see Turner, pp. 294–98; *NIDNTT*, vol. 2, pp. 705–10; *TDNT*, vol. 6, pp. 745–58; vol. 7, pp. 339–58).

It is not surprising that such a verse would find a prominent place in Peter's mind, for he would ever remember Jesus' words to him: "I tell you that you are Peter (*Petros*), and on this rock (*petra*) I will build my church" (Matt. 16:18), to be followed (when Peter sought to deflect him from the way of the cross) by the rebuke, "Get behind me, Satan! You are a stumbling block (*skandalon*) to me; you do not have in mind the things of God, but the things of men" (Matt. 16:23).

Destined: The NT nowhere teaches a rigid predestination to eternal perdition. The possibility of salvation which personal repentance turns into reality is open to all in this life; cf. Rom. 11:11, 23, regarding Israel's present unbelief, not necessarily final but still retrievable through a change of heart.

§9   The New People of God (1 Pet. 2:9–10)

2:9 / But you! With an almost audible sigh of relief, Peter turns away from contemplating the dark and inescapable lot of those who disobey God's command to believe on the Lord Jesus Christ (Acts 16:31), to consider the bright and very different prospect of believers.

Peter draws expressions from the Greek OT (LXX) which there are addressed to Israel as the people of God. The apostle is thus boldly claiming that privileged status on behalf of the Christian church of believers. It is they who are now the **chosen people** (*genos eklekton*), a phrase echoing Deuteronomy 14:2 LXX: "The Lord your God has chosen you to be his special property from all the nations on the face of the earth."

In his opening greeting, Peter addressed his readers as "elect" (*eklektois*); the same Greek word is here translated **chosen**. Now Peter adds **people**, *genos*, a term denoting race and blood relationship, and involving the idea of hereditary privilege. It is a further reminder of the new birth (1:23), whereby Christians have been brought into the divine family and thus share in all that such a relationship means (2:4–7).

Furthermore, believers are **a royal priesthood** and **a holy nation**, phrases quoted from Exodus 19:6; 23:22 LXX, which promise such a standing before God to those who are loyal to his covenant. The **priesthood** here spoken of is one applying to all Peter's readers, that is, to believers in general (not to a hierarchy of a select few set apart), as in verse 5, where Christian priestly duties have already been touched upon.

As members of **a holy nation**, all believers are *set apart* for God (the sense of **holy**), but without geographic boundaries or without being limited to particular cultures, ages, or ethnic groups. This is a worldwide, spiritual **people belonging to God** (*laos eis peripoiēsin*, lit. "a people for [his] possession," language reminiscent of such verses as Exod. 19:5; Deut. 7:6; 14:2; Mal.

3:17). Peter probably has in mind Isaiah 43:21 LXX, since that verse also goes on to refer to God's chosen people who are to tell forth his "praises" (*aretas*), the word used by Peter in the next clause: **that you may declare the praises (*aretas*) of him who called you out of darkness into his wonderful light.**

That you may declare the praises of him who called you indicates the purpose for which God has chosen his people: they are to proclaim his **praises**, *aretas*, excellencies (NASB), glorious deeds (REB), triumphs (NEB). The translations seek to express aspects of the meaning of *aretas*, which include moral worth of the divine action in bringing about salvation and the resultant worship by those who recognize and respond to what God in Christ has done for them individually and collectively. While the declaration of such praises would include the proclaiming of God's glory in preaching, the primary sense is of adoring worship by believers.

Peter reminds his readers that God has called them **out of darkness**, that is, they are called to leave the darkness due to their earlier ignorance of God (1:14), which had kept them not only from a knowledge of his character, but also from realizing the immense love he had for them and the great blessings he had in store for their eternal benefit.

The divine call is **into his wonderful light**. To Jews, **light** was a familiar image of Messiah's kingdom and spoke of the presence and active leading of God (Exod. 13:21; 14:20; Num. 6:25; Ps. 104:2). **Light** is the unexpected third element that makes a trio with the themes of *precious stones* and *priesthood* in the present chapter.

The **light** of the divine presence is often associated in Scripture with precious stones (Ezek. 1:16, 26; 10:1; Rev. 4:3, 6; 21:18–26). Whatever may be the relationship of the stones listed in Revelation 21 with the twelve stones set in the high priest's breastpiece (Exod. 28:17–20; 39:10–14), the same association of priesthood and precious stones occurs here and in verses 5 and 9.

One of the values of the precious stones in the high priest's breastpiece was their ability to reflect light, and the light most readily associated in the Jewish mind in this context would be the light of the Shekinah, the divine presence.

2:10 / The status of Peter's Christian readers is again defined, but in different terms. Formerly, before their conversion, they were **not a people**, a not-people, so to speak: those who did not count in God's program. But there has been a fundamental change: **now**, after undergoing a new spiritual birth (1:3), they have been brought into the divine family as full members.

Though once a not-people, they are now part of **the people of God**. The transformation is described yet again, this time in terms of forgiveness and reconciliation: **once you had not received mercy**, being outside the covenant of grace, **but now you have received mercy**, on account of the redeeming work of Christ (1:3).

Readers of Peter's words with a knowledge of the Jewish Scriptures would at once recognize them as a skillful selection of phrases from Hosea 1–2. For the prophet Hosea, the restoration of relationships with his estranged wife spoke of repentant Israel being brought back to God. For Christian teachers, the episode was seen as foreshadowing the admission of Gentiles into the one true church. It is perhaps surprising that such a strongly negative phrase in the Hosea passage as **not a people** was interpreted by the rabbis as referring to Israel and not to Gentiles, despite hints that God had something special in mind for the latter (as in Isa. 9:1–2; 11:10; 42:6; 49:6; 60:5–6; Mal. 1:11).

Verse 10 rounds off a passage (from v. 4) in which Peter has been spelling out the blessings, originally promised to Israel, that are now the privilege of the church of believers in Christ. The Jerusalem temple of stone is now replaced by the living stones of the new spiritual temple of believers. The priesthood, formerly limited to the tribe of Aaron and engaged in offering animal sacrifices as the means of approaching God, is now a royal priesthood shared by all believers, who enjoy direct personal access to God. They are individually able to offer spiritual sacrifices, acceptable to God because they are made through the perfect sacrifice of Christ. God's chosen people are no longer confined to the physical descendants of Abraham, the nation of Israel, but by divine decision they are now the body of Christian believers. It is not that ethnic Israel has been irrevocably rejected by God and replaced by Gentiles (Paul makes that clear in Rom. 9–11); rather, for both Jew and Gentile the divine blessings to God's people are available through Jesus the Messiah.

Additional Notes   §9

2:9 / Peter apparently has in mind Isa. 43:20–21 LXX, for he uses a string of Greek expressions from that passage: *genos eklekton,* chosen race; *laos,* people; *peripoiēsamēn,* possessed, owned; *aretas,* praises. The first of these, **a chosen people,** *genos eklekton,* is a frequent OT expression: Deut. 4:37; 7:6; 14:2; Isa. 41:8–9; 43:10, 21; 44:1–2; 45:4; Ps. 105:6, 43. Peter himself several times reiterates that believers are *eklektoi,* divinely chosen: 1:2; 2:4, 6, 9; 5:13.

A royal priesthood: Peter quotes the Greek rendering of Exod. 19:6; 23:22 LXX. The Hebrew has "a kingdom of priests," which is not dissimilar. Both expressions involve royal and priestly status, duties, and privileges (Rev. 1:6; 5:10; 20:6).

A holy nation is another phrase from Exod. 19:6; 23:22 LXX.

A people belonging to God (*laos eis peripoiēsin*). The sense of *peripoiēsin* suggests a collector who has set his heart upon a rare prize of great value, as in Jesus' parables of the hidden treasure and the pearl (Matt. 13:44–46). Peter's phrase recalls Isa. 43:21; Mal. 3:17 LXX; cf. Ps. 134:4 LXX: "For the Lord has chosen Jacob for himself, and Israel for his special property." Israel was distinguished from all other nations on earth as God's treasured possession. Such is the sense of the Hebrew of Exod. 19:5; Deut. 7:6, where the LXX uses the *periousios*. This was translated in the Vulgate by the Latin *peculiaris,* hence the KJV renderings "peculiar treasure" (Exod. 19:5), "special people" (Deut. 7:6), "peculiar people" (Deut. 14:2; 1 Pet. 2:9), "jewels" (Mal. 3:17). The word "peculiar," which to the King James translators meant "special, highly valued property," can be misunderstood by modern readers of KJV as having the current sense of "possessing strange and unconventional characteristics." The corresponding Hebrew term is twice used of the personal treasure of a king, as distinct from the national revenues that he controlled (1 Chron. 29:3; Eccl. 2:8).

That you may declare his praises (*aretas*): In contemporary pagan usage, a god's *aretai* were his miracles. Peter's use of the term can be rendered "victorious achievements," which would echo the practice of the early Christian preachers in proclaiming the resurrection of Christ, his "victorious achievements" over death and sin, the saving facts of the gospel (1:3; Acts 2:32; 3:15; 4:2).

Called: The call of God is a favorite theme in this letter: in 1:15, believers are called to strive for holiness and to follow the divine example; in 2:9, out of darkness, into light; in 2:21, to suffer on account of loyalty to Christ and to follow his pattern and leadership; in 3:9, to inherit blessing; in 5:10, to share in the eternal divine glory. The very term "call" implies the divine saving initiative and the duty of the believer to respond.

Out of darkness: That is, out of spiritual darkness, which may be due to ignorance of God (1:14), to unbelief (2 Cor. 6:14; Eph. 5:8), to opposition to God's rule (Eph. 6:12), or to false teaching (2 Pet. 2:17; Jude 13). The change from unbelief to faith is often pictured in the NT as a change from darkness to light (Matt. 4:16; 6:22–23; Luke 1:79; Acts 26:18; 2 Cor. 4:6; 6:14; Eph. 5:8; Col. 1:12; 1 Thess. 5:4; 1 John 1:6).

Isaiah's prophecy about "Galilee of the Gentiles" declares that "the people walking in darkness have seen a great light, on those . . . a light has dawned" (Isa. 9:1–2). The prophecy is taken up in the Gospels (Matt. 4:15–16; Luke 2:32). Jesus himself claimed to be the light of the world, i.e., of both Jews and Gentiles (John 1:8–9; 3:19; 8:12; 9:5; 12:46). The description is also ascribed to believers in Christ (Matt. 5:14; Acts 13:47; 26:18) and is interpreted in terms of the light of witness and of separation (2 Cor. 6:14–15).

Paul too picks up the theme: "For God, who said, 'Let light shine out of darkness [Gen. 1:3, the first fiat of creation, from which all else flowed],' made his light shine in our hearts to give us the light of the knowledge of the glory of God in the face of Christ" (2 Cor. 4:6; cf. 2 Cor. 5:17; Gal. 6:15). One of Paul's interpretations of this light is in terms of witness and of separation (2 Cor. 6:14–15).

2:10 / **Not a people . . . people of God**: Like Peter, Paul also alludes to Hosea, but independently. In Rom. 9:25 he uses Hos. 2:23 and 1:10 (in that order), whereas Peter has made his own appropriate selection of phrases from Hos. 1:6, 9; 2:1, 23. The restoration of relationships between the prophet Hosea and his wife evidently appealed to early Christian preachers as a vivid illustration of the result of Christ's reconciling work in bringing men and women back to God. The liturgies of the early church, by then mainly comprised of Gentiles, showed appreciation of the privilege of addressing God as *Abba, Father*, by introducing the Lord's Prayer with "We *make bold* to say, Our Father." Modern liturgies have reintroduced this ancient practice.

§10   Living the New Life among Others (1 Pet. 2:11–12)

2:11 / Having detailed the theological standing of believers, Peter turns to consider their practical, everyday behavior among those living around them who have no such relationship with God. This section runs as far as 3:12.

Dear friends is a rather insipid translation of *agapētoi*, a word embodying the love (*agapē*) of God. Peter addresses his readers as those who are bound (1:22) to one another and to him, not simply by natural affection but by their common sharing in God's great love (*agapē*) for them as believers in Jesus Christ, God's beloved (*agapētos*) Son (Mark 1:11). It is the working out of that divine love within them in their relationship toward others to which Peter now directs their attention.

I urge you is, again, hardly robust enough as a translation. The verb *parakalein* is formed from *para*, alongside, and *kalein*, to call. The picture conveyed is of the writer's wishing he were alongside his friends, personally calling them to respond wholeheartedly to his pressing exhortation.

As far as society around them is concerned, Christian believers are in a spiritual sense different. They live in this world as **aliens and strangers** (*paroikous kai parepidēmous*, "aliens and exiles," RSV). The phrase echoes God's command to the Israelites never to sell the promised land to outsiders, "for the land is mine; for you are strangers and sojourners with me" (Lev. 25:23, RSV). The Israelites are depicted in Leviticus as no longer wandering in the wilderness but as having reached the promised land. Yet even so, their *status* is to remain that of sojourners and pilgrims. In relation to the society in which they are living, Christian believers are **aliens**. They are pilgrims in a world that is either apathetic or hostile. Their true home is in heaven with their Lord.

Nevertheless, Christians presently live among unbelievers. So how are they to behave? The comparative difference in their lives must be evident to unbelievers. To that end, Christians are **to abstain from sinful desires,** a somewhat delicate rendering of *tōn sarkikōn epithymiōn,* literally fleshly lusts. Already, in 1:14, Peter has warned his readers not to respond to "evil desires" (*epithymiai*), and later (in 4:3) he will give examples of what he has in mind: "living in debauchery, lust, drunkenness, orgies, carousing and detestable idolatry." Self-gratifying conduct belongs to the darkness from which they have been summoned by the call of God (2:9).

From such sinful passions they are to **abstain:** the use of the present tense for **abstain** implies the need to maintain a constant guard against succumbing to the repeated blandishments of the so-called "natural" (and, thus it is implied, allowable) desires of the human heart.

The reason for Christians to heed Peter's warning is that evil desires **war against** the **soul,** and consequently against a believer's best interests, which concern eternity, rather than time, and the spiritual, rather than the natural life.

2:12 / To heed the warning not to yield an inch to impulses to engage in self-indulgence is necessary not only for the Christian's own well-being, but as a positive witness to unbelievers. Peter's readers are instructed to **live such good lives** that opponents can never have any well-grounded justification for pointing the accusing finger. The most saintly and innocent behavior is not going to prevent slanderous allegations being made— even Jesus himself suffered calumny. But the Christian response is to rebut such false charges by the quality of daily conduct. In the end, an unbelieving society will have to admit that **your good deeds** cannot be gainsaid. That, Peter tells his readers, will lead their opponents to acknowledge the Christians' Lord and Master, for they will **glorify God on the day he visits us,** that is, on the final day when the Lord returns in power and great glory.

The promise of divine visitation appears constantly in the OT (e.g., Jer. 6:15; 10:15 LXX) and suggests God's intervention in support of his people in mercy and in judgment. Peter's words may be taken as meaning that on that climactic day unbelievers will be won over by acknowledging the beauty of the Christians' lives. The eyes of opponents will be opened to the rightness of the believers' conduct and thus to the glory of the God whom Christians honor.

Additional Notes §10

2:11 / **Dear friends** translates *agapētoi*, lit. "beloved ones," that is, "beloved by God, and beloved by me because we share in the same divine love (*agapē*)." Although *agapētoi* was an expression in general use at the time, Christians gave the term a new depth of meaning, for it described the quality of the Father's feeling for Jesus: "This is my beloved (*agapētos*) Son" (Matt. 3:17, KJV, RSV). The writer's address to his readers as *agapētoi* also occurs in 4:12; 2 Pet. 3:1, 14, 17; cf. Jude 3, 17, 20; it appears in Paul's letters, although he usually prefers *adelphoi*, brothers (and sisters).

Urge, *parakalein*, is found again in 5:1 ("appeal") and in 5:12 ("encourage"). The RSV translation, "beseech," may be dated, but it conveys the stronger sense that Peter intends (cf. Rom. 12:1; 1 Cor. 1:10; 1 Thess. 4:1).

Aliens and strangers (*paroikous kai parepidēmous*): Perhaps Peter has Abraham's words in mind ("I am a stranger and a sojourner [*paroikos kai parepidēmos*] among you," Gen. 23:4 LXX, RSV), for the Genesis passage concerns Sarah, to be mentioned by Peter in 3:6. In the OT, *paroikos* is regularly used as the LXX translation of Heb. *gēr*, a foreigner living among Israelites as a resident alien. See Davies, *Paul and Rabbinic Judaism*, p. 114. "The Christians dwell in their own countries, but only as sojourners. As citizens, they share in all things with others, and yet endure all things as foreigners. Every foreign land is to them as a native country, and every land of their birth as a land of strangers" (*Epistle to Diognetus*; Anon., 2nd cent.).

The clear difference in Christian lives must be evident to the unbelieving world around, a point well brought out some years ago when converts in the southern Sudan needed a word for "parish." The English term comes from Peter's *paroikos*. When the derivation was mentioned, the Sudanese Christians were delighted. In their own language an expression very close in sound to the Greek meant "your life is different." Peter would have approved.

Abstain (*apechesthai*) is a present tense: "continue to keep away from." The practice will need to be maintained. But the implication is also that, given the believer's will and God's grace, such abstinence is a practical possibility for the Christian—however much the world may claim that such inward desires are (in its view) natural and their satisfaction legitimate.

Sinful desires is *tōn sarkikōn epithymiōn*, lit. "fleshly lusts." The adjective *sarkikōn* is from *sarx*, flesh, and here takes on the usual Pauline meaning of "the seat of human passion and frailty which leaves God out of account." On *sarx*, see Turner, pp. 176–78, 297, 418.

On *epithymia*, lust, see Additional Note on 1:14.

War against your soul: The NT often uses the imagery of warfare to depict the inner human moral struggle (Rom. 7:23; 2 Cor. 10:3; James 4:1) which corresponds to the rabbinic wrestling between "good and evil inclinations."

2:12 / **You live ... good lives** (*tēn anastrophēn hymōn ... echontes kalōn*): *Anastrophē* (manner of life, behavior, conduct) is a frequent term in this letter. See Additional Note on 1:15. *Echontes* is a present participle: go on having, i.e., maintain always. *Kalēn* is "good" in the sense of "attractive," as in Jesus' claim "I am the good (*kalos*) shepherd" (John 10:11, 14), with its consequence that "I will *draw* all (people) to myself" (John 12:32).

Among the pagans (*en tois ethnesin*): Normally this would be rendered "among the Gentiles." The NIV translation "pagans" rightly interprets *ethnesin* as meaning Gentiles who were not Christians (so also in 4:3). Peter's readers included both Gentile and Jewish believers.

Of doing wrong (*kakopoiōn*): The accusation of wrongdoing, to use that mild term, continued to be made by unbelievers in Nero's day. Christians were suspected of being those "given to a new and malefic superstition." The Latin *maleficus* corresponds to the *kakopoios* (Suetonius, *Life of Nero* 16.2).

That they may see your good deeds: Godly conduct was recognized as a missionary instrument. Simeon ben Shatah (early 1st cent. B.C.) gave as a reason for dealing honestly with an Arab that he preferred hearing the Arab say, "Blessed be the God of the Jews" [*whose followers are so honest*], to all the gain of this world (J. *Baba Meṣi'a* 8c). Peter alludes to the theme again in 3:1 (wives winning husbands by their behavior). Some OT writers looked forward to the time when pagan nations would "fear God" and acknowledge his sovereign power and holiness (Ps. 22:27–28; 67:7; Isa. 52:10).

And glorify God can be taken to mean "they will justify God: he was right after all" (Rev. 11:13).

On the day he visits us: lit. "on [the] day of visitation" (*en hēmera episkopēs*), a frequent biblical phrase (Isa. 10:3). God "visits" to comfort or to deliver (Gen. 50:24; Exod. 3:16; 1 Sam. 2:21; Job 10:12), or to punish (Exod. 32:34). The basic idea is that of a judicial investigation (Ps. 17:3), to reward or to punish, according to the divine findings. The theme of attention to daily conduct in view of the final reckoning is found in the Dead Sea Scrolls. Members of the Qumran community were to "be zealous to carry out every ordinance punctiliously, against the Day of Requital" (1QS 9.23).

2:13 / What living the Christian life entails is now spelled out in some practical detail. Peter applies the admonition **Submit yourselves** to a series of relationships: to civil government (vv. 13–17), to slavery (vv. 18–20), to Christ himself (vv. 21–25), and to marriage (3:1–7).

The relationship of Christians to the state was one which soon became problematic, for in the early centuries of the church all states not only were governed by pagans but included pagan worship within their social, economic, and political systems. A collision with the church, owing its primary allegiance not to the state but to Jesus Christ, was inevitable. Added to this was the fact that even before Christianity broke completely with Judaism, the Jewish hierarchy perceived a powerful rival in the followers of "The Way," and its leaders were not slow to stir up trouble with the civil authorities whenever the opportunity arose. But Jews and Christians alike appreciated the value of settled government, and each faith sought to follow its religious practices within the existing civil framework whenever possible. One rabbinic writer bids Jews "Pray for the welfare of the government, since without the fear of it people would devour one another alive" (m. *Aboth* 3.2). Both Peter (in this chapter) and Paul (Rom. 13:6–7) express a similar sentiment in less colorful terms.

Therefore, despite the fact that the current emperor in Rome was Nero, Peter could still press his readers to be good citizens and obey the government, to submit **to every authority instituted among men.** But being advised to obey the civil authorities does not mean "under any circumstances." There are many biblical examples of God's people being commended for *disobeying* human governments (Exod. 1:17; Dan. 3:13–18; 6:10–24; Acts 4:18–20; 5:27–29; Heb. 11:23). These are occasions when obeying the civil law would involve breaking the divine law. That aside, there is a fundamental difference between the despotic state universal in NT times and the democratic state of today. The NT authoritarian state took for granted the total and unquestioned obedience of its subjects. The modern democracy is intended to be run as a cooperative government between leaders and citizens, though still, of course, the Christians' first loyalty is to their Lord.

The point is nicely expressed by Peter's choice of *ktisis*, here translated **authority**, which in secular Greek refers to the (human) founding of something (a city, a sect, the games, an altar). Biblical Greek, however, uses *ktisis* to mean the divine creation. Peter's implication here is, therefore, that God, not humanity, is behind the setting up of the civil authorities: they are for the regulation of social life, as God intends, and this is reflected in the reason Peter adds: submission is **for the Lord's sake**.

The civil power may be represented by **the supreme authority**, which in the case of the Roman Empire is the emperor—although in the absence of a word for emperor the Greek has to use the term **king** (*basileus*), as again in verse 17.

2:14 / That power may also be delegated to **governors** in the various provinces of the empire. Their commission as governors is, first, **to punish those who do wrong**. The Greek word here for **punish** includes the note of retribution: the wrongdoer is to be made to suffer for any misdeeds. There is no suggestion of more modern ideas of trying to reform the criminal as part of the judicial process. The governor's duty is to exact recompense: that is his appointed task (Rom. 13:4). Not so for the individual Christian believer who is the victim of a crime: vengeance is not the believer's prerogative (vv. 19–23); it must be left to higher authority—to God himself (Rom. 12:19), or to governors, those delegated under the divinely established framework of government (John 19:11).

The governors' second duty, however, is a positive one: they are **to commend those who do right**. This is more than an encouragement to good citizenship, to advance the general welfare of society, and thus to benefit the state as a whole. Peter is thinking beyond obedience to laws and is advising believers to be model citizens: the government expected that of all subjects as a matter of course. The commendation (*epainos*, praise) of **those who do right** is a reference to the special quality of Christian lives.

2:15 / The purpose of Christian conduct, that is, **God's will** for believers, is **that by doing good you should silence the ignorant talk of foolish men**. In this context **ignorant talk** means the making of groundless accusations against believers by those who are unaware of the spiritual motive for the way Christians behave, for to be **foolish**, in biblical terms, means to leave God out of account (Ps. 14:1; Luke 12:20). It was only too easy for Christian practices to be misconstrued as anti-social or even as treasonous. Peter expects Roman justice to be much more far-sighted than that of a mob. Yet should officialdom fail in its God-given duty, the apostle is confident that God himself will intervene in the interests of his perfect justice—even if this must await God's final day of visitation (1:5; 2:12).

2:16 / Peter's emphasis on submission—a theme he will repeat a number of times (2:18; 3:1, 5, 22)—is at once balanced by his reminder that paradoxically Christian believers should realize that they are to **live as free men**, for that is what they are, irrespective of their worldly status. They have been liberated by Christ from the bondage of past sin, and released by means of the new birth (1:3) into life on a spiritual plane which is in a different realm from that of the natural order.

The paradox of submission and liberty is brought out by Peter's description of believers as **servants** (*douloi*, bondslaves) **of God**. Complete submission in perfect obedience to their Master results in complete freedom of spirit: "whose service is perfect freedom," as the church collect puts it. Peter's Jewish-Christian readers in particular would see his point. In the Passover-eve liturgy, which celebrates the exodus deliverance from Egyptian bondage, one emphasis is on a change of master which results in liberty. Israelites now enjoy freedom because they are bondslaves of God. The Passover meal is eaten lying at table, after the manner of free subjects in the Greco-Roman world, not sitting, as did slaves for their meals. "Even the poorest in Israel must recline on a couch" (m. *Pesaḥ.* 10.1). It was a note struck at the Last Supper, set in a room "with couches spread" (Moffatt; Mark 14:15; Luke 22:12).

With Christian liberty comes responsibility: **do not use your freedom as a cover-up for evil**. It was evidently by no means a warning irrelevant even in NT times (Gal. 5:13; 2 Pet. 2:19). Christians are free solely because they are the bondslaves of God: they have been purchased by the price paid by his Son

(1:18–19). Since they are now God's property, they are to carry out God's will. "Christian freedom does not mean being free to do as we like; it means being free to do as we ought" (Barclay [DSB], p. 207).

2:17 / **Show proper respect to everyone** (*pantes timēsate*). The Greek imperative is in the aorist tense, yet it is followed by three *present* imperatives, **love . . . fear . . . honor**. The meaning seems to be: Take up once for all (aorist imperative) as a permanent stance the attitude of respect for all. In practice this works out as continuously (present imperatives) loving **the brotherhood of believers**, fearing **God**, and honoring **the king**. Christians may increasingly appreciate their special status and privileges as children of God, but that is no reason for looking down on others. All that believers are and can become is solely by God's grace. To guard against such false suppositions of superiority, they are to make sure that they **show proper respect** to all. Respect is due to others as fellow human beings irrespective of any particular position they may hold. And, in any case, what right has one person to judge the spiritual condition of another? "Trample not on any: there may be some work of grace there that thou knowest not of" (Leighton, vol. 1, p. 367).

Additional Notes   §11

2:13 / Similar codes of conduct are frequently included in early Christian writings: Eph. 5:21—6:9; Col. 3:18—4:1; 1 Tim. 2:8–15; Titus 2:1–10; Didache 4.9–11; 1 Clement 1.3; 21.6–9; Barnabas 19.1–7; Polycarp, *To the Philippians* 4.2–6.2.

Submit yourselves: The verb *hypotassein* was originally a military term, "to rank under, place under the command of." The instruction was not novel. "Rabbi Ishmael said, 'Be submissive to a superior, affable to a junior, and receive all with cheerfulness' " (m. *Aboth* 3.13). Ishmael, a high priest's grandson, was taken captive to Rome after the fall of Jerusalem in A.D. 70, though he was later released. Living at a time when Rome's hand was heavy upon Jews, he advised his contemporaries to accept harsh political realities with cheerfulness.

Authority (*ktisis*): see Turner, pp. 288–89. About the same time that the book of Revelation pictures the Roman Empire as a satanic beast or a blasphemous harlot, Clement of Rome can pray for political rulers: "Give them, Lord, health, peace, concord, stability, in order that they may administer without offence the government that you have given them" (1 Clement 61.1–2; cf. Titus 3:1–2).

2:14 / **Governors** translates *hēgemōn*, the title used of Pontius Pilate (Matt. 27:2) and Felix (Acts 23:24). Jesus warned his disciples that they would be called to witness for him before the highest civil authorities, kings and governors (Matt. 10:18; Mark 13:9; Luke 21:12).

To punish: The Greek *ekdikēsis*, punishment, involves the state's taking vengeance on the culprit (Rom. 13:3–4). The disciple, however, is not to consider taking the law into his or her own hands (Matt. 5:38–48; Rom. 12:17–21).

2:15 / **God's will**, mentioned here for the first time in this letter, is a theme reappearing in 3:17, 4:2, 19, usually in the context of suffering, actual or anticipated.

You should silence: The verb *phimoun* means lit. to muzzle. The quality of Christian lives is to stop opponents' bark and bite. The same verb describes the stilling of the storm (Mark 4:39): "Shut your mouth!", which contrasts ill with the meek and mild "Peace, be still" of KJV. Jesus evidently recognized the action of Satan behind that storm, an attempt to swallow up the little party in the boat (cf. Mark 1:25, where the same verb occurs). Antagonism against truly Christian standards of conduct, even though channelled through human opponents, is fundamentally satanic.

Ignorant refers to the opponents' lack of spiritual understanding of Christian values. It described the position of Peter's readers before their conversion (1:14).

2:16 / **Live as free men**: The greatest of the pagan thinkers also appreciated that freedom and obedience cannot be separated. "Liberty consists in obeying God" (Seneca). "We are servants of laws so that we can be free" (Cicero). "No bad man can ever be free" (Epictetus). "Every bad man is a slave" (Plutarch). See Barclay (DSB), p. 207; Daube, *Exodus Pattern*, pp. 45–46.

Cover-up: The Greek *epikalumma* means a veil or cloak. So the NIV translation is more apt than the RSV's "pretext."

2:17 / **Show proper respect to everyone**: "Let your neighbor's honor be as precious to you as your own" (m. *Aboth* 2.10). "Who is honored? He who honors mankind" (m. *Aboth* 4.1). The rabbinic collection *Aboth* ("Sayings of the Fathers") was compiled between A.D. 70 and 170.

Fear God, honor the king is virtually a quotation from Prov. 24:21, although Peter reserves "fear" for God (as in 1:17). "Whoever fears the Holy One, blessed be He, will ultimately become a king" (*Midrash Rabbah* 15.14 on Prov. 24:21). Paul deals with the theme in Rom. 13:7–10.

The Greek verb to **honor** (*timan*) actually occurs twice in this verse, once translated as **show proper respect** (to all), and the second time as **honor** (the king). While the different renderings by NIV are not unreasonable in this context, perhaps Peter is engaging in mild irony. For all his pomp and power, any emperor in Rome, even though he may claim divine status, is in God's eyes on a level with all other human beings. Both the emperor and a next-door neighbor are to be equally treated by believers—with proper respect. Peter uses the corresponding noun (*timē*) in 1:7; 2:7; 3:7; 2 Pet 1:17.

Brotherhood (*adelphotēs*): This term occurs in the NT only here and in 5:9. In 1 Macc. 12:10, 17, the word again describes family ties established by covenant relationship, which is indeed the basis of Christian fellowship.

2:18 / The second topic under the theme of submission bears upon the relationship of **slaves** (*oiketai*, not the more frequent *douloi*, bondslaves) to their **masters**. It was a matter of immediate and personal concern for many of the early believers. Besides living in a pagan society, Christian *oiketai*, which may be roughly translated "unfree house servants" (there is no exact term in English—see Additional Note) probably had pagan masters, who at best would be unsympathetic to a novel religion preaching "freedom" and speaking of another and superior Master. Peter wants to encourage Christians to face the suffering that in varying degrees would inevitably be their lot in such circumstances. They are to treat their situation as a daily opportunity to witness by bearing up, as Jesus did, under every grade of persecution, from a small injustice to actual bodily harm. This is the attitude to which they have been called (v. 21).

Masters fall into two main types. Some **are good and considerate** in their dealings with their servants, who therefore do not find it difficult to submit. For servants having to deal day after day with masters **who are harsh** and mean, and who mistreat those who serve them, however, it is another story. Yet in both situations Peter tells his readers that it is their Christian duty to submit cheerfully. Their constancy in bearing whatever they have to suffer in the course of duty is a powerful sign to those over them that they possess inner resources beyond the natural. This positive attitude may indeed cause annoyance to an uncomprehending pagan master who expects a very different response. That in itself witnesses to the special grace believers are given and could be the means of prompting a desire in the master to share the believers' secret.

2:19 / Not to be sullen or rebellious, as would be the normal reaction of an unbelieving slave in painful or unjust circumstances, is **commendable**, a fine thing in God's sight, for such an attitude is what he expects of his children toward all others (v. 17), whatever their status or power.

2:20 / Peter gives an example of what he has in mind, thereby introducing his comments on Christ's attitude toward suffering (vv. 21–24). Bearing up stoically under punishment for, say, insubordination or inefficiency, is hardly meritorious, since the penalty is deserved. But on occasions punishment may be meted out when some good action is misconstrued, either by accident or by design. It is in such a situation that believers are to reveal their Christ-centered life. The faithful are to **endure it**, accepting the undeserved pain, physical, mental, or emotional, as an inevitable consequence of living a God-honoring life in an environment that is not only godless but is, for that very reason, antagonistic to anything which exposes its own lower standards. Such acceptance of unjust suffering **is commendable before God.**

2:21 / **To this** attitude of patient endurance in the face of undeserved suffering **you were called.** Whatever other tasks believers are given to do, all share in one Christian vocation, to follow the supreme **example** set when **Christ suffered for you.** Although the NT often speaks of Christ's sufferings when it means his death, here the emphasis is on the unwarranted afflictions of Jesus, for Peter is referring to Christian slaves being beaten, not killed.

Peter first reminds his readers that **Christ suffered for you**, then expands this statement concerning Christ's sufferings by a series of comments saturated with citations and allusions from the main OT prophecy of Christ's sufferings, Isaiah 53. Peter does not say he is quoting, but his language reflects a mind filled with the content of that OT prophecy of a suffering Messiah.

By the way he faced his experiences, Christ has left **an example** (*hypogrammos*), **that you should follow in his steps.** Peter once heard the call of Jesus to follow (Matt. 5:11). At a later critical moment, after Jesus' arrest, Peter had followed "afar off" (Matt. 26:58, KJV). Now, as if mindful of his failure to keep close enough to his Master, Peter exhorts his friends to **follow** (*epakolouthein*, to follow *closely*) and emphasizes the exactness that is required by adding **in his steps**, in his very footprints (*ichnesin*) as it were. The apostle is not suggesting that disciples must expect to face exactly the same kinds of suffering as their Master, but they are to accept the call to suffering for Christ's sake (in whatever way it may be presented to any individual believer) and to follow it through on the lines traced out by Jesus as the supreme exemplar: "for he gave us this model example (*hypogrammos*, Peter's word) in his own person" (Polycarp, *To the Philippians* 8.2).

2:22 / To fill out his exhortation, Peter now begins to make use of a stream of phrases from Isaiah 53:4–12 LXX, although he gives no direct indication that he is quoting (v. 22, Isa. 53:9; v. 24a, Isa. 53:12; v. 24b, Isa. 53:5; v. 25, Isa. 53:6). Jesus, says Peter, **committed no sin** (Isa. 53:9), and the statement reiterates Jesus' innocence (1:19)—not only of the accusations leveled at him by human opponents, but also in the sight of God, a point brought out by other NT writers (John 8:46; 2 Cor. 5:21; Heb. 7:26; 1 John 3:5). As **committed no sin** relates to wrong actions, so the second part of the quotation from Isaiah 53:9, **no deceit was found in his mouth**, refers to wrong speech. Together the two clauses cover all of life, whether expressed in deeds or in words.

Peter is here not so much setting up the perfection of Christ as drawing attention to the totally undeserved nature of his suffering. A Christ on a moral pedestal, far out of reach of imperfect ordinary mortals, can be no encouragement to men and women facing everyday provocation and persecution for their faith. But a Christ who, despite his sheer and unquestioned goodness, has himself suffered, is a true sympathizer, standing alongside lesser characters.

2:23 / The silence of Jesus before his accusers and antagonists (Matt. 26:63), which provoked Pilate into bewildered irritation (Matt. 27:12–14), had also deeply impressed the early Christians. As they well knew from the Gospel story, though **he suffered**, Jesus refused to react to his opponents' **insults** (Mark 15:32) or to threaten divine vengeance at the coming day of judgment (Mark 14:65). Lest silence suggest merely a negative attitude, Peter at once adds the positive aspect: **he entrusted himself to him who judges justly**. The example of Christ is one for his disciples to follow (v. 21), and later Peter will reiterate the lesson (4:19). Believers are not left to face suffering solely in their own strength, which might well prove inadequate. In the same confidence that Jesus had, they are to hand over their whole situation to God, for God, as all-knowing and all-seeing, **judges justly**. He alone can be relied upon to view all the evidence and to understand all the motives which lie behind every human action—and in the final analysis to dispense perfect justice (Gen. 18:25). But it is noteworthy that Peter uses the present tense: God, he says, **judges justly**. At all times and in every situation, God's discernment is perfect and his verdict just and true.

2:24 / The teaching that Jesus **himself bore our sins**, that the righteous and innocent one suffered the penalty for the misdeeds of the ungodly and guilty, is elaborated in this verse by means of language soaked with terms from the Suffering Servant passage of Isaiah 53 (LXX). Yet Peter sends his readers no signal that he is about to quote from the OT. That Peter weaves Isaiah's words so naturally into what he writes suggests that the passage must have been the subject of much meditation on Peter's part as he pondered the meaning of the death of Christ. He has so absorbed the prophet's message that it has molded his own thinking. Furthermore, since he can use Isaiah's language without seeing any need to offer his readers an explanation, it also suggests that the early Christians in general habitually applied Isaiah 53 to the passion of Jesus.

Although Peter began this section by addressing Christian slaves (2:18), his words have a far wider and more general application. Hence he can here refer to Christ bearing **our** sins, that is, whatever our social status in life happens to be, slaves or free.

Peter's description of the cross of Christ as a tree (*xylon*) is a favorite expression of his, for it recurs in his addresses in Acts (5:30; 10:39). According to Deuteronomy 21:22–23 LXX, one who broke the Mosaic law was to be hanged on a tree (*xylon*), so Peter's use of the term is appropriate as it alludes to the alleged breaking of the law by Jesus (Mark 2:24; John 19:7). In the eyes of his enemies, he received the right penalty. But Peter's reference is more profound. For a reader familiar with the OT background, "to be hanged on a tree" is more meaningful than "to be crucified," for the implication of the former expression is that by dying in that manner Jesus bears the punishment for all who break the divine law.

The purpose of Christ's death upon the cross is clearly spelled out: **so that we might die to sins and live for righteousness**. Negatively, the death of Jesus takes away the believer's sins: the word translated **die** occurs only here in the NT and has the sense of separation (lit. "to be away from, have no part in"). Positively, Christ's death enables believers, now separated from their old sins, to live a life that is right with God, in accord with the divine will. Or, as Mrs. Alexander's famous hymn has it,

he died to make us good.

Again Peter supports his words by an allusion to Isaiah 53 (v. 5): **by his wounds you have been healed**. Physical healing is certainly not excluded, as Matthew 8:17 shows by applying the Isaianic prophecy to the Lord's healing ministry. But primarily Peter's thought here is spiritual and refers to the healing of sin-affected souls, as his following sentence makes clear.

2:25 / The shepherd/sheep image, used regularly in the OT for the relationship of God with his people, is taken up by nearly all the NT writers and applied to Christ and believers. Not surprisingly, with the risen Lord's charge to Peter indelibly impressed upon the apostle's memory (John 21:15–17), this letter includes many pastoral figures of speech, most explicitly here and in 5:2–4.

You were like sheep going astray paraphrases Isaiah 53:6 and reminds Peter's readers of their situation before they became believers (1:14, 18; 2:10). **Now you have returned**, been converted (turned around) to Christ, **the Shepherd and Overseer of your souls**, to the one who recovers the strayed sheep and cares for them. Conversion to Christ completely reverses the aimless straying of the purposelessness of the unregenerate life. A person is converted when that individual's life attains a purpose, a direction, following acceptance of the divine leadership.

Additional Notes §12

2:18 / **Slaves** (*oiketai*): Unfree household servants (a milder Greek term than *douloi*, bondslaves) were by the first century mainly those who had been born into slave families, the descendants of people captured in earlier wars. Although without civil rights, they were the subject of a mass of Roman legislation. Generally well treated, they were often to be found in responsible household or professional posts; they received some payment for their services and could eventually expect to be able to purchase their liberty. There is no true equivalent in English for *oiketai*; "slaves" bears too harsh overtones.

The Greek translated **submit** is *hypotassomenoi*, a participle with imperative force ("slaves must submit themselves . . . "). The unusual grammatical construction is confined in the NT to passages concerning early Christian codes of conduct (Rom. 12:9–19; Eph. 4:2–3; Heb. 13:5; other examples in 1 Peter are in 3:1, 7, 9; 4:8–10). The corresponding rabbinic idiom is common in similar codes in Judaism. See Daube, "Participle and Imperative in 1 Peter," in Selwyn, pp. 467–88.

Considerate (*epieikēs*): gentle, fair; in the moral sense, reasonable; applied to authorities, lenient, equitable; applied to God, it refers to his gracious forbearance (1 Kings 12:22–24; Ps. 85:5).

Harsh translates *skolios*, which strictly speaking means crooked, bent; metaphorically, awkward to deal with (" you never know which way he is going to turn"). Used again by Peter in his address in Acts 2:40 ("this *corrupt* generation").

2:19 / **Commendable**: "a fine thing" (NEB). The Greek is *charis*, usually rendered "grace." In biblical usage, *charis* can cover both gracious action and the recipient's grateful appreciation ("thanks" in Col. 3:16).

Because he is conscious of God is problematic in the Greek: *ei* (if) *dia syneidēsin* (by reason of conscience) *theou* (of God). The noun *syneidēsis*, usually translated "conscience," is literally "a knowing (*eidēsis*) with (*syn*)" and here probably refers to a knowledge, an understanding, of God's will shared with other believers, since clearly we cannot speak of "God's conscience," which is what the Greek appears at first sight to suggest.

2:20 / **Credit**, *kleos*, occurs only here in the NT. The Greek word can mean good report, fame, glory: the general notion is praiseworthiness.

Beating: The Greek verb basically means "to strike with the fist" but is applied to physical violence in general. Used of Jesus during his trial (Mark 14:65), the word provides an apt link with Peter's following commentary on Christ's own sufferings (vv. 21–24).

If you suffer for doing good, i.e., "when in fact you were working well."

Commendable is again *charis*, as in v. 19.

2:21 / **Called**, that is, God's summons in Christ, a favorite theme in this letter; see Additional Note on 1:15, and the commentary on 2:9.

Christ as a title occurs by itself 13 times in this letter: 1:11 (twice), 1:19; 2:21; 3:15, 16, 18; 4:1, 13, 14; 5:1, 10 (some MSS), 14 (some MSS). The name Jesus does not occur except (11 times) in conjunction with Christ: 1:1, 2, 3 (twice), 7, 13; 2:5; 3:21; 4:11; 5:10 (some MSS), 14 (some MSS). It is as though Peter by this time is so aware of the divine glory of his risen Lord that he automatically associates the title Christ (Messiah) with the One he had formerly known only in his human form.

Follow: Invariably in the OT "to follow" in the religious sense has God as object, as in Num. 14:24: "My servant Caleb . . . follows me wholeheartedly." Even Samuel, whose integrity could not be challenged

(1 Sam. 12:3–5), did not encourage personal disciples, but warned his hearers, "Do not turn away from the Lord, but serve the Lord with all your heart" (1 Sam 12:20).

Suffered: The theme of suffering pervades the whole letter. The verb *paschein*, to suffer, occurs twelve times (2:19, 20, 21, 23; 3:14, 17, 18; 4:1 [twice], 15, 19; 5:10), and the noun *pathēma*, suffering), four times (1:11; 4:13; 5:1, 9).

The concept of Jesus as the Suffering Servant of the OT dominates Peter's thinking. In 2:21–24 and 3:18 he quotes phrases from Isa. 53:4–12; 1 Pet. 2:25 alludes to Isa. 53:6; 55:7; 60:7; Peter's speech in Acts 10 again echoes Isaiah: v. 36, Isa. 52:7; v. 38, Isa. 61:1; v. 39, Isa. 43:10; v. 42, Isa. 43:9–12; v. 43, Isa. 55:7. It is strange that the redemptive Suffering Servant theme of the OT, most clearly brought out in Isa. 53, is not used more frequently by NT writers, or indeed by the early church fathers. In the NT it is virtually restricted to Luke 22:37; Acts 8:32; and to this passage, 1 Pet. 2:21–25. C. F. D. Moule remarks that it is "a phenomenon that still awaits explanation" (*Birth of the New Testament*, p. 83). It may well be that the answer lies in the hint of 1 Cor. 1:23 that the central message of Christ crucified was incomprehensible in any appeal to Jews and Gentiles alike. But for all that, the Spirit-quickened mind, from whatever religious background, appreciated the truth that "Christ died for our sins"—and, of course, Peter is here addressing believers. See R. N. Longenecker, *The Christology of Early Jewish Christianity* (London: SCM, 1970), pp. 108–9. Peter was no rabbi, but like Paul (Rom. 9:33) he knew the reaction that direct preaching of Christ crucified would produce: blind unbelief on the part of Jews in rejecting the cornerstone (1 Pet. 2:7) and a cause of stumbling to Greeks (1 Pet. 2:8).

For you: The rabbis interpreted death as a sin-offering. The death of an individual atoned for that one's sins (b. *Sanh.* 44b), or for the sins of others (b. *Sukkah* 20a; b. *Yebam.* 70a). The death of a high priest liberated one guilty of manslaughter from his city of refuge (Num. 35:25). Nobody suggested that the high priest Caiaphas was saying something out of the ordinary when he told the Jews "it would be good if one man died for the people" (John 18:14).

Example translates *hypogrammos*, a rare word occurring only here in the NT. It is used for a child's copy-writing of the Greek alphabet. Clement of Alexandria (*Strom.* 5.575) uses *hypogrammos* as a technical term for a copyhead traced out for children to write over. Each of the three examples he gives contains all the letters of the Greek alphabet. This throws vivid light on Peter's use of the word. The disciple must not only follow, but so completely copy the example of Jesus Christ from A to Z that it means reproducing every stroke of every letter of the Lord's character, thus making a facsimile of the Master. Peter echoes the thought again in 4:1.

The apostolic fathers took up Peter's use of the word. Clement of Rome speaks of Paul's departure from this world as a notable *hypogrammos* (pattern) of patient endurance (1 Clement 5.7), and of Christ's good works as a *hypogrammos* "to which we should conform ourselves" (1 Clement 33.8).

2:22 / **He committed no sin**: In quoting from Isa. 53:9 LXX, Peter uses **sin** (*hamartia*) where the OT has "violence" (*anomia*, lawlessness). The distinction is unimportant, for 1 John 3:4 uses them as synonyms.

Deceit (*dolos*): a lie. Peter again refers to the sin of the lips in 3:10, where he is citing Ps. 34:12–16, another passage he has much in mind during the writing of this letter.

2:23 / **Insults**: Verbal abuse against Peter's readers was evidently a notorious feature of their daily experience, judging by the number of times it is mentioned in this letter (2:12, 15; 3:9, 16; 4:4, 14).

He made no threats: On the silence of Jesus, see Jeremias, *Central Message*, pp. 88–89. "The holy man is merciful to his reviler, and holds his peace" (*T. Benj.* 5.4); cf. 1 Pet. 3:9. The attitude of Jesus is reflected in rabbinic writings: "Those who are insulted but do not insult, hear themselves reviled without answering, act through love and rejoice in suffering, of them Scripture says, They who love him [God] are as the sun when he goes forth in his strength [Judg. 5:31]" (b. *Šabb.* 88b; similarly in b. *Giṭ.* 36b; b. *Yoma* 23a).

He entrusted himself to him who judges justly: Since the word **himself** is not in the Greek, **entrusted** could equally refer to Christ's adversaries; Jesus was content to leave it to the Father to judge justly. But on the analogy of 4:19, where Peter applies a similar thought to believers, the translators who add **himself** (i.e., Christ) in 2:23 are probably correctly interpreting the writer's meaning. "Leaving it to God" is, in any case, a familiar biblical attitude (Deut. 32:35; Judg. 11:36; Ps. 31:5; 37:5; 94:1; 96:13; Isa. 35:4; Rom. 12:19; Heb. 10:30).

2:24 / **By his wounds** (*mōlōpi*) **you have been healed** (*iathēte*) comes from Isa. 53:6 LXX, slightly modified: "by his bruises (*mōlōpi*) we were healed (*iathēmen*)." The theme of one suffering on behalf of the sins of others is repeated in Isa. 53:4, 5, 11, 12. Matthew interprets Isa. 53:4 LXX ("He bears our sins and is pained for us") as referring both to spiritual and to physical sickness (Matt. 8:17), and Peter is adopting a similar line. In the Talmud, Isa. 53:4 is taken to mean that Messiah is "the Leprous One" and "the Sick One" (b. *Sanh.* 98b).

He himself bore (*anenenke*) the **sins** (*hamartias*) of many. In the OT, to "bear iniquity" (Lev. 5:17; Num. 14:34 RSV) means to suffer the penalty of its consequences. The sacrificial significance comes out in such passages as Lam. 5:7; Ezek. 4:4.

The **tree** is the gibbet on which a breaker of the Mosaic law was hanged (Deut. 21:22–23; quoted by Paul, Gal. 3:13). See Turner, pp. 463–64; C. J. Hemer, *The Letters to the Seven Churches of Asia in their Local Setting* (Sheffield: JSOT Press, 1986), pp. 41–47. Irenaeus comments that Christ "remedied the disobedience concerning the tree of knowledge [Gen. 3:11] by the obedience of the tree of Calvary." Revelation 22:2 speaks of the tree of life being for the *healing* of the nations.

So that we might die to sins: cf. Rom. 6:11; 2 Cor. 5:14–15.

2:25 / **Sheep . . . Shepherd**: This figure of speech for God and his people is very frequent in the OT (e.g., Num. 27:17; 1 Kings 22:17; Ps.

23:1; 100:3; Isa. 40:11; 63:11; Jer. 3:15; 10:21; Ezek. 34:23; 37:24; Mic. 5:2–9; Nah. 3:18; Zech. 11:4–9, 15–17; 13:7) and is used similarly by most NT writers (e.g., Matt. 10:6; Mark 6:34; Heb. 13:20; Rev. 7:17). It can also be an image of the Christian ministry: Acts 20:28; 1 Cor. 9:7; Eph. 4:11; so in 1 Clement 44.3; Ignatius, *To the Philadelphians* 2.1; *To the Romans* 9.1. Christians are pictured as sheep in Matt. 10:16; Mark 14:27; Luke 12:32; Acts 20:28; 1 Cor. 9:7; Heb. 13:20. See C. K. Barrett, *The Gospel According to John* (London: SPCK, 1955), p. 310.

Pastoral images in 1 Peter abound, doubtless prompted by the risen Lord's threefold commission to the apostle (John 21:15–17): *scattered* (1:1); *kept* by the vigilance of God (1:5); a *lamb* without blemish (1:19); *follow* in his steps (2:21); straying *sheep*, now returned to the *Shepherd* (2:25); elders bidden to tend the *flock* of God (5:2); and to be examples to the *flock* (5:3); chief *Shepherd* (5:4); watch out for roaring *lion* (5:8).

You were . . . going astray (imperfect, indicating past habitual action) **but now you have returned** (aorist middle, lit. "have turned yourself to") by a deliberate response at the time of conversion. The words recall Christ's charge to Peter, "When you have turned back, strengthen your brothers" (Luke 22:32). 1 Enoch 89:10 speaks of Israel at the exodus as sheep escaping from the wolves of Egypt. Later the story is picked up again in similar terms by describing the wanderings in the wilderness: "I saw the Lord of the sheep pasturing them and giving them water and grass" (1 Enoch 89:28).

Shepherd and Overseer is probably to be taken as "overseeing Shepherd," a hendiadys, the literary figure whereby one idea is expressed by two (or occasionally three) nouns linked by a simple "and." The first noun is treated as the main substantive, with the second (and third) taken adjectivally. Other possible examples in 1 Peter are "respectful gentleness" (3:15); "authoritative powerful angels" (3:22); "glorious divine Spirit" (4:14).

An eschatological note is sounded in 2 Esdras 2:34, "Await your shepherd; he will give you everlasting rest, because he who will come at the end of the age is close at hand."

Overseer is *episkopos* (from which the later ecclesiastical title *bishop* is derived). In Rhodes five (civil) *episkopoi* guarded the rights and privileges of the whole community. God, says Philo, is the *episkopos* of the universe, and heaven is the *episkopos* of all people, for the stars are a thousand eyes that look down and keep watch (*Allegorical Interpretation* 3.43; *On Dreams* 1.91). So to Peter, the Lord Jesus Christ is the Guardian and Protector of believing **souls**, by which term the writer usually means "lives" as a whole, not just the spiritual aspect. The Greek word (*psychai*) is variously translated in NIV as "yourselves" (1:22); "people" (3:20); "themselves" (4:19).

3:1 / Peter's linking phrase **in the same way** occurs again in verse 7, as he turns to speak to husbands. So the expression is not to be taken as being too significant in itself: in verse 7 there is no question of husbands being admonished to be submissive to their wives. Neither is Peter implying that **wives** are to be **submissive** in the way expected of the slaves he has just been addressing (2:18), for the husband/wife relationship is on a different plane. Each wife is instructed to be submissive to *her own* husband (as the Greek indicates)—that is to say, this is not a general directive to all women to be subject to men, but to each wife to be faithful in conjugal relations solely to her husband. The reference to Sarah in verse 6 has the same sexual implication. The occasion when she is recorded in Scripture as addressing Abraham as "her master" is when she learns that despite their advanced ages, she is to bear him a son. Her submissive response is a laughing "My lord is rather old!" (Gen. 18:12 LXX). Thus both in verse 1 and in verse 5 the meaning of the wife's submission to her husband concerns the sexual relationship and should not be taken in a more general and oppressive sense.

It is noticeable that much more advice is addressed to wives (six verses) than to husbands (just v. 7), for the former were in far more need of support and guidance in what could be a tricky situation. The position of women in the ancient world was never an easy one. In Roman, Greek, and Jewish cultures women were subject to the authority of their husbands. If a husband were converted to Christ, it automatically followed that he brought his wife into the church as well. But the other way around posed a very different situation. For a wife to become a Christian, while an unsympathetic husband remained a pagan, threatened the stability of the marriage relationship as understood in the ancient world, permeated as it was with pagan religious practices in which a Christian could not engage.

Acute problems, therefore, face Christian wives whose husbands **do not believe the word** of the gospel message, and Peter seeks to offer such women wise advice. He does not tell them to leave their husbands, any more than Paul does when dealing with the same difficulty (1 Cor. 7:13–16). Peter encourages them to persevere in seeking to win their husbands to Christ. Wives are not to try to achieve this end by preaching at them or by nagging. The situation requires not pressing words but testifying conduct.

3:2 / Lives lived in **purity and reverence** will prove to be an effective missionary instrument (2:12). The **purity** of which Peter speaks is not the cultic cleanness looked for from OT ritual, but the moral purity and sincerity that result from a wholehearted inward dedication to Jesus Christ and are the consequence of a spiritual life (1 John 3:3).

3:3 / The attractive beauty of the Christian wife is not to depend on **outward adornment**. It is certainly right for every Christian to be neatly dressed: a dowdy, unkempt appearance is no advertisement for a gospel of grace. But Peter has in mind unnecessary extravagances in his reference to **braided hair and the wearing of gold jewelry and fine clothes.**

The apostle is not forbidding Christian women from having hairdos or from wearing ornaments. His language is to be taken as more figurative than literal, since grammatically (by a *hendiadys*: see Additional Note on 2:25) he means "gold-braided hair," after the fashionable and extravagant hairstyling of the day among the wealthy, and which amounted to virtually submerging the hair in lavish gold spangles. Surface show aside, elaborate hairdos consumed much time, and Christians had more important matters of the Spirit to which to devote themselves (1:18).

3:4 / On the contrary, instead of ostentatious outward show, what really matters is the attractiveness of the **inner self**: that inward lovely light which shines through the window of the human frame. Even unbelievers are able to recognize this **beauty**, even if they cannot appreciate its source. It is a **beauty** which is **unfading**: there is nothing superficial about it, since it is the fruit of a spiritual life that is ageless, "a beauty that the years cannot wither" (Barclay). Neither is it transient, like all that belongs to the world and its fleeting fashions and fads. This is the inner loveliness that is born of a **gentle and quiet spirit**, and it is that which counts in God's eyes as being of real value in setting forward his work—in this instance, of winning unbelieving husbands to faith in Christ.

3:5–6 / The advice to wives on how to be truly beautiful is not just some man's well-meaning opinion. Scripture itself reveals that this is the way it was achieved by **the holy women of the past**, that is, by those who demonstrated by their lives that they truly belonged to the holy people of God. Such women **put their hope in God**, and women believing in Christ through their new birth have similarly embraced a living hope (1:3, 21).

The way in which godly OT wives showed that **they were submissive to their own husbands** is illustrated by the example of Sarah. The occasion on which we are told that Sarah called Abraham **her master** is when she reveals her incredulity that, despite their advanced years, she was to bear her husband a son (Gen. 18:12 LXX). But her "submission" to Abraham when she **called him her master** is not to be understood in any slavish fashion—as is made clear by Sarah's later refusal to allow Hagar and Ishmael to remain in the home, despite her husband's protests (Gen. 21:10, 12). The term translated **master** (*kyrios*, lord) was simply a deferential mode of address, along the lines of our "sir" today. Sarah's response to Abraham on that occasion was an amused "My lord is rather old!"

Christian women whose obedience matches Sarah's can claim to be **her daughters**. By their trust in God they **do what is right** and so exhibit a spiritual family likeness to one who is included among the outstanding examples of faith (Heb. 11:11; cf. Isa. 51:2; Rom. 4:19; 9:9). Believing women have no reason to **give way to fear**, when they are threatened, from whatever unbelieving quarter, for in truth they belong to a kingdom not of this world.

Additional Notes   §13

3:1 / The NT writers regularly include instruction on Christian family life; on **wives** specifically, see also Eph. 5:22; Col. 3:18; Titus 2:4.

Submissive: As explained in the commentary, the application here (and also in v. 6) refers to the conjugal relationship. See Horsley, *New Documents*, vol. 1, p. 36.

Although women generally lacked official status, their influence was well recognized. As Edersheim notes, the rabbis commented on the creation of woman from a rib of Adam: "It is as if Adam had exchanged a pot of earth for a precious jewel." More caustically, the Jewish wit had it: "God has cursed woman, yet all the world runs after her. He has cursed the ground, yet all the world lives off it." See Edersheim, *Sketches of Jewish Social Life*, p. 140.

They may be won over: The Greek verb *kerdainein*, whenever used in the NT with this meaning, always represents humility as an instrument of conversion. See Daube, *New Testament and Rabbinic Judaism*, pp. 352–54.

Without words: When Augustine's mother Monica "came to marriageable age, she was given to a husband and served him as her lord, and did all she could to win him to you, speaking of you to him by her deportment, through which you made her beautiful and reverently lovable to her husband . . . Finally, when her husband was coming to the very end of his earthly life, she won him to you" (Augustine, *Confessions* 9.19, 22).

3:2 / **Purity** (*hagnos*, consecrated): The word expresses separation from the world and has sacrificial overtones. See Turner, pp. 82–83.

3:3 / **Braided hair . . . gold jewelry**: An example of the extravagance that Peter is warning against is the *safa* of the time, a coiffure with countless gold spangles almost entirely hiding the hair, and glittering and tinkling with every movement of the head. See James Neil, *Everyday Life in the Holy Land* (London: Church Missions to Jews, 1930), pp. 200–201. Paul has the same thing in mind in 1 Tim. 2:9. Contemporary Roman sculptures show such elaborate coiffures rising several inches above the head. Extravagant female finery was no new source of outraged protest: see Isa. 3:18–24.

Wearing of . . . fine clothes is lit. "putting on . . . garments," but in this context the simple Greek words are obviously intended to suggest elaborate dresses and even perhaps hint at a staff of servants waiting on a fine lady.

3:4 / **Your inner self** is lit. "the hidden person of the heart" (Rom. 7:22; 2 Cor. 4:16; Eph. 3:16).

Unfading here translates *aphthartos*, imperishable. The same term is used in 1:23 in speaking of the new birth. The inner beauty Peter is commending is a fruit of the new life in Christ.

Gentle (*praüs*): mild, benevolent, not pushing or insisting on one's own rights; elsewhere in the NT the term depicts the Christ-character (Matt. 5:5; 11:29; 21:5).

Quiet: the Greek word *hēsychios* (tranquil, calm) is found only here and in 1 Tim. 2:2.

Of great worth: The same Greek word is used of the *very expensive* perfume of Mark 14:3, and of the *expensive* clothes of 1 Tim. 2:9.

In God's sight: Cf. 1 Sam. 16:7, concerning the divine choice of David, to the surprise of onlookers.

3:5 / **Holy women**: The association of married life and holiness, here made by Peter quite incidentally, is genuinely Jewish. "As a divine institution, marriage is viewed in a twofold light. First, as the means intended for the propagation of the human race. Secondly, as an ideal state for the promotion of sanctity and purity of life." I. Epstein, *Judaism* (London: Epworth Press, 1945), p. 54.

Of the past: The unspoken assumption is that the Christian church is a continuation of and heir to the divine revelation in the OT.

Who put their hope in God, that is, by trusting that his promises would be fulfilled.

They were submissive to their own husbands. "A certain wise woman said to her daughter: 'My child, stand before your husband and minister to him. If you will act as his maiden, he will be your slave, and honor you as his mistress. But if you exalt yourself against him, he will be your master, and you will become vile in his eyes, like one of the maidservants.' " (Edersheim, *Sketches of Jewish Social Life*, p. 140)

3:6 / **Sarah**, together with Rebekah, Leah, and Rachel, was deemed in Judaism to be one of the four mothers of the chosen people.

Called him her master: A different slant from that usually taken by commentators on the incident in Gen. 18:12 is given in *Apostolic Constitutions* (6.29): "She honored him inasmuch as *she would not call him by his name*, but styled him lord, when saying, 'My lord is old.' " There is another example in 1 Sam. 1:8 LXX, when Hannah answers her husband Elkanah. See E. Nestle, *ExpT* 10 (1898–99), pp. 282–83.

You are her daughters, says Peter, even if the women he addresses had previously been pagan and not Jewish (Rom. 4:11; Gal. 3:7). In the case of women converted from Judaism, Peter is in effect saying that they truly reveal a spiritual family likeness to Sarah only when they reproduce her character (Rom. 4:12).

Do what is right and do not give way to fear alludes to Prov. 3:25 LXX, where both Proverbs and Peter use the rare Greek verb *ptoein*, to agitate with alarm (not found elsewhere in the NT).

§14   To Husbands (1 Pet. 3:7)

3:7 / Marriage has reciprocal obligations that form the foundation of a loving relationship. Having addressed Christian wives on their responsibilities, Peter now turns to the husbands. For marriage to be described in terms of a mutual partnership may appear unremarkable to modern Western minds, but this Christian teaching broke upon the ancient world as a novelty. Women had few legal rights. We might have assumed that Jewish husbands would have a more enlightened attitude toward marriage in view of centuries of living as the people of God with all their opportunities of revealed truth. Yet in Jewish law a woman was deemed to be a thing. A man owned sheep and cattle—and his wife. *She* could not leave him, but *he* could despatch her at a moment's notice, if he felt so inclined—although a rejected wife did have to be given a divorce certificate, enabling her to remarry.

The teaching of the NT brought about a revolutionary concept of marriage between believers. Now the union involved a new and liberating attitude. While Christian wives were still bidden to be faithful to their spouses, Christian **husbands** also must now take on obligations toward their wives.

Believing husbands are to **be considerate**, understanding, and sensitive to their wives' feelings. They must be courteous in their behavior and **treat** their wives **with respect as the weaker partner.** This again sounds unremarkable to Western ears, but it was a revolutionary doctrine in NT times. Even today in the East, as in Bible times, it is nothing unusual to see a man riding on a donkey while his wife trudges along by his side on foot.

Christian husbands and wives share spiritual rights and privileges as equals, for they are alike living stones being built into a spiritual house for God's service (2:5). They are together **heirs . . . of the gracious gift of life**, which in this context is probably not limited to a reference to the eternal life they both have as Christian believers (3:9), but alludes to the more intimate concerns of their own family life.

The reason for this whole new attitude toward the marriage contract between Christian believers is **so that nothing will hinder your prayers.** Herein lies a spiritual principle which extends beyond the husband/wife relationship. For prayer to reach the throne of God means that those who pray must be right with others (Matt. 5:24; 18:15). In the present verse the specific subject of prayer by husbands and wives may well allude in particular to the procreation of children. But the need for harmony when a couple prays together applies across the board of topics, if such prayers are to achieve their objectives.

Additional Notes   §14

3:7 / **In the same way** is not to be taken as referring to another example of submission (2:13, 18; 3:1), which would be inappropriate in relation to husbands. The phrase is virtually a colorless connective expression for "next on the list."

As you live with your wives (the Greek verb occurs in the NT only here) is a clause covering a couple's day-to-day relationship generally, but it has particular reference to sexual intercourse, and this colors the sense of the remainder of the verse.

The revolutionary nature of the NT's teaching on Christian marriage is highlighted by the Jewish attitude toward divorce. The OT grounds for divorce (Deut. 24:1–4) were couched in terms so general as to require interpretation. In NT days the conservative Jewish school of Shammai restricted legitimate cause for divorce to a wife's unfaithfulness, but the more liberal school of Hillel extended it to include anything the husband deemed displeasing. See *IBD*, vol. 2, pp. 957–58.

Considerate is lit. "according to knowledge," i.e., getting to know her needs and feelings, and acting in a courteous and understanding way as a result; cf. Eph. 5:25; 1 Thess. 4:4.

Treat . . . with respect (*aponemontes timēn*, apportioning honor): The verb occurs in the NT only here; cf. Prov. 31:29.

Weaker refers to physical strength, not to intellectual powers, moral courage, or spiritual standards.

Partner is *skeuos*, vessel, instrument; but the word is to be taken as simply meaning a person (as in Acts 9:15; 2 Tim. 2:21), or a woman in particular (1 Thess. 4:4). The term is not intended to suggest that women are simply tools for men to use! That would be contrary to the spirit of the whole verse.

Hinder: The verb *enkoptein*, to block, is used of making a road impassable by means of barricades or potholes. The rabbis were keenly aware of the possibility of prayer being hindered. "Whenever you find a dwelling mentioned, Satan becomes active [by the Hebrew word for dwelling the rabbis understood *to live in tranquillity*]. Wherever you find contentment, Satan brings accusations [so as to disturb it]" (*Midrash Rabbah* 38.7 on Gen. 11:2).

Your prayers, that is, of both partners praying separately or together (1 Cor. 7:5). "There is a time for intercourse with one's wife, and a time for abstinence so that one can pray" (*T. Naphtali* 8.8). A rabbinic saying in our Lord's day declared: "Prolix prayer prolongs life." See Edersheim, *Sketches of Jewish Social Life*, p. 273.

3:8 / **Finally** (not to end the letter but to complete this passage) there comes a general exhortation to the whole Christian community, married and unmarried alike. Peter commends a set of attitudes which together depict what relationships within the Christian fellowship should be.

Christian believers must **live in harmony with one another**, literally, "being of one mind" (a single word in the Greek). The term is intended to convey a unity of aim and purpose, a oneness in attitude. Idealistic? But this was the actuality at the very beginning of the Christian church, rejoicing in the glow of the early days of the outpouring of the Holy Spirit at Pentecost when "believers were together and had everything in common" (Acts 4:32). On a purely practical level, unity among Christians was in any case highly necessary in the hostile environment in which they were living.

They must **be sympathetic**, sharing one another's feeling. Believers' hearts should go out to one another in love, during times of joy as well as sorrow (Rom. 12:15). The truly sympathetic attitude is the antithesis of selfishness.

They must **love** each other **as brothers** and sisters (1:22), for in truth they all belong to the one family of God in Christ. They are to treat one another (and both male and female are included under **brothers**) as having an equal standing in the sight of God—a notion that challenges the competitive nature of so much in the modern Western world. Such a sensitiveness to the feelings of other Christians will follow from a growing appreciation of belonging to the one body of believers (1 Cor. 12:26). Peter is simply relaying the teaching of Jesus that he heard in the Upper Room: "By this all . . . will know that you are my disciples, if you love one another" (John 13:35). The vertical relationship, God's love for men and women in Christ, creates a horizontal relationship, the love between those who know themselves to be the objects of divine love (Cranfield, p. 76).

They must be **compassionate**, tenderhearted, caring deeply for one another—a powerful and rich term in the Greek for which there is no adequate English translation. All the emotions are involved.

They must be **humble** toward one another. The idea of humility as a desirable characteristic is promoted in the NT as a virtue of Christlike living (Gal. 5:23; Eph. 4:2; Phil. 2:3) and follows the teaching of Jesus himself (Matt. 11:29). To the Hellenistic world such a notion came as a startling novelty, for Greeks had always considered humility as a sign of weakness. Yet in truth, as the believer grows in the Christian life, there come constant reminders that an attitude of humility is entirely appropriate. Human abilities and wisdom all too often prove to be insufficient to cope with life's ordinary experiences and relationships, let alone when the Christian is faced with the standard of perfection set by Jesus in both his teaching and example (Matt. 5:48; John 8:46). Peter will repeat the admonition to be humble later when he addresses young men in particular (5:5).

3:9 / To treat others in such a charitable manner is not likely to prove impossibly difficult when a similar response is forthcoming, as it certainly should be within the Christian fellowship. But if it is not? Peter is no doubt thinking now of outsiders. Then the demand of Christ's ethic for his followers is still to maintain a positive attitude, despite any adverse reaction. It would be a betrayal of the high moral standard expected by Jesus of those claiming to be his disciples if they **repay evil with evil or insult with insult.** Certainly evil and insults will come the believers' way, for such will be part and parcel of the lot Christians are called upon to bear. It was not a new or unexpected turn of events for those seeking to live a godly life to attract undeserved suffering. The people of God have always been liable to face persecution; such is the malignant character of the spiritual world of evil opposed to God. But at the same time, those attuned to God's mind on the subject have long admonished believers not to pursue the settlement of accounts: vengeance, when and where necessary, is the divine prerogative (Deut. 32:35). The believers' sole task is to keep facing the light and to seek to reflect that light to others by their lives. They are to "get even" by **blessing** those who are antagonistic. In this they will be following both the example of their Master (2:23) and his teaching (Matt. 5:43–48), for by **blessing** we are to understand "seeking the highest good" of others, that is, by what we are and what we say advancing, not setting back, what God intends in his perfect plan for them.

Peter explains why believers are not to retaliate, but to bless. No doubt there are occasions when silence is the appropriate response, as in the example of Christ himself (2:23). But to **bless** involves speech, and there will be other circumstances in which the disciple should speak. Only a sensitiveness to the prompting of the Spirit as to the right reaction in any given situation will indicate which attitude to take.

To bless is one aspect of the Christian vocation: **to this you were called**. Jesus Christ looks to his followers to display his character in their lives, for this is the only opportunity non-believers have of glimpsing what he is like. But more than this, Peter tells his Christian readers to bless so that they themselves may **inherit a blessing**. The choice of term is significant: strictly speaking an inheritance is a gift, not something that can be earned or deserved.

3:10 / Following his practice of supporting teaching with Scripture, Peter backs up his warning not to retaliate by citing a favorite psalm of his, and one which lends itself to the theme of the whole letter (see Additional Note on 2:3). The quotation, from Psalm 34:12–16 LXX, slightly modified for the purpose, is introduced simply by the conjunction **For**, without further indication of its source. Peter is not bothered about footnotes for scholars. The words he quotes carry their own authority.

When the psalmist addresses **whoever would love life and see good days**, he is in effect asking, "Who would like to live a long and happy life?" The apostle is more realistically not holding out the possibility of a trouble-free existence in this world. Peter uses the psalmist's phrase to mean "Do you want to love life?" He is extending the OT words to include a spiritual sense, and he applies them not to quantity of life but to quality—to eternal life, the life worth having (v. 7), and to the ultimate full salvation in Christ which is to be revealed at the climax of history (1:5). All the same, the blessing which believers will inherit in the next life (v. 9) is not to exclude a foretaste for Christians in the here and now.

The psalmist's words spell out the practical conditions involved. The heirs of blessing must keep the **tongue from evil**, avoid malicious and bitter words that disparage another person and are calculated to hurt. They are to keep their **lips from deceitful speech**: not to tell lies or be economical with the truth, for lies are calculated to deceive (2:1, 22). The tongue, for all its smallness in physical size (James 3:5), has always been recognized as a power for good, or more usually for ill, and needing to be kept under tight control (James 1:26). Words can achieve a temporary victory, but inflict lasting hurt, wrecking a relationship and spoiling a believer's witness to Jesus Christ.

3:11 / From referring to speech, Peter's thought turns to actions, but the two aspects of words and deeds are not to be separated. Believers **must turn from evil**, and the Greek implies "not to lean toward" evil, not even to give it a passing thought as to whether some advantageous end might result from unworthy means. On the contrary, and positively, far from sitting back, content with supposedly nurturing their own souls quietly in a corner, Christians are to be actively engaged in God's work: they are to **do good**. But the admonition equally covers both the Martha deeds of busy hands and the Mary devotion of hands together that, for example, leads to prayer for others: "To pray is to work."

Again, there must be intense and persistent efforts to **seek peace and pursue it**. Personal relationships, of course, not politics, are primarily in view here. The phraseology is echoed by other NT writers (Rom. 14:19; 2 Tim. 2:22; Heb. 12:14), for the theme is plainly one close to the spirit of Jesus himself (Matt. 5:9), and indeed is the heart of his work of salvation in securing reconciliation between men and women and God. Peace in any sphere of life can never be taken for granted, but Christians must actively and persistently strive for it until it is achieved.

3:12 / The psalm quotation goes on to reassure the loyal people of God who walk in his ways that the divine watchful care is unceasing. **The eyes of the Lord are on the righteous** is a colorful biblical way of describing God's personal concern for his own, as is the companion phrase **his ears are attentive to their prayer**. The vivid metaphors may appear to couch divinity in physical terms, but such picture-language is used simply to bring home the intimacy of God's relationship with his people, not to apply any human traits—and limitations—to the Lord.

In contrast to **the righteous**, those who follow the right ways of God, the psalmist speaks of **those who do evil** as having the might of a holy God ranged against them. **The face of the Lord** is an OT phrase to express a relationship of God to people, either his gracious turning toward them or his disappointed turning away from them, the latter implying his withdrawal of grace and a refusal to hear any prayer they may offer.

Peter stops short of completing the quotation by omitting the closing clause of Psalm 34:16, "to cut off the memory of them [those who do evil] from the earth." The ultimate fate of those who continue to do evil is not Peter's concern in this letter, and as a Christian he would not want to suggest that the grace of God cannot reach evildoers beyond a certain point. While earthly life remains, so does an opportunity for repentance and salvation, as the penitent thief bears witness (Luke 23:43).

Additional Notes   §15

3:8 / **Live in harmony with one another** is a single word in the Greek: *homophrones*; the word occurs in the NT only here, although Paul touches on a similar notion in Rom. 15:5 and Phil. 2:2. Unity is, of course, one of the major themes of our Lord's high priestly prayer (John 17:21). The wide application of Peter's term is brought out in the various translations: "of one mind" (KJV); "have unity of spirit" (RSV); "agree among yourselves" (JB); "united" (REB); "one in your attitude to life" (Barclay); "like one big happy family" (LB). The theme of unity among Christians is stressed again and again in the NT, not as an optional luxury but as an essential characteristic of Christianity.

Be sympathetic (*sympatheis*; the only occurrence in the NT): lit. "suffer with," i.e., share feelings; happier experiences are not excluded, for we are to rejoice with the joyful as well as to weep with the mournful (Rom. 12:15; 1 Cor. 12:26; Heb. 10:34).

Live as brothers (*philadelphoi*): Only here in the NT, although the similar term *philadelphia* occurs in 1:22.

Compassionate: The Greek *eusplanchnoi* (only elsewhere in the NT at Eph. 4:32) is derived from *eu*, well, and *splanchna*, the internal organs that were viewed as the seat of the emotions. As attempts at translation, "a tender heart" (RSV) and "kindly" (NEB) are passive, and "pitiful" (KJV) is condescending. The NIV's **compassionate** is probably as near as English can get to a word so replete with feeling. The corresponding verb refers in the NT to the actions of the Good Samaritan (Luke 10:33) and the Prodigal's father (Luke 15:20). Usually it describes Jesus himself being moved with compassion (as in Mark 1:41, when he touches and heals the leper).

Be . . . humble (*tapeinophrones*): This is yet again a word that Peter alone uses in the NT.

Self-assertion is not always as profitable as it might promise. "A man that will walk abroad in a crowded street cannot choose but be often jostled; but he that contracts himself passes through more easily" (Leighton, vol. 1, p. 370).

3:9 / The whole verse echoes the words of Jesus (Matt. 5:43–44; Luke 6:27–28; cf. Rom. 12:17; 1 Cor. 4:12; 1 Thess. 5:15).

Evil with evil: An adversary aware of the Jewish Scriptures would do well to recollect that "if a man pays back evil for good, evil will never leave his house" (Prov. 17:13; cf. Matt. 7:2).

Insult (*loidoria*; in the NT only here and in 1 Tim. 5:14: The corresponding verb *loidorein* in 2:23 referred to Jesus' refusal to retaliate in kind.

Repay . . . with blessing: Christ's admonition to pray for one's enemies (Matt. 5:44) is echoed in Judaism, so it would not have sounded novel to Jewish converts at any rate. "If any man seeks to do evil to you, do well to him and pray for him, and you will be redeemed by the Lord from all evil" (*T. Joseph* 18:2). "The holy man is merciful to his reviler and holds his peace" (*T. Benjamin* 5.4). When Rabbi Meir (about A.D. 150) was accosted by highwaymen he at first prayed for their destruction. But his wife taught him better ways, to pray for their repentance, and the rabbi records that he did, for he saw that was always the right course to take (b. *Ber.* 10a).

Blessing (*eulogountes*) adversaries means seeking their highest spiritual good, defined by Jesus in terms of intercession, lifting them up to God to bring to pass in their lives what he sees is required (Matt. 5:44; Luke 6:28), a marked advance on the usual classical Greek sense of *eulogein* as merely "speaking well of." In the present world order, *temporal* blessings, such as sun, rain, and crops, are bestowed upon all, irrespective of their attitude toward God (Matt. 5:45; Acts 14:17). Peter here has in mind *spiritual* blessings.

Called: The Christian's call is a frequent theme in this letter (1:15; 2:9, 21; 3:9; 5:10).

Inherit: The Christian's inheritance is preserved inviolate in heaven (1:4). See Turner, pp. 133–34.

3:10 / The extended quotation from Ps. 34:12–16 LXX is but the most obvious example of Peter's appreciation of the aptness of this psalm for his message. Echoes of Ps. 34 abound in 1 Peter (see Introduction, p. 00) and in the liturgy of the early church, for it was recognized from the first as being particularly appropriate for a community of God's people facing undeserved suffering. See Kelly, p. 87; Gene L. Green, "The Use of the Old Testament for Christian Ethics in 1 Peter," *TynB* 41 (2, 1990), pp. 278–82.

Whoever would love life: The Greek verb *agapan*, besides its usual meaning of "to love," can also be translated "to choose, strive after, prefer" (Kelly, p. 138).

Tongue: The influence of words for good or ill is frequently mentioned in this letter: 1:10, 12, 25; 2:1, 9, 12, 15, 22, 23; 3:1, 7, 9, 10, 12, 15, 16, 19; 4:4, 5, 6, 7, 9, 11, 14, 16; 5:1.

Evil (*kakon*): What is morally base or mean.

Deceitful speech (*dolon*, guile): No deceit was found in Christ's mouth (2:22), and he is the believers' example.

3:11 / The admonition **do good**, or its equivalent, comes surprisingly often in this letter, apparently as an echo of Ps. 34 (1:15; 2:12–15, 20, 24; 3:6, 9, 11, 13, 17; 4:2, 17, 19). The Greek implies "carry out what is good in action."

Seek peace and pursue it: a thought repeated in Rom. 12:18; 14:19; Heb. 12:14. The command is adapted in 2 Clement 10:2 to run: "If we are zealous to do good, peace will pursue us."

Commenting on Ps. 34:14, the rabbis declared: "The Torah did not insist that we should actually go in pursuit of the commandment but said, 'If you meet . . . (Exod. 23:4); if you see . . . (Exod. 23:5); when you beat . . . (Deut. 24:20); when you gather . . . (Deut. 24:21); when you come . . . (Deut. 23:25).' In all these cases, if they come your way, you are commanded to perform the duties connected with them. But you need not go in *pursuit* of them. In the case of peace, however, seek peace (wherever you happen to be) and pursue it (if it is elsewhere)" (*Midrash Rabbah* 19.2 on Num. 21:21).

3:12 / **The eyes of the Lord are on the righteous**, not simply to see what they are up to! The implication is "for their good." Cf. Ps. 1:1–6.

The face of the Lord: In biblical terms, to seek the face of God is to draw near to him in prayer. See *NIDNTT*, vol. 1, pp. 585–87.

§16   Do Good, Even If You Suffer for It
(1 Pet. 3:13–17)

3:13 / Who among the perpetrators of evil are able **to harm** believers, provided they for their part are **eager to do good**, concentrating on doing God's righteous will? The rhetorical question expects the answer "Nobody!" This is not to deny the possibility that persecution, difficulty, and suffering will be encountered by the people of God, and Peter has already recognized this (1:6). The apostle does not view the situation solely in terms of the immediate present, but he considers the position of faithful believers in relation to eternity. No temporal suffering can do them permanent harm or alter their standing with God (2:20–21), for spiritual life is on a different plane from the physical. Neither can it affect the believers' inheritance, safely out of harm's way in heaven (1:4).

The believers' eagerness **to do good** is a matter of obedience to God's will. Their benevolent activities should by rights have the support of the civil authorities (2:14). But there is certainly no guarantee that the world will view what they do in the same favorable light. In fact, their very moral goodness will provoke antagonism. The scene on Calvary illustrates the point. The world seeks to eliminate both those who fall below average behavior (criminals) and any who exhibit an uncomfortably higher standard (saviors). The fact of their "doing good," plain for all to see, may rob opponents of any real reason for their attacks, but it will not prevent their trumping up some other excuse, as was the case with Jesus himself (Acts 10:38).

3:14–15a / But even if believers, like their Master, should suffer in spite of their right conduct, then there is still a spiritual plus which adversaries cannot filch from them: they are **blessed**. The term is that used at the beginning of the Sermon on the Mount (Matt. 5:3–11). The Beatitudes listed there spell out an ethical standard far beyond the unaided capabilities of any human being. In every case divine grace is essential for any believer even to approach such moral demands. Similarly, in times of persecution and suffering, Christians are to keep in mind that they are not left to their own devices—so often inadequate in a testing situation. At all times and in all circumstances they have available the powers of an understanding God, always at their side sharing his people's lot. As believers draw on those divine reserves, they find as an unexpected bonus that they are being spiritually blessed: they are learning to grow in grace and in the knowledge of their Lord (2 Pet. 3:18). For this reason, there is no need for them to be afraid.

Once again, Peter supports his words with a quotation from the ot. Isaiah 8:12–13 lxx reads: "Do not fear what they fear, neither be frightened. Set apart [as holy; the Greek word means to sanctify] the Lord himself and he shall be your fear." Isaiah's words, spoken in the context of a threatened Assyrian invasion, were to encourage Judah. A parallel situation in the spiritual realm was being faced by Peter's readers in the form of persecution. Initially it was probably local in character, but it may have started to become Roman government policy. Caesar brooked no rival king. By adding the words **in your hearts**, Peter could well be pointing out that individual personal devotion to Christ is the believer's source of strength whenever it proves impossible to meet with others in worship—and not only, of course, in times of persecution.

In quoting the passage from Isaiah, Peter is doing more than simply claiming the ot promise on behalf of the early Christian community as it faced antagonism in its own day, like Judah of old. He is also, though quite incidentally, claiming divine honor for Jesus Christ with his use of the term **Lord**.

Do not fear what they fear. While Christians are not exempt from troubles, neither are they the only ones who face them. But there is a great difference: believers are aware that there are divine resources available to faith. So, unlike nonbelievers, they have no need to be afraid. Nor are they to **be frightened**—the word means to be greatly disturbed in spirit ("stormtossed"). Their spirit is the very place where they are to maintain the divine peace, for it is that which will carry them through. And how is that peace achieved? The way to counter fear is to displace it with a greater power. The believer is to submit wholeheartedly to the lordship of Christ and let him be the garrison of the heart (Phil. 4:7).

3:15b / The calm poise of a Christian in the midst of an onslaught may well be baffling to nonbelievers, whose own natural reaction in a similar situation would be very different. What is the secret of an unruffled heart? That question will come sooner or later, and fear of opening the mouth is not to keep the Christian silent. **Always be prepared to give an answer.** But Peter probably has in mind being ready to respond to accusations of alleged wrongdoing, for the Greek word translated **answer** is *apologia*, meaning a defense. It would be the term familiar in a court of law (Acts 22:1), but Peter's use here of the general expression "*always be prepared to give an answer to everyone*" suggests he means accusations from any quarter, official or otherwise. In either case, whether being challenged about the secret of peace of mind or being accused of evil practices, Christians must be ready to **give the reason for** their **hope** in the living God (1:21). Believers are not called upon to respond by preaching to their interrogators. They are expected to be able to say what Christ means to them. They are to answer **with gentleness and respect**. A quiet dignity is far more effective than any amount of argument or belligerence. The subject itself, faith in God, also demands **respect**, i.e., reverence. The Greek word is *phobos*, often translated "fear." Fear of God is meant here, for Peter still has in mind the quotation from Isaiah 8:13, "He [God] shall be your fear."

3:16 / Christian lips must be corroborated by Christian lives. When believers are challenged, what they answer in words has to be supported by character. Hypocrisy is soon exposed for what it is. Their day-to-day conduct as professing followers of Christ must be such that they can face any false accusation with **a clear conscience**. Provided they are right with God and obedient to his promptings, then those who engage in scurrilous charges must sooner or later come to realize that such indictments are groundless. Truth will prevail. It may be that as a consequence the slanderers will become **ashamed** in the here and now, even if they are reluctant to own up to it. But certainly such people will be put to shame when they face the day of God's perfect judgment.

3:17 / For the present, the reaction of persecutors may not be so much a feeling of shame as of being incensed. If believers still have to suffer undeservedly for their Christian stand, **it is better**, if God should allow events to take their course just now, to put up with the injustice (2:20).

Such patient endurance is **better** because, being so un-expected to unbelievers and so unnatural in their view, it constitutes a convincing witness to the power of the gospel to transform and empower human lives. That indeed may be one reason why God trusts his believing servants to bear undeserved suffering: it has the value in God's sight of issuing in good for his wider purposes (2 Cor. 1:4; 4:17).

But **better** has a more profound significance. All through his letter, and not least at this point, Peter is keeping in mind what is important beyond the present age. The Christian should be cherishing the longer prospect and remembering that God's verdict on the day of final judgment is what matters.

The supreme exemplar of creative suffering is, of course, Jesus Christ himself, and Peter now turns to this aspect of the theme, for here is the sure foundation of the believer's confidence in the ultimate triumph of good over evil.

Additional Notes   §16

3:13 / Undeserved suffering by believers, touched on earlier (1:6; 2:19), is addressed more fully both now and later (4:12–19).

Harm is the verbal form of "evil" in v. 12. The word is used in Acts 12:1 of Herod's intention to *persecute* the church.

Eager (lit. zealous) **to do good**: cf. Titus 2:14.

3:14 / **Blessed** (*makarioi*): This same word occurs in the Beatitudes (Matt. 5:10); the term describes a benefit bestowed by a superior on another, but in the Bible always with the spiritual dimension prominent: a gift of the divine favor to human beings. The blessing may not necessarily extend to pleasant feelings at the time!

Do not fear what they fear is lit. "do not fear the fear of them," i.e., the fear that they [people in general] have when faced with similar troubles, for unbelievers lack an appreciation of divine resources available to a trusting soul. Peter's quotation, based on Isa. 8:12–13, extends to the next verse (3:15).

Isaiah 8 was a favorite passage among the early Christians, since they found so many allusions there to Jesus the Messiah. Verses from it are quoted in Matt. 1:23 (Isa. 8:8, 10); Luke 2:34; Rom. 9:32; 1 Pet. 2:8 (Isa. 8:14); Rom. 2:9 (Isa. 8:22); Heb. 2:13 (Isa. 8:17; 8:18); 1 Pet. 3:14–15 (Isa. 8:12–13); Rev. 16:10 (Isa. 8:22). See Dodd, *According to the Scriptures*, pp. 78–79.

Do not be frightened recalls John 14:1 and 14:27, where the same Greek verb ("stormtossed") is used.

3:15 / **Be prepared**: The notion of readiness occurs twice more in 1 Peter, of "salvation ready to be revealed" (1:5) and of Christ standing "ready to judge the living and the dead" (4:5).

Always be prepared to give an answer: "Rabbi Eleazar said, 'Be eager to study the Torah, and know what answer you should give to the Epicurean [heretic]. And know before whom you toil and who is your employer [God] who will pay you the reward of your labor' " (m. *Aboth* 2.14). Eleazar's enthusiasm for studying the Mosaic law may have been prompted by an experience he had. After the death of the great spiritual teacher Rabbi Johanan ben Zakkai (late 1st cent. A.D.), he left the company of his fellow students and went to live in Emmaus because it was a pleasant resort. In a short time he realized he was forgetting much of his learning.

A sure and certain **hope** (1:3) is what distinguishes Christians, for unbelievers have none (Eph. 2:12).

Gentleness is a fundamental Christian virtue, frequently mentioned in the NT (1 Cor. 4:21; 2 Cor. 10:1; Gal. 5:23; 6:1; Eph. 4:2; Col. 3:12; 2 Tim. 2:25; Titus 3:2; James 1:21; 3:13).

With gentleness and respect: A similar notion is found in the Dead Sea Scrolls: "teaching understanding to them that murmur that they may answer meekly before the haughty in spirit and humbly before men of injustice" (1QS 11.1).

The two qualities go closely together. Grammatically Peter's expression may be a hendiadys for "respectful gentleness." See Additional Note on 2:25.

3:16 / To maintain **a clear conscience**, vital to Christian living, is frequently stressed in the NT (Acts 23:1; 24:16; 1 Cor. 4:4; 1 Tim. 1:5, 19; 3:9; 2 Tim. 1:3; Heb. 13:18). The subject occurs again in 2:19 and 3:21.

Speak maliciously against your good behavior echoes 2:12. The Greek is literally "in the matter in which you are spoken against," i.e., the insults, threats, and abuse are specifically on account of their Christian life and witness.

The Christian's **behavior** (*anastrophē*) is a main theme of this letter (1:15, 18; 2:12; 3:1, 2, 16; the corresponding verb occurs in 1:17).

In Christ, frequent in Paul's writings, occurs in 1 Peter here and in 5:10, 14.

§17   Christ's Saving Work (1 Pet. 3:18–22)

3:18a   /   No person was less deserving of suffering than Jesus Christ, who went about doing so much good (Acts 2:22; 10:38). Even the belief popular in that day, and not unknown in modern times, that suffering must be due to sin (John 9:2), did not apply to him, for his sharpest adversaries could pin nothing on him on that score (John 8:46). In the end, it was a trumped-up charge by frustrated foes that secured his illegal execution (Acts 2:23). Yet God allowed him to die, **the righteous** one **for the unrighteous** many, for the divine purpose embraced the whole world (John 3:16).

Christ died for sins, that is, as a perfect sin-offering for the sins of others; he himself was sinless (1:19; 2:22). In the OT, sin-offerings were made repeatedly. But Christ's sacrifice of himself was of a different order. His death was **once for all**. He died only the once (Rom. 6:10), and that death is effective **for all** time, so that no further sacrifices for sins will ever again be needed (Heb. 9:26).

Winning people for God has been Peter's theme in this chapter. He has shown wives how to bring their husbands to faith in Christ (3:1). Malicious opponents are to be disarmed and reached for Christ by a spirit of gentleness and respect (3:15). It was with the same motive that Christ himself died: **to bring you to God**, for apart from his sacrifice Peter's readers would be without hope and without God (1:3, 21). On behalf of all believers, Christ opened up direct access to God (Eph. 2:18), and by taking away their sins he established their right relationship with God.

3:18b   /   Verses 3:18b–4:6 form one of the most obscure and difficult passages in the NT. This is not least because much of the background and many of the allusions, to say nothing of what are to us strange notions in the popular religious literature of the intertestamental period, all no doubt clear enough to the first readers, are largely lost to later minds.

Every portion of Scripture must be viewed in its context. What has led up to 3:18—4:6 concerns the encouragement of Christians facing potential or actual persecution, and possibly even martyrdom. The preceding verses (3:13–17) have exhorted the readers to maintain their loyalty to Christ, both in keeping to his standards of behavior toward others and in holding firm to their faith toward God. (This stress on loyalty will be resumed in 4:1–6.) Verse 3:18b sounds the triumphant note of Christ's victory over suffering and death. This sets the scene for verses 19–22, which describe the extent of that triumph.

While it is true that Christ **was put to death in the body**, that is, physically killed at the instigation of sinful men, it is also gloriously true that he was **made alive by the Spirit** (Rom. 8:11), raised from the dead by the power of God. Christ was no longer constrained by his human frame (Luke 12:50 RSV), or by the realization that he must experience death to complete his saving work on earth. Now **death in the body** has been conquered and Jesus is liberated to work freely in the spiritual realm.

3:19 / The shortness of this verse belies the number of problems it contains. Martin Luther, no less, cheerfully commented that this was "a more obscure passage perhaps than any other in the New Testament, so I do not know for a certainty just what Peter means."

The statement that **through whom also he** (Jesus) **went and preached to the spirits in prison** prompts a series of questions.

1. What does **through whom** mean?
2. What does **also** signify?
3. *When* did Jesus go and preach?
4. *What* did he preach, salvation or judgment?
5. *Who* are the **spirits in prison**?
6. *Where* was their prison?

First, what does **through whom** (*en hō*) mean? The Greek phrase can be translated **through whom** (i.e., through the Holy Spirit, as NIV), "in which [spiritual state]," or even "when" (i.e., on which occasion, as in 1:6; 2:12; 3:16; 4:4). The preceding words, literally "made alive by (or in) spirit," suggest that what Peter is saying is that after going through the experience of death, Jesus was liberated to act in the spiritual realm, free from the restriction of his earthly body. The encouragement this interpretation would give to Peter's readers is that the risen exalted Christ, who is with them and in them, sharing their day-to-day experiences, is mighty to save, fully able to deal with any situation they may have to face, spiritually or morally as individuals, or politically or economically as members of the society in which they live.

Second, what is the significance of the **also (through whom** *also* **he went and preached**)? The meaning seems to be that, in addition to knowing liberation from physical restrictions after his death, Jesus **also**, in this new spiritual liberty, went off and did something—which Peter goes on to define as preaching to certain beings who were themselves in a spiritual, not a physical, form.

Third, when did Jesus go and preach? There are at least three possibilities. It could have been at some time before his human birth at Bethlehem; i.e., it was the preexistent Christ who did the preaching (1:11). But this answer seems to be ruled out by the context, which is the suffering of Christ during his earthly ministry. Or it could have been in the hours between his death (mentioned in v. 18) and his resurrection (mentioned in v. 21). This assumes that "made alive by the Spirit" refers not to resurrection but to an earlier state. Yet another suggestion is that this preaching took place during or after his ascension.

Fourth, what did Jesus preach on this occasion? Was it an offer of salvation or the announcement of condemnation? If the meaning is that he proclaimed judgment, Jesus was declaring that the power of evil had been finally broken, and that those who had exercised its power faced certain and total ruin. Such an interpretation would greatly increase the confidence of Peter's readers to believe in their ultimate triumph by sharing in Christ's victory, however testing their present or anticipated situation.

The alternative view that Jesus preached salvation is supported by the fact that, although the Greek verb *kēryssein* used here is a neutral term for any public pronouncement, in the NT it is almost always used in the sense of proclaiming the saving good news of the gospel. Again, if this is Peter's meaning, his readers would find encouragement to believe that despite the apparent intransigence of adversaries, it was still possible to win them to Christ. The best way to overcome an enemy is, after all, to make that person an ally.

Fifth, who are the imprisoned spirits? There are three main possibilities. The **long ago** may indicate that Peter is referring to the fallen angels of Genesis 6:1–4, linking up with the disobedience to God mentioned in verse 20. This would be in line with highly popular traditions in Jewish literature prolific in the period between the OT and the NT. These disobedient angels were also considered to be representative of heathen rulers. Christ's preaching to them would encourage Christians to follow his example by proclaiming the gospel to the pagan rulers of their own day, when they were summoned before them to answer charges.

Alternatively, the imprisoned spirits may be the godless people who perished in the Flood, the **long ago** in this case meaning "in Noah's day." That generation was branded in Judaism as the worst of sinners, who could never be saved. "The generation of the Flood have no share in the world to come, now shall they stand in the judgment" (m. *Sanh.* 10.3). That Christ preached even to them indicates that the gospel is capable of saving the worst of sinners—assuming that **preached** here refers to salvation rather than to the proclamation of condemnation.

Some have suggested that the imprisoned spirits are OT believers, that is, those who, although men and women of faith, under the old dispensation were confined to what was called "Sheol" in Hebrew and "Hades" in Greek, the abode of the dead. The reference to "disobedience" in verse 20 appears to rule out this possibility, and to restrict the preaching to the wicked. Yet 4:6 makes it clear that the gospel brought not only judgment to the dead but new life in God. The whole passage 3:18—4:6 is a unity, as its chiastic literary form indicates (see Additional Notes), and 4:6 implies that the total mission of Christ included the OT dead. The reference to "the spirits in prison" therefore is not restricted to the wicked dead but includes all who under the OT dispensation were confined to Sheol/Hades, the place of the dead, until Christ's own triumph over death. This was the line taken, for example, by Tertullian (*On the Soul* 55).

Sixth, where was the spirits' prison? In the ancient world this was considered to be in the lower regions of the earth, "Sheol"/"Hades." This place of the dead, often described as a prison house (Rev. 18:2; 20:1–7), applied both to human beings and to fallen angels, the latter in particular being confined to an intense darkness (2 Pet. 2:17; Jude 6; 1 Enoch 10:4–5; cf. Rev. 20:3) somewhere in the depths of the earth (Jub. 5:6).

3:20 / The spirits singled out for Christ's preaching, specified as those who **disobeyed long ago** in the days of Noah, are the angels whose fall is narrated in Genesis 6:1–4. The patient endurance of God (Gen. 6:3) is frequently mentioned in biblical and other Jewish writings, but it is a divine restraint that offers a limited opportunity for repentance before eventual and certain punishment falls.

The Flood in **the days of Noah** is frequently mentioned as an example of divine judgment, even if God will not use that particular method again (Isa. 54:9). But the incident serves to indicate the relative paucity of godly people compared with the vast majority of unbelievers, a point which Peter's readers would readily appreciate. The reference to the building of the ark against the Flood will also introduce the subject of water, and thus of Christian baptism (v. 21).

3:21 / Just as Noah was saved from the hostility of the godless, and water was involved in his deliverance, so Christian believers should appreciate that they too are saved from evil through water —the water of **baptism**. Their new status as forgiven servants of the living God should make them confident to stand before godless opponents without fear. That confidence is based not on some outward ritual washing, which could at best only remove dirt from the skin, but on a **good conscience toward God**. The significance of baptism is that it is the public acknowledgment of an inward spiritual purity brought about in the individual by the work of God in Christ. The **pledge** made by believers in their baptism to serve God and so maintain that **good conscience** is their expression of faith that through accepting the work of Jesus on the cross they have been forgiven and made right with God; they have a clear conscience before him. But to avoid any possible misunderstanding, Peter makes it clear that the effective power of Christian baptism is due not to any ceremony but to **the resurrection of Jesus Christ**. That event set the seal on his triumph over death and evil. It is the foundation of all Christian life.

3:22 / The resurrection was followed by Christ's triumphant return to **heaven**. There he was accorded the supreme place of honor **at God's right hand**. The metaphor, a quotation from Psalm 110:1, expresses the Father's bestowal of the highest dignity and power upon his Son. In this position Christ now rules with God over **angels, authorities and powers,** an omnibus expression to include all spiritual agencies. Peter is thus further emphasizing the supreme and all-sufficient lordship of Jesus Christ that will aid his followers in whatever testing situation they may find themselves as they live for God.

Additional Notes   §17

3:18 / **For sins** is a phrase commonly used in the OT for the sin-offering (Lev. 5:7; 6:30; Ezek. 43:21).

The righteous: The Righteous (or Just) One was a well-known messianic title (e.g., Wisd. of Sol. 2:18; 1 Enoch 38:2). In the NT it was applied to Jesus: Acts 3:14 (by Peter); 7:52 (by Stephen); 22:14 (by Paul).

The unrighteous: The Greek term (*adikos*) basically concerns law rather than ethics; here it has the sense of "those who break God's law."

Bring you (*prosagein*) **to God:** The verb, found in the NT only here, is used of having the right of access to a tribunal or a royal court. In the Greek OT (LXX) it describes the act of offering sacrifices to God (Exod. 29:10) or of consecrating people to God's service (Exod. 40:12). The Greek verb corresponds to the Hebrew *hiqrîḇ*, the technical term for "to prose-lytize," i.e., to make a member of the chosen people one who was not so by natural birth. In rabbinic terminology such converts were also styled "newborn children" (cf. 2:2).

The balanced phrases **put to death ... made alive** may echo a piece of an early Christian hymn, for something similar occurs in Rom. 1:3–4 and 1 Tim. 3:16.

The phrases **in the body . . . by the Spirit** translate two Greek datives of identical form, which one would expect to be reflected in an identical English translation. The Greek can be rendered "as far as the physical body was concerned" . . . "as far as the spirit [of Jesus] was concerned."

3:19 / For much more detailed discussion of this problematic verse, see Selwyn, pp. 314–62; R. T. France, "Exegesis in Practice: Two Samples," in Marshall, ed., *New Testament Interpretation*, pp. 264–78; on the whole passage, see Grudem, pp. 203–39; Dalton, *Christ's Proclamation*; Reicke, *Disobedient Spirits*.

Went: The preexistence of Christ is referred to in 1:11, and elsewhere in the NT it is mentioned in John 1:1; 8:58; 17:5, 24; Phil. 2:6–7. That Christ was active in some way between his death and resurrection is hinted at in Matt. 12:40; Acts 2:25–27 (one of Peter's addresses); 13:35; Rom. 10:7; Eph. 4:9; Rev. 1:18.

Christ's descent into Sheol/Hades, inferred from Ps. 16:8–11, also appears in Acts 2:27, 31; 13:35; Rom. 10:6–8; Eph. 4:8–10. The misleading statement about Christ's descending into "Hell" (the place of punishment; Sheol/Hades is meant, the "neutral" place of departed spirits) was not included in the Apostles' Creed until the sixth century. It was inserted to stress the real humanity of Jesus Christ, against those who taught that he only appeared to suffer and to die.

Preached: The fact of the dead hearing the gospel is alluded to in John 5:25; Phil. 2:10; cf. Eph. 4:9.

Some scholars speculate that the original MS of 1 Peter mentioned Enoch as the preacher. The suggestion was first put forward in Bowyer's Greek Testament in the 1772 edition and supported the next year by the apparently providential discovery of the Ethiopic Book of Enoch. In 1 Enoch 12–14 we read of Enoch's mission to preach to the fallen angels of Gen. 6:1–4, who were disobedient in Noah's day. (Enoch is specified in this connection in Jude 14.) The basis of the proposal was that the original MS could have read "in which also Enoch . . . " The Greek for "in which also" (*en hō kai*) is almost the same as for the name *Enoch*, and the latter could easily have been accidentally omitted by a later copyist. The Greek text of the time had no spaces between words, so a slip of the eye was entirely feasible. But there is no surviving MS evidence of the proposed emendation. However attractive the suggestion, it seems unlikely to be correct, since it would make the passage more unintelligible, not less (as an emendation should). The sudden and unexplained intrusion of Enoch would in any case interrupt Peter's argument, for Christ is the subject both of v. 18 and v. 22.

Spirits in prison: According to the book of Enoch, popular in Peter's day, these spirits were patrons of powerful kings of the earth and as such promoted heathenism. Their punishment in the Flood was considered the prototype of the coming judgment of all heathen rulers who oppressed the people of God. "This judgment wherewith the [imprisoned] angels are judged is a testimony for the kings and mighty ones who possess the earth" (1 Enoch 67:12). The tradition, based on Gen. 6:1–4, of angelic disobedience was firmly established in Jewish thought (1 Enoch 6:1–8; 12:1–16:4; 19:1; 2 Baruch 56:12) and was placed just before the Flood (1 Enoch 10:2). The tradition is clearly alluded to in 2 Pet. 2:4; Jude 6.

The place of the dead (Sheol/Hades) is referred to in Matt. 11:23; 16:18; Luke 16:23; Acts 2:27; Rev. 1:18; 6:8; 20:13.

The whole passage 3:18—4:6 is a literary unity (*chiasmus*), with 3:18–20 inversely paralleled by 3:21—4:6. Note, for example, the following:

> 3:18 dead in body . . . alive in spirit
>> 3:19 went . . . spirits
>>> 3:20 saved . . . water
>>> 3:21 saved . . . water
>> 3:22 went . . . spirits
> 4:6 dead in body . . . alive in spirit

See S. E. Johnson, "The Preaching to the Dead," *JBL* 79 (1960), pp. 48–51.

3:20 / **God waited patiently**: The divine longsuffering prior to eventual judgment is a common theme (Isa. 48:9; 1 Enoch 60:5; *Pirqe Aboth* 5.2; Acts 17:30; Rom. 2:4; 2 Pet. 3:9).

The events of **the days of Noah** are often quoted as offering spiritual lessons (Isa. 54:9; Matt. 24:37; Luke 17:26; Heb. 11:7; 2 Pet. 2:5).

While **eight** undoubtedly stresses how few were saved in the deluge, the numeral itself was already significant in Judaism and was taken up by the early church. Circumcision was to be on the eighth day (Gen. 17:12; Luke 2:21); Noah himself was the eighth person saved (2 Pet. 2:5, KJV and Greek); David was the eighth son of Jesse (1 Sam. 16:10–11); a healed leper was declared "clean" on the eighth day (Lev. 14:10); the Feast of Tabernacles climaxed on the eighth day (Lev. 23:36; John 7:37); the Lord's Day early became known as the Eighth Day (Justin, *Dialogue with Trypho* 138.1). In every example there is an association with the notion of a new beginning.

Through water (*di' hydatos*): The Greek preposition *dia* can be taken as local or instrumental, meaning that he was saved *from* the peril of water, or *by means of* [floating on] the water in the ark. The distinction is unimportant. Either way, Noah was saved from godless opponents and water was involved.

3:21 / **Symbolizes** translates a Greek noun, *antitypon*, a type or figure fulfilled in the life and work of Christ. See Turner, pp. 168–73, 363.

Pledge: The Greek *eperōtēma* occurs in the NT only here. Strictly speaking the word means "question," but this is hardly appropriate in a baptismal context. The candidate for baptism would be expected to *answer*, not ask. The response to a question is probably what is meant, hence many modern translators agree with the NIV rendering. See Turner, pp. 342–44.

3:22 / **Gone into heaven**: The ascension of Christ is also mentioned in the longer ending of Mark [16:19]; Luke 24:51; Acts 1:9; Eph. 4:8; Heb. 4:14; 9:24.

At God's right hand alludes to Ps. 110:1, the most quoted OT passage in the NT (Matt. 22:44; 26:64; Mark 12:36; 14:62; [16:19]; Luke 20:42; 22:69; Acts 2:34; 5:31; 7:55; Rom. 8:34; Eph. 1:20; Col. 3:1; Heb. 1:3, 13; 8:1; 10:12; 12:2). See Dodd, *According to the Scriptures*, pp. 34–35; 120–21.

Jews, in common with most Eastern peoples, were careful to distinguish between the right and left hands. The right hand is used exclusively for blessing, salutation, giving (Ps. 16:11; Prov. 3:16), eating, and for receiving and showing honor. See Derrett, *Law in the New Testament*, pp. xlv–xlvi.

Angels, authorities and powers may be taken as the literary figure of hendiadys and mean "angels, authoritative and powerful as they are," which would avoid our having to puzzle over the identity of "authorities" and "powers" in heavenly places. For hendiadys, see Additional Note on 2:25.

In submission to him probably alludes to Ps. 8:4–6. Christians understood this to indicate that Christ in his incarnation as Son of Man was temporarily reduced to a status inferior to that of angels, only to be raised to sovereign authority over all beings, including angels, following his death and resurrection (1 Cor. 15:27; Eph. 1:22; Phil. 3:21; Heb. 2:6–8).

§18   Live Wholly for God (1 Pet. 4:1–6)

4:1 / What are the practical implications for Christians of Christ's suffering and consequent triumph over death and the powers of evil? Recalling the opening of this section, back in 3:18, Peter reverts to the death of Christ. This is the example that believers should follow. They must turn their backs on the immoral practices of their pagan neighbors, formerly their own life-style, and wholeheartedly follow their Master by copying him. **Christ suffered in his body**, that is, he gave his all, including his very life, in carrying out the will of God. His followers must resolve to go to the same lengths: **Arm yourselves also with the same attitude**—a military metaphor; but the NT is not averse to using such language, for believers are indeed engaged in warfare, albeit in the spiritual realm.

By his death, Jesus **is done with sin**. The meaning, of course, is not that Jesus now stopped sinning—Peter has already reminded his readers of Christ's sinlessness (2:22)—but that he dealt once and for all with the world's sin when he took it upon himself on the cross (2:24). The problem of dealing with sin is now over and done with. Peter's readers are to adopt the same attitude. Believers are to recognize that in view of their new birth spiritually (1:3), by which they now partake in the risen life of Christ, they are to reckon themselves dead to the blandishments of sin, presented to them by their "evil human desires," but alive to the creative and positive urgings of God. It is the same thought that Paul puts forward: "Count yourselves dead to sin but alive to God in Christ Jesus. Therefore do not let sin reign in your mortal body so that you obey its evil desires" (Rom. 6:11–12). That is the "will of God" for all believers.

4:2 / As they **live the rest of** their **earthly life**, they must constantly remind themselves that the power of the risen Christ is sufficient to enable them to pass each day in a manner pleasing to God. To strive to be perfect in God's sight was Christ's instruction (Matt. 5:48) and this must be their aim, even if they cannot achieve sinlessness in this life (1 John 1:8). At least they can be assured that as Christians they now possess the spiritual power to resist sin. They must resolve to make use of it.

4:3 / This verse implies that Peter's readers came from a pagan background. But it would be wrong to infer from the way he writes that they were all Gentiles. The many references to the Hebrew OT suggest otherwise, for Peter would hardly inject an important letter with frequent allusions which his readers might have little chance to appreciate.

With a touch of ironical understatement, Peter reminds them that they **have spent enough time in the past** filling their hours with immoral pagan practices. What those practices were accurately reflects what is known of the contemporary situation in Asia Minor. The acts of immorality listed fall into three groups: sexual misconduct (**debauchery, lust**), intemperance (**drunkenness, orgies, carousing**), and misdirected worship (**detestable idolatry**). The last would often have involved all the other malpractices. The Christians' unconverted lives have in that respect been utterly wasted. Less of their earthly life now remains for the Lord's work to be carried out, so the fulfilling of God's will is all the more urgent.

4:4 / The lives of the Christians have been so turned around by their conversion to Jesus Christ that pagan neighbors are thoroughly bewildered. They cannot understand how it is that their former boon companions are no longer wanting to join them in the old reckless rush into a **flood of dissipation**, a way of life abandoned to debauchery. And since they cannot comprehend what has happened, their resentful response is to **heap abuse on you**. Vilification was an aspect of suffering evidently all too common an experience for Peter's readers, for he mentions it no less than four times in this letter.

4:5 / Those who assail God's servants will one day undoubtedly **have to give account** at the divine tribunal when they stand before **him who is ready to judge**. The charge they will have to try to answer relates both to their own God-ignoring lives and to their reviling of Christ's followers. The identity of the one who is **to judge** is left unclear. It may be God himself (1:17; 2:23) or, as many references in the rest of the NT indicate, the glorified

Christ (e.g., Matt. 25:32; Rom. 2:16; 2 Tim. 4:1). The distinction matters little since God has committed judgment to the Son (John 5:22), who will therefore be acting with the Father's authority. The statement that the divine judge stands **ready** to act is in line with the topic coloring the whole letter: the imminent return of Christ in power and great glory (4:7). The judgment will involve **the living and the dead** (Acts 10:42, an address of Peter's). Whenever the moment of Christ's second coming arrives, some people of course will on that particular day in history be alive on the earth, others will have died—all will have to face judgment. But all can be assured that the divine judgment will be impartial (1:17), fair (2:23), inexorable (4:5), and full (4:6). Christians already have had their sins dealt with by the sacrifice of Christ upon the cross (2:24). The judgment of believers, therefore, concerns not their past sins but what they have achieved for God in their lives following their conversion to Christ (2 Cor. 5:10).

4:6 / In verse 5, Peter has mentioned the coming judgment of the living and the dead. Now he adds what amounts to a postscript concerning **those who are now dead**. It must be said straight away that no fully satisfactory explanation of this verse has ever been given. We can but seek to sense the drift of Peter's meaning.

Although Peter has previously referred to the preaching to some who were no longer on earth (the "spirits in prison," 3:19), we should not assume that the preaching here in 4:6 harks back to exactly the same topic. In 3:19, the Greek verb for "preach" is *kēryssein*, to proclaim; here in 4:6 it is *euangelizesthai*, to evangelize, preach good news. While the former Greek term is often used in the sense of "proclaim the gospel," the use in 4:6 of *euangelizesthai*, the more usual NT verb for preaching the gospel, is almost certainly deliberate (it also appears in 1:12, 25, where Peter refers to the first preaching heard by his readers). By **those who are now dead** Peter appears to have in mind men and women who were once friends and relatives of his present readers, who heard the gospel in their lifetime and responded to it, but who have since died. What is their situation?

On the one hand, as is the case with all human beings, they too face judgment (**according to men in regard to the body**: lit. "according to men in flesh"). But on the other hand, something else applies to believers who have passed on from this life, **those who are now dead**. Because they responded to the gospel during their earthly lives, they enjoy the supreme benefit of that gospel—eternal life: **they . . . live according to God in regard to the spirit**. So those who have been left behind on earth for a while longer need have no anxiety about their dead loved ones in Christ. They are safe with him and enjoying a full life in the spirit. Death is certainly not the last word for the Christian, any more than it was for Christ.

Additional Notes §18

4:1 / **Arm yourselves**: The NT makes use of military metaphors, for Christians are involved in spiritual warfare (Rom. 6:13; 13:12; 2 Cor. 6:7; 10:4; Eph. 6:11–17; 1 Thess. 5:8; 1 Tim. 1:18; 6:12; 2 Tim. 2:4; Rev. 12:17).

He who has suffered in his body: cf. Gal. 2:19–20.

Is done with sin: cf. Rom. 6:7.

4:2 / **Evil human desires** (*anthrōpōn epithymiais*): lit. "for impulses of human beings." NIV adds **evil** by way of interpretation since this is clearly what is meant (v. 3). The human impulses are based on ignorance of God's standards (1:14) and are antagonistic to the soul's welfare (2:11); cf. 1 John 2:16.

The will of God is a regular theme in this letter (2:15; 3:17; 4:2, 19).

4:3 / **Pagans** translates *ethnōn*, nations, the usual biblical term when non-Jews are meant.

Living is *peporeumenous*, from *poreuesthai*, to go along. Pagans travel a road in life which is filled with all kinds of immoral engagements.

Debauchery (*aselgeiai*): sexual excesses, resulting in grossly indecent behavior.

Lust (*epithymiai*): translated "evil human desires" in v. 2. The word also occurs in 1:14; 2:11.

Drunkenness: The Greek *oinophlygiai* implies habitual intoxication (from *oinos*, wine; *phlyein*, to bubble up, overflow).

Orgies (*kōmoi*): the result of excessive drinking ("wild parties," JB).

Carousing (*potoi*): This word can refer to drinking competitions to see who can down the most.

Detestable idolatries (*athemitoi eidōlolatriai*, "lawless idolatry" [RSV]): practices forbidden by the Mosaic law (Acts 10:28), "which outrage common decency" (Barclay).

4:4 / **Plunge** (lit. "run together") paints a picture of people rushing forward from all directions in order to see something untoward (Mark 6:33; Acts 3:11).

Flood of dissipation: *Anachysis* means a pouring out, an excess; *asōtia*, a life given up to profligacy (Eph. 5:18; Titus 1:6), implying a waste of time, energy, and resources. The cognate term *asōtōs* is used of the prodigal son's "wild living," which included lavishing his money on harlots (Luke 15:13). In *T. Asher* 5.1 *asōtia* is significantly contrasted with "wedlock."

Heap abuse on you translates one word, lit. "blaspheme." The Greek means to speak lightly or profanely of sacred things, especially of God; but it can also, as here, refer to the reviling of people. Evil-speaking against Christian believers is mentioned several times in this letter (2:12; 3:9; 4:4, 14). It was by no means a novel experience for the godly: see Wisd. of Sol. 2:12–20, where the situation is graphically described.

4:5 / Give account is an expression used in the NT of an employee in relation to his employer (Luke 16:2) and of rioters being answerable to civil authorities (Acts 19:40); and, in the spiritual field, it can describe Christian leaders in respect of their flock (Heb. 13:17). Each individual bears responsibility for his or her life and actions and will eventually have to answer for both.

The living and the dead: On whatever date in history Christ makes his return, many people will be alive on the earth, of course, and many others will have died. A similar thought lies behind Christ's statement to Martha: "I am the resurrection [in respect to dead believers] and the life [in respect to those living on earth at the second coming, and who will not need to go through the experience of death]" (John 11:25–26). The fate of believers who had already died before the second coming may have been causing concern to their surviving loved ones, as in the case of the Thessalonian Christians (1 Thess. 4:13–17). Peter's words here may in part be intended to encourage any of his readers faced with such a worry. Cf. Wisd. of Sol. 3:1–4.

4:6 / The gospel was preached. The verb *euangelizesthai* is used also in 1:12, 25, where it refers to the first preaching of the gospel to Peter's readers. The verb *kēryssein*, to proclaim, occurs in Peter's writings only in 3:19.

To those who are now dead has been taken in several ways. It might mean (1) the spiritually dead (Eph. 2:1); but this involves giving a different sense to the "dead" in v. 5. (2) OT saints, who waited in the abode of the dead ("Hades") for Christ (= Messiah) to come. His preaching enabled them to respond to the gospel. This interpretation, like the first, also requires a different meaning for "dead" in v. 5. (3) The dead in general, taking "the spirits in prison" of 3:19–20 to be good and bad people alike, waiting in the abode of the dead. Or (4), the Christian dead, i.e., those who responded to the gospel during their lifetime.

Judged according to men could perhaps relate to judgment at the hands of the civil authorities that Christians (now dead) had suffered during their days on earth. This might also suggest that some believers had therefore died as martyrs. Or the phrase may simply be a reference to the experience of death through which all human beings have to pass (Rom. 5:12; Heb. 9:27).

4:7 / **The end of all things is near**: The second coming is not in view here as much as is the transience of all that pertains to the closing present age. When he goes on to admonish readers to be **clear minded and self-controlled**, Peter is not seeking to calm over-excited readers keyed up by the anticipation of Christ's return, a situation Paul once had to address (2 Thess. 2:1–2). The readers are bidden to hold loosely to earthly commitments and not to let their attention be unduly absorbed by them. They are to be **clear minded** about their true priorities **and self-controlled**, calm, in their consideration of all that concerns their life. The reason for this watchful self-discipline? **So . . . you can pray**. This maintains uncluttered lines of communication with the Lord, both to discern his will and to receive his directions for carrying it out. Being too caught up with worldly affairs and being confused by their attendant worries can ruin prayer-life and spoil spiritual relationships, both with God and with fellow Christians.

4:8 / **Above all**, as far as fellow believers are concerned, right relationships between them are paramount. The importance of the old tag "unity is strength" became increasingly obvious to the early Christians as members of their community faced hardening antagonism from neighbors and officials. The vital link between Christians is expressed by Peter's admonition to his readers: **above all, love each other deeply**. And by way of supporting explanation, he once again turns to the OT for a proof-text: **because love covers over a multitude of sins** (Prov. 10:12). As a proverb, the expression perhaps originally meant "Love is blind to the faults of others." It came to be interpreted by Jews as referring to deeds of love, especially almsgiving, that in the Jewish view helped to atone for an individual's own sins. Significantly, in taking over the OT citation Peter changes the word for "love" to the usual NT term (*agapē*), and so points to the Christian understanding of the proverb. Love here refers to Christ's love. At best, a Christian's love is but a reflection of that of the Lord Jesus, and that is unique because it alone can "cover over sins." Only Christ's love is able to hide an individual's sins from God's consciousness (Rom. 5:9).

4:9 / Love is to be expressed in practical ways. For example, Christians are to **offer hospitality to one another**. In the early days of the church especially, hospitality was far from being merely a matter of occasional friendly entertainment. Peter bids his readers to be ready to open their homes and offer a necessary service to fellow Christians. In a world dominated by paganism in employment and culture, living the Christian faith would often entail temporal loss. Mutual support was therefore vital. Traveling missionaries in particular were dependent upon local believers for their food and lodging. But in the absence of church buildings, believers met for worship in private houses (Rom. 16:5; 1 Cor. 16:10, 19; Col. 4:15), and this is probably what Peter primarily has in mind when he speaks here of offering hospitality **to one another**. He is mainly addressing the local situation. Having to stretch resources to provide for others could on occasions lead to irritation, so Peter adds the warning **without grumbling**. "True Christian hospitality is making people feel at home, when you wish they were at home" (Donald Coggan, former Archbishop of Canterbury).

4:10 / Christian service takes a multitude of forms, and everyone in God's family has a part to play. Whatever may be the feelings of inadequacy, none is too weak or incapable of contributing something to the community, for the Lord has seen to it that each believer has one **gift** or another to employ for the common good. Peter does not mention the Holy Spirit in this connection, as Paul does when he discusses the subject of gifts (1 Cor. 12–14). But he uses the Greek word (*charisma*) and makes it clear that every such gift comes from God. The purpose of his bestowing such gifts on Christians is to enable them **to serve others** in the community of believers, a service of trust that they are supposed to carry out **faithfully**, as good administrators of the divine estate **in its various forms** (Matt. 25:14; Rom. 12:6; 1 Cor. 4:2).

4:11 / Not everyone has the gift of preaching. But each believer who does have that God-given ability should always use it bearing in mind the awesome responsibility that goes with it.

He or she opens the mouth **as one speaking the very words of God**. To one conscious of being inspired by the gift of prophecy (1 Cor. 14:1), it should not be difficult to remember the divine source, even though a human channel is being used. But the **speaking** referred to here covers any public pronouncements of Christian truth. All who claim to be speaking in the name of God should do so only if they are aware of having a divine commission.

A believer's ministry may lie not in words but in what we tend to regard as more practical fields. **If anyone serves**, then that service is to be carried out **with the strength God provides**, though not thoughtlessly taking on any and every job that sails into view. God gives strength for the tasks he wants particular individuals to carry out. The word for **serving** is a general one and covers all manner of contributions to the good of the Christian community. From the first days of the early church, such free and cheerful service included providing for the hungry, caring for the sick and needy, succoring those suffering for their faith, and welcoming strangers (Matt. 10:8; 25:35; Acts 2:45).

At the end of the day, the right and successful application of all gifts depends not on the individual's natural abilities but on God working in and through the believer. As Christians come to appreciate that any success attending their labors is due to the effectiveness of divine resources rather than to any innate abilities, then they will see that the praise is addressed to the one to whom it is due, to **God**. The employment of gifts in service is not to promote any pride in human achievement (1 Cor. 4:7), but to further God's glory **through Jesus Christ**. Peter brings the thought back yet again to his Lord, who is at the heart of every Christian life and whose glory is the object of all Christian work. The sounding out of a paean of praise in a doxology therefore follows naturally: **To him be the glory and the power for ever and ever. Amen.** Attention is turned away from any human effort to the divine figure who has both prompted and brought to fruition a portion of service.

Additional Notes §19

4:7 / **Be clear minded**: The Greek verb *sōphronein* means to have a sober attitude, to keep one's head—it can contrast being demon-possessed (Mark 5:15) or being out of one's mind (2 Cor. 5:13), or overproud, too high-minded (Rom. 12:3).

Self-controlled, from *nēphein*, to abstain from wine; metaphorically, to be calm, circumspect. The verb is also used in 1:13 and 5:8.

4:8 / **Deeply** (*ektenē*): "Stretched out," in today's jargon, "going all out," like a sportsman or a race car driver. The corresponding adverb occurs in 1:22, again in reference to Christian love between believers.

Love covers over a multitude of sins. The quotation (for a NT writer, unusually cited from the Hebrew not the Greek OT) is from Prov. 10:12 (also used in James 5:20). A similar thought is in *T. Joseph* 17.2, "Therefore love one another, brethren, and with longsuffering hide one another's faults." On a Christian interpretation of the proverb, see S. Kierkegaard, *For Self-Examination, and Judge for Yourselves* (Oxford: Oxford University Press, 1941), pp. 18–25.

4:9 / Israel was always distinguished for its hospitality. It was said that during the great national feasts, no pilgrim in Jerusalem ever wanted for hospitality without charge. Nearby Bethphage and Bethany were renowned for their generosity in this respect. The rabbis declared that hospitality involved even greater merit than early morning attendance at an academy of learning—praise indeed from such a source. Understandably, the rabbis also taught that to entertain a sage and to send him away with presents was as meritorious as offering the daily sacrifices (b. *Ber.* 10b). See Edersheim, *Sketches of Jewish Social Life*, pp. 47–48.

Without grumbling: The splendidly onomatopoeic *gongysmos* is the word used of the murmuring of the Israelites in the wilderness (Num. 17:5, 10 LXX).

4:10 / **Gift** is *charisma*, a gift of *charis*, grace, i.e., something bestowed freely and without merit on the believer by God that is to be used for the good of the community of believers. See Rom. 12:3–8; 1 Cor. 12:4–11, 27–31.

Faithfully administering is the NIV rendering of *hōs kaloi oikonomoi*, "as good managers." Many translations use the term "stewards." In the Greek world of NT times, the steward was a slave who was entrusted with managing his master's household and estate (Luke 12:42; 16:1–8).

Grace (*charis*) can be a synonym for **gift** (*charisma*); the latter term occurs only here in 1 Peter, and otherwise in the NT only in Pauline writings (17 times).

In its various forms translates *poikiloi* , lit. multicolored. Christian gifts of service come in many varieties, but exercised together they form a harmonious pattern. The Greek term is used only in one other place in this letter, in referring to "*all kinds* of trials." See commentary on 1:6.

4:11 / **Words** is *logia*, sayings, divine oracles.

Serves translates *diakonein*, the usual NT verb for Christian ministry in all its forms (also in 1:12; 4:10).

With the strength God provides: The Greek verb is *chorēgein* (which occurs in the NT only here and in 2 Cor. 9:10). It is used of defraying the expenses of the Greek chorus in dramatic productions, an act of munificence possible only to the wealthiest citizens. The word therefore conveys the idea of liberal giving for the public good.

In the doxology **power** (*kratos*) refers to the all-sufficient and inexhaustible divine ability to create and control (Eph. 1:19; 6:10; Col. 1:11).

Amen ("So it is!" or "It is true!") usually concludes doxologies (5:11; Rom. 11:36; 16:27; Gal. 1:5; Eph. 3:21; Phil. 4:20; 1 Tim. 1:17; 6:16; Heb. 13:21; 2 Pet. 3:18; Jude 25; Rev. 1:6; 7:12).

4:12 / **Dear friends** signals the beginning of a new section, as Peter returns to the subject of suffering, though in particular to suffering on account of being a Christian. That a **painful trial** should come to those who have committed their lives to God's keeping should not cause surprise. Conversion does not bring exemption *from* troubles, though it does assure believers of divine assistance *through* troubles. To have been born again into new spiritual life (1:3) will inevitably arouse opposition (1:6). This is because spiritual agencies antagonistic to Christ stir up the enmity of pagan neighbors and authorities. Believers should not conclude that **something strange** is **happening** to them. Now that Jesus himself is no longer on earth in human form, the spiritual onslaught falls upon his followers.

The **painful trial** is a less dramatic rendering than the Greek warrants, for the expression suggests an ordeal by fire—a purifying in a furnace (a "fiery trial," KJV). Evidently Peter had heard of some experience of suffering his readers were facing beyond what might be expected in the course of their everyday life among unsympathetic pagans, who naturally disliked people who were different. It could possibly indicate some form of more or less official persecution.

4:13 / A further cause of pagan bewilderment at the way Christians behave is their cheerful attitude toward suffering. When Peter tells his readers to **rejoice** in such circumstances, he is not only alluding to an earlier remark (1:6) but remembering his own experience of years before (Acts 5:41). He assures his friends that they can joyfully accept persecution on account of their faith because what they go through is a sharing **in the sufferings of Christ**. What happened to him is happening to them. Far from being upset by such treatment, Christians should be glad that they are considered worthy to be set alongside their Master in this respect. But there is more to it than the fact that their suffering, like his, is unmerited.

To share in Christ's sufferings means also to benefit from their consequences (Rom. 8:17; 2 Cor. 4:10; Phil. 3:10), for **when his glory is revealed** at the second coming, believers will have every reason to be **overjoyed**. They will not simply be spectators, so to speak, but be privileged in some way to partake in Christ's glory (Peter spells this out in 5:10). Even the English terms "rejoice" and "be overjoyed" make it clear that Peter is far from merely advising his Christian friends to fix on a brave smile when suffering for Christ comes their way. The Greek words convey the idea of overwhelming delight, a great burst of joy that will fill the jubilant hearts of God's people to overflowing when they greet Christ on his triumphant return in glory (1:6).

4:14 / One form of suffering may be verbal abuse hurled at them because they are associated with **the name of Christ**: "they belong to that evil gang!" Jesus forewarned the disciples of this type of persecution (Matt. 5:11; John 15:2), and it came to pass from the earliest days (Acts 5:41; 9:16; 21:13; James 5:10; 3 John 7; Rev. 2:3).

The proverb may claim that "Hard words break no bones," but something more injurious is meant by Peter's reference to Christians being **insulted**. Their very characters are being assailed, and this in itself could easily lead on to mistrust or worse. Many social and civic activities of the day involved pagan practices in which Christians could not in conscience take part (4:4). This led not merely to misunderstanding and resentment by uncomprehending pagan neighbors; it could readily be interpreted as antisocial at best or treasonable at worst.

All the same, being reviled for the name of Christ is still to be viewed positively when it comes. The experience, far from being a negative and useless one, brings a blessing with it through divine action, **for the Spirit of glory and of God rests on** believers who suffer in this way. The expression alludes to the messianic passage "The Spirit of the Lord will rest on him" (Isa. 11:2). This text was, of course, one which Jesus claimed in the Nazareth synagogue to be fulfilled in himself (Luke 4:18). Now Peter boldly applies the same prophecy to Christians, but with a significant amplification. The Spirit is **the Spirit of glory**, literally of *the* **glory**, which almost certainly is an allusion to the *Shekinah*, the glory cloud signifying the divine presence (Exod. 40:34–35; 1 Kings 8:11; Matt. 17:5). This makes it clear why believers are to realize that they are **blessed**: the very reviling is a proof that Christ is in them, and God's enemies intuitively recognize this and react accordingly. It is worthy of notice that Peter declares that the divine Spirit of glory **rests** on believers. The expression implies a contrast between the storm of abuse and calumny raging around a Christian life and the peace enjoyed within the soul where the Spirit of God makes his resting place.

4:15 / There is perhaps a little smile on Peter's face as he continues: "Only make sure you don't deserve suffering!" Anyone who commits crimes like murder or theft can expect to pay the penalty—nothing unjust about that. Let any suffering faced by Christians be for the right reason: their loyalty to God in faithfully following Jesus Christ.

4:16 / While it is obviously a disgrace if a professing believer is guilty of besmirching the name of Christ by getting involved in any sort of civil crime, there is no cause for shame if suffering is due solely on account of being a Christian. The earliest disciples were known as Nazarenes, after the home-town of their Master Jesus (Acts 24:5). The nickname **Christian** was first popularly applied to his followers at Antioch on the Orontes in Syria (Acts 11:26). That was no doubt due to the name Christ being frequently used by believers when referring to their Master, but it will also reflect the fact that the messiahship of Jesus was recognized by the general public as a prominent factor in the apostolic preaching ("Christ" is, of course, simply the Greek version of the Hebrew term "Messiah"). Whatever the reason for opponents calling them by the name **Christian**, let believers **praise God** when they are so labeled.

By the translation **that you bear that name**, the NIV has paraphrased the Greek (which literally is simply "in this name") and assumes **that name** refers back to the title **Christian** earlier in the verse. For readers familiar with the OT, however, **name** can be a technical term for the presence of God (Deut. 12:11; Ps. 74:7; Isa. 18:7; Jer. 7:10–14 and passim). Peter's assurance that you can **praise God** "in this name" may therefore be intended to convey the meaning "the divine presence is evident in your lives, and you can rejoice in relying on the presence of God being with you through whatever suffering you may face on account of your faith."

4:17 / Peter returns to the theme of divine **judgment** (4:5–6). That judgment is imminent. The last times are here. Furthermore, and this may have come as a surprise to Peter's readers in view of all they were already going through, the judgment will **begin with the family of God**. Christians are not exempt. But what is the purpose behind the judgment of believers? Peter has already touched on this at the beginning of his letter: it is to refine faith, for faith in God's sight is infinitely precious. On the human level, even gold has to go through the crucible (1:7).

But there is another aspect to the judgment faced by believers. They will have to give account of the response they have made to the privilege of knowing God and his grace: "Every one to whom much is given, of him will much be required" (Luke 12:48 RSV). The judgment that begins at the house of God will mean a refining of God's people (Mal. 3:3). No purifying process can ever be painless, but believers can take heart from the knowledge that all that they suffer has an end, a goal: it is for their ultimate good in the purposes of God (Rom. 8:18).

Judgment is to be universal. It will also extend to unbelievers, which would of course include those persecuting Peter's readers, and **the outcome** for them can scarcely be imagined. The offer of the good news of the **gospel of God** is not an offer of good advice, to be accepted or disregarded at will. It is a matter of obeying a divine order. God has *commanded* all people everywhere to repent (Acts 17:30), so **those who do not obey the gospel of God**, and persist in their disobedience, are rebels against the Most High, and they will be treated as such. A clear understanding that there is a life to come in the immediate presence of the Lord provides a powerful stimulus to living a godly life in the present world. Conversely, a lack of belief in any hereafter will confirm the godless in applying their thoughts and actions to making the best they can of their own material situation in the present world, for this, in their view, is all that there is. There is no place in their scheme of things for an ultimate reckoning.

4:18 / Once again Peter supports his statement with a quotation, this time from Prov. 11:31 LXX. **"If it is hard for the righteous to be saved . . . "** does not, of course, imply that it is difficult for God to save, or that there is any uncertainty about the destiny of believers. The words mean that the believer must not expect the road to ultimate full salvation to be uneventfully smooth and easy. Spiritual adversaries will see to that, quite apart from the common ills to which anyone living in this world may be subject. But if it is far from roses all the way for the godly, the quotation goes on with the rhetorical question **"what will become of the ungodly and the sinner?"** What indeed! The outlook for one who acts contemptuously toward God (such is the implication of the word for **ungodly**: impious) is left hanging threateningly in the air.

4:19 / Summing up, Peter declares that all this means that believers **who suffer** in the course of following **God's will** are to express their trust in the Lord by a deliberate handing over of their lives to him. Meanwhile, regardless of discouragements, they are to carry on with the good work he wants them to do.

Those who **commit themselves** to God can be assured that, far more faithfully than the most loyal of human beings, he will accept each one of them individually as a sacred and inviolate trust. Believers can be as utterly confident about this as their Master was, when on the cross he committed his spirit to his Father (Luke 23:46). Their own act of committal is **to their faithful Creator**, to one who not only brought them into this world in the first place, but was responsible for their second birth, when they were reborn of the Spirit (1:3). They are therefore doubly God's and can unreservedly depend upon his care and protection. God is **faithful**. He always keeps his promises to do what he says he will do. For their part, believers are not to droop in a resigned fashion under persecution, but to respond to it positively, however difficult that may be, by continuing to **do good**—and perhaps having Christ's words in mind Peter means "especially to persecutors" (2:12; 3:9; Matt. 5:16; Luke 6:27).

Additional Notes   §20

4:12 / **Dear friends** translates *agapētoi*, beloved (by God), as in 2:11; 2 Pet. 3:1, 8, 14, 17. See Additional Note on 2:11.

Surprised (*xenizein*): to astonish by the unexpected.

Painful trial renders *pyrōsis*, a refining or trial by fire. "Fire (*pyrōsis*) is the trial for silver and gold" (Prov. 27:21). In the Dead Sea Scrolls the corresponding Hebrew word *maṣrēp*, which occurs quite frequently, has shifted in meaning to become virtually a technical term in the Qumran community for the eschatological ordeal, after which the elect will be saved. This is the sense reflected by Peter.

Suffering is part of the inescapable order of things in the present world. Christians will have their share (5:9). But in their case the purpose in suffering is the proving of faith. But for all the value that Peter sees in the suffering of Christians, he is under no illusions as to whose sufferings were needed to bring us to God (3:18). This contrasts with the view in Judaism. Rabbis viewed personal sufferings as a means of atonement. "A man should rejoice at chastisements more than at prosperity, for chastisements bring forgiveness for his transgressions" (*Sifre Deut.* 32 on Deut. 6:5). "Beloved are chastisements, for just as sacrifices atone, so also chastisements atone" (*Midrash Ps.* 94.2).

4:13 / **Sufferings** for Christ's sake is also a prominent theme in Paul's letters (Rom. 8:17; 2 Cor. 1:5, 7; Phil. 1:29; 3:10; Col. 1:24; 2 Tim. 2:12).

Sufferings of Christ is lit. "sufferings of *the* Christ," and could be taken as a reference to the "messianic woes," a time of suffering preceding Messiah's advent, which was expected in Judaism. The emphasis in rabbinic teaching, however, was not on the sufferings of Messiah himself but on the experience of Israel during years of great distress (b. *Šabb.* 118a) and suffering (b. *Pesaḥ.* 118a), for this is the period of Mother Zion's "birthpangs" ushering in a new era. The parallels with NT teaching about the second coming of Christ are patent. See G. F. Moore, *Judaism* (Cambridge, Mass.: Harvard University Press, 1927), vol. 2, p. 361.

Be overjoyed (*charēte agalliōmenoi*, lit. "you may rejoice exulting"): This recalls Christ's "rejoice (*chairete*) and be glad (*agalliasthe*)" in Matt. 5:12, where again the context concerns persecution. Peter has also combined the two terms in 1:8. See commentary and Additional Note on 1:6.

4:14 / **Insulted** (*oneidizein*): to revile, slander. This particular term occurs only here in 1 Peter, but the theme of verbal abuse suffered by believers is mentioned several times. Evidently it was an all too common experience (2:12, 15; 3:16; 4:4).

Blessed (*makarioi*): The same word is used in the Beatitudes (Matt. 5:3); see commentary and Additional Note on 3:14.

The Spirit of glory and of God may be an example of hendiadys, and so be translated "the glorious divine Spirit." On the literary figure of hendiadys, see Additional Note on 2:25.

The presence of the Spirit is promised to believers in times of persecution (Matt. 10:20; Mark 13:11; Luke 12:11–12; John 14:26; 16:7–11). Before the Sanhedrin, Stephen's face is said be like an angel's (Acts 6:15); and at Stephen's subsequent martyrdom, the Spirit and the glory of God are specially mentioned (Acts 7:55).

Rests (*anapauetai*): "makes for himself a place of rest." "The Holy Spirit does not rest where there is idleness, or sadness, or ribaldry, or frivolity, or empty speech, but only where there is joy" (*Midrash Psalms* 24.3.3).

4:15 / The list of misdemeanors includes the obvious like murder and theft, a general term *kakopoios*, evildoer (rendered by NIV as **any other kind of criminal**), and a fourth word, the meaning of which is something of a puzzle. The term *allotriepiskopos* is unique in Greek literature—apart from references to this verse in the early fathers—and may even be a word Peter has coined. The translators vary widely in their efforts: from *busybody* (KJV) and *mischief-maker* (RSV) to *informer* (JB) and *sorcery* (NEB). The Greek word itself is made up of terms meaning roughly "one who looks upon what is rightly the business of others," "a self-appointed overseer." So NIV's **meddler** is as good a suggestion as any, even if the nature of the meddling is left obscure to us. See Turner, p. 332; *NIDNTT*, vol. 2, p. 742; *TDNT*, vol. 2, pp. 620–22.

4:16 / **Christian**: The followers of Jesus are called by various names in the early days, as recorded in Acts: saved (Acts 2:47), disciples (6:1), saints (9:13), brothers (9:30), believers (10:45), Nazarenes (24:5), Christians (26:28). Perhaps the earliest reference to "Christian" in non-Christian literature is in Josephus, *Ant*. 18.63–64, where "the tribe of Christians" is said to be named after "the so-called Christ." Even the Josephus reference, however, is part of a passage generally thought to be a Christian addition (*Testimonium Flavianum*). The emperor Claudius banished Jews from Rome in A.D. 49 for rioting "at the instigation of Chrestus," according to Suetonius (*Life of Claudius* 25.4), by which the writer (seventy years after the event) appears to think that the leader of the Christians was in Rome at the time.

Nearly fifty years after the probable date of 1 Peter, Pliny the Younger (A.D. 62–113), the Roman governor of Bithynia-Pontus (109–111), one of the provinces to which this letter was addressed, wrote to the emperor Trajan for advice on how to deal with Christians:

> "I have never taken part in investigations of Christians, so I do not know what charge is usually brought against them. Neither do I know whether punishment is given just for the name [*of Christian*], apart from secret crimes connected with the name. This is the course I have taken: I asked them if they were Christians. If they said yes, I asked them a second and a third time, with threats of punishment. If they still said yes, I ordered them to be executed. Those who denied being Christians, I thought it right to let go. They recited a prayer to the gods at my dictation, offered incense and wine to your statue, and cursed Christ. Those who are really Christians cannot be made to do these things." (Pliny, *Letters* 10.96)

4:17 / **Time** (*kairos*): a definite fixed time or season.

For judgment to begin alludes to Mal. 3:1–3. The Greek word for **judgment** here is not condemnation but rather a judicial decision made on the evidence. God will reward or punish as he sees fit.

Family of God (*oikos tou theou*): lit. house of God. Peter has the spiritual temple in view (2:4–5). That judgment begins with God's own people is an OT theme (Jer. 25:29; 49:12; Ezek. 9:6; Mal. 3:1–5). Paul refers to this as the judgment seat of Christ (2 Cor. 5:10).

If it begins with us, not "with *you*," as would be expected if Peter were referring to some particular local persecution faced by his readers.

"Then shall all people rise, some to glory and some to shame [Dan. 12:2]. And the Lord shall judge Israel first, for their unrighteousness" (*T. Benjamin* 10.8), to which a later Christian hand has added: "for when He appeared as God in the flesh to deliver them, they believed Him not."

"If the earth trembled when he gave life to the world [a reference to the giving of the law on Mount Sinai, Exod. 19:16, 18], how much the more so when He comes to punish the wicked for transgressing the words of the law? If no creature can stand before Him when He is pleased [at the giving of revelation], then who can stand before Him when He rises in His fierce wrath?" (*Midrash Rabbah* 29.9 on Exod. 20:1).

The phrase **the gospel of God** (the revelation made by God of his own character and his required response from human beings) appears in this letter only here (also Mark 1:14; six times in Paul), although the corresponding verb occurs in 1:12, 25; 4:6).

4:18 / **The righteous** is singular, the righteous one. In 1 Enoch 38:2 the term is a messianic title: "When the Righteous One appears before the eyes of the elect righteous whose works are wrought in dependence upon the Lord of Spirits . . . where then will be the dwelling of sinners or the resting place of those who have denied the Lord of Spirits?"

4:19 / **God's will** is a repeated theme of the letter: explicitly in 2:15; 3:17; 4:2 and implicitly in 2:19; 3:16, 21.

The Greek verb in **commit themselves** means "to make a deposit," as in the safe-keeping of a bank. The same Greek verb is used of Jesus on the cross committing his spirit to his Father (Luke 23:46). Peter spoke from experience. When in prison facing execution (Acts 12:6), he was soundly asleep, unworried and undisturbed. A blow from the angel was necessary to awaken him.

The theme of believers committing themselves in trust to God is frequent in the Bible: Ps. 31:5; 34:22; 37:5; Prov. 3:5; Acts 7:59; 1 Cor. 10:13; 1 Thess. 5:23–24; 2 Thess. 3:3; 2 Tim. 1:12; 2:13; Heb. 10:23.

Creator: Only here in the NT is God so called. The one who is responsible for the whole of creation and for its care can be relied upon to provide the needs of all who put their trust in him (Matt. 6:25–33).

5:1 / Peter now turns to address the local church leaders, **the elders among you**. The term **elders** can indicate those senior in age (as in v. 5) or as here, senior in experience. In the nature of the case, of course, the latter meaning will often include the former. Hints of the function of elders can be gleaned from verses 2–3. Their duties include leading and pastoring church members, taking financial responsibility, and living exemplary lives that match up to Christian teaching. With many of the first believers coming from a background of Judaism, it would be natural for the early churches to be organized on the well-established model found in the Diaspora, Jewish settlements scattered abroad. This was the Sanhedrin, a council of elders under a president, who together looked after the corporate life of the Jewish community. Later in Asia Minor, the area to which 1 Peter is addressed, a clearer hierarchical structure has been established, according to the letters of Ignatius (martyred ca. A.D. 107), but the present letter does not suggest a rigid ecclesiastical system.

Peter makes his appeal to the church leaders as a **fellow elder**, one of them in some respects, although as an apostle (1:1) he is able to speak with special authority. Referring to himself as a **fellow elder** expresses a certain humility, although he does go on to refer to the privilege he has of being a firsthand **witness of Christ's sufferings** (Acts 10:39). But Peter's use of the term **fellow elder** is probably intended to convey that he too considers himself to be a pastor; thus he can speak from experience and with a sympathetic understanding of their responsibilities.

While **a witness of Christ's sufferings** will include the sense of being an eyewitness of what went on, the term **witness** also means "one who testifies." Peter qualifies on both counts.

Furthermore, he can claim to be **one who also will share in the glory to be revealed**. The reference may be to the second coming of Christ at which his glory, glimpsed during his earthly life at the transfiguration (Matt. 17:2; 2 Pet. 1:18), will be made manifest to believing eyes. Or Peter may have in mind the glory that believers themselves will together enjoy when they finally go to be with the Lord. Either way, the shortness of the time-factor is evident from the Greek, which literally means "*about* to be revealed." The sufferings that Christ went through ended in glory. So will it be for faithful believers (4:13–14).

5:2 / Not surprisingly, after his unforgettable interview with the risen Lord on the shore (John 21:15–17), Peter again employs pastoral language. The church leaders are to **be shepherds of God's flock that is under your care** (lit. "to shepherd God's flock among you"). The symbol of shepherd/sheep appeared in 2:25, where it corresponds to Christ/Christians, echoing the frequent OT picture of God as the Shepherd of his people (Ps. 23:1; 80:1; Isa. 40:11; Zech. 9:16). But the image is also applied in the NT to Christian leaders/other believers (Acts 20:28; Eph. 4:11). The transfer is natural enough, for Christian leaders are acting on behalf of the Chief Shepherd, Jesus himself (5:4), and they are to pattern their ministry after his.

A shepherd is responsible for the total well-being of the flock committed by an employer into his charge. He must see to it that the sheep are fed, watered, and protected at all times, and that, as necessary, they are led from place to place to find fresh pasture. The task can involve not simply the personal inconvenience of putting the sheep before his own comfort, but hardship and danger, even at the risk to his own life (John 10:11). The appropriateness of the metaphor is apparent in the harsh and wild rural economy of Bible days, even if the city-dweller of today may have to make a special effort to appreciate its application to a modern situation.

The **flock** of church members is described as **God's**. The flock belongs to him: it is his property. Elders in their shepherding are to keep that fact always in mind, for they are engaged in fulfilling a divine trust, and in due course they will be answerable to God for what they do—or fail to do—with it.

The elders do not own the sheep, but are **serving as overseers**, exercising oversight in the church fellowship. But they are not to carry out this responsibility with any unworthy motives. It must be voluntary service (not because you must) and willingly and eagerly given, for such is the true nature of Christian love.

Neither must there be any idea of doing for getting, no notion of serving only for what they can squeeze out of it: **not greedy for money** (1 Tim. 3:8; Titus 1:7). The inclusion of such a warning suggests that it was not unnecessary. Probably since being known as a committed believer meant almost certain ostracism from employment and social life in the general pagan community, the opportunities for grasping money entrusted to Christians in a position of authority might become all too tempting.

5:3 / Neither must elders display any misplaced attitude of overbearing superiority by **lording it over those entrusted to** them. On the contrary, the life of each elder must be a shining example to the rest of the fellowship, for if that example is to reflect Christ (as it should), then the note sounded will rather be one of humility. They are not to be high-handed or autocratic. The Greek for **those entrusted to you** is literally "the lots." One implication of the choice of such a term could be that the care of a group of believers in the Christian community was allocated to each elder—though it must be added that there is no evidence from other sources that this sort of organization existed.

More profoundly, the Greek word for "lot" is applied in the OT to God's choice of Israel: it is as if God assigned Israel to himself as his special responsibility (Deut. 9:29). Now in the Christian dispensation, God is handing on a similar charge to elders called to look after the people of the new covenant inaugurated by Jesus Christ. It follows that each elder's attitude toward the members of the church allocated to the elder for oversight must reflect the divine attitude—and show God's love, forbearance, forgiveness, sympathetic understanding, not to mention God's tireless service at all times. It is a tall order for any elder. No wonder Peter has made a special point of it all in these few words.

5:4 / The elders' reward will not be in terms of this world but in a form appropriate to the life to come. At the opening of the books at the last judgment, the faithful elder will be abundantly recompensed. The elder will receive reward far beyond the value of any earthly remuneration, which, however great, would be liable to moth and rust and thieves (Matt. 6:19), and which would be useless in a spiritual sphere.

The reference to the occasion **when the Chief Shepherd appears** is a reminder that elders are not acting independently.

They are answerable to the One who has delegated the work to them. But the reward for faithful service will surpass our imagining. At the second coming, when all Christians are summoned before the judgment seat of Christ (2 Cor. 5:10), the elders who have been true to their commission **will receive the crown of glory**. That can never be subject to the ravages of time, for it belongs to another world-order, and it can **never**, like earthly things, **fade away** (1:4). What form a **crown of glory** will take is not explained, and indeed it could not be. Earthly words are totally inadequate to describe spiritual realities of the next life. The grammar of the expression **crown of glory** allows for interpretations that include a crown which is in some way composed of glory (4:14), a glorious crown (one that will never lose its dazzling brightness), or a crown symbolizing a share in the divine glory (2 Pet. 1:4). There may even be a hint, if a *royal* crown is in mind, of greater responsibilities in the world to come (Matt. 19:28; 25:21; cf. 1 Pet. 2:9). Whatever the nature of that crown, it is clearly intended as a symbol of triumph and represents a sharing in the victory of Jesus Christ over all suffering and over death itself (5:1).

5:5a / **Young men** are to **be submissive to those who are older**. The nouns **young men** and **older** can, of course, refer to relative age. But in the context of a charge to elders as church officials, it seems more likely that here the term **young men** (lit. *"younger* men") means those more recently appointed to the office of elder. They are warned not to let their new position go to their heads, but to be prepared to bow to the experience and guidance of **those who are older**, senior in experience.

Additional Notes §21

5:1–3 / Qualifications for a Jewish sanhedrin (governing council) are echoed in these verses. According to rabbinic writings, members of a sanhedrin must be God-fearing (cf. 1 Pet. 5:1), not greedy for money (5:2), and humble and modest (5:3). They were termed elders (5:1), overseers (5:2), shepherds of the flock (5:2), guides (5:3, examples). See Edersheim, *Sketches of Jewish Social Life*, p. 282.

5:1 / **Elders** are frequently mentioned; e.g., in Jewish communities: Exod. 3:16; Lev. 9:1; Num. 11:24; 1 Sam. 4:3; Ezek. 8:1; Matt. 26:47; Acts 4:5); and in Christian fellowships: Acts 15:2; 1 Tim. 4:14; Titus 1:5. The term is also applied to certain heavenly beings (e.g., Rev. 4:4; 5:8; 7:11; 11:16).

Appeal is the Greek verb *parakalein*, to exhort.

Fellow elder: This verse, together with 1:1, offer the only direct clues to the identity of the author of 1 Peter.

Witness (*martys*): not necessarily an eyewitness (as it is in Acts 1:22; 2:32; 3:15), but one who gives testimony (as in Matt. 26:65; Acts 7:58; 2 Cor. 13:1). In the latter sense, *martys* eventually came to be used in the early church to mean "martyr," one who held firm to testimony to Jesus even at the cost of life (Rev. 2:13).

Christ's sufferings is lit. "the sufferings of *the* Christ" and could be another reference to the messianic woes, the period of suffering prior to the return of Christ (Messiah). The word **witness** in this case would carry the meaning of "one who testifies." See Additional Note on 4:13.

5:2 / **Be shepherds**: Peter, a fisherman, has been recommissioned as a shepherd (John 21:15–17).

Serving as overseers (*episkopountes*): (Not in some important MSS: it may be a later exegetical expansion based on 2:25). The corresponding noun *episkopos*, overseer, later gave us the title "bishop." A near parallel is found in the Dead Sea Scrolls, where the *mebaqqer*, or overseer, "shall love them [the members of the Qumran community] as a father loves his children, and shall carry them in all their distress like a shepherd his sheep" (CD 13.7).

Not because you must (*mē anankastōs*): Not by way of compulsion; the Greek word is rare, and in the NT only here. The direct opposite of *hekousiōs*, voluntarily, **because you are willing**: Christian service of every kind must be freely given out of love and not wrung unwillingly from reluctant hands.

Not greedy for money (*mē aischrokerdōs*): Not from eagerness for sordid gain. The corresponding adjective occurs in 1 Tim. 3:8 and Titus 1:7, both in a similar context of a character-sketch of a worthy Christian office-bearer. At least some church leaders were supported financially from the early days (Matt. 10:10; 1 Cor. 9:12; 1 Tim. 5:17–18).

Eager to serve translates one Greek word *prothymōs*, zealously. Emotion is implied because in ministering to God's people they are in truth serving God himself.

5:3 / **Lording it**: The Greek verb *katakyrieunein* includes a derivative of *kyrios*, lord, plus the prefix *kata*, down upon, the two together implying an overbearing and oppressive attitude.

Those entrusted to you renders one Greek word *klērōn*, lots, allocations; its earlier sense of "dice" occurs in Matt. 27:35. In secular Greek *klēros* meant an estate. Peter may have in mind Deut. 9:29 LXX, in which the people of Israel are called God's *klēros*, since that verse includes the phrase "the mighty hand of God," which Peter goes on to use in v. 6.

5:4 / The **Chief Shepherd** is described in Heb. 13:20 as the "great Shepherd of the sheep." In the OT, the promised Messiah is termed the shepherd of God's people (like David, Ezek. 34:23). The messianic prophecy of Mic. 5:4 speaks of the ruler of Israel coming from Bethlehem to shepherd God's flock. In Matt. 26:31, Jesus applies to himself the reference in Zech. 13:7 to the shepherd being struck down and the sheep scattered, a prophecy understood by the Qumran community as referring to some eschatological figure (CD 19.5–9).

The book of Enoch speaks of Israel in the days of the exodus as sheep escaping from the wolves of Egypt (1 Enoch 89:10), and goes on in similar terms to describe the wanderings in the wilderness: "The sheep escaped from that water [the Red Sea that overwhelmed the wolves of Egypt pursuing Israel], and went forth into the wilderness, where there was no water and no grass . . . and I saw the Lord of the sheep pasturing them and giving them water and grass . . . His appearance was great and terrible and majestic" (1 Enoch 89:28–30).

You will receive: *Komizein* (occurring again in 1:9) is a verb regularly used in the NT for the bestowing of the ultimate recompense of reward or punishment at the last judgment (2 Cor. 5:10; Eph. 6:8; Col. 3:25; Heb. 10:36; 2 Pet. 2:13).

Crown (*stephanos*, derived from *stephein*, to encircle): The word can mean a wreath, garland, or chaplet awarded as the winner's prize, or an honor for distinguished public service, or a golden royal crown. A laurel wreath can soon wither, public acclaim can be short-lived, and a royal crown lost. But the **crown of glory**, in whatever form that may take, is unfading, eternal in quality. There could also be a link with the joy of the wedding supper of the Lamb (Rev. 19:7), for a crown was also worn by Jewish bridegrooms. Also in the Greek world crowns denoted the joy that comes at weddings, and they were common objects in pagan religions (*TDNT*, vol. 7, pp. 616–24). For both Jew and Greek, the dominant idea was of the recognition of victorious achievement, with its associated themes of honoring and joyful celebration, rather than any reference to a symbol of the autocratic rule of a king.

That will never fade away (*amarantinos*): unfading, unlike the garlands of flowers and leaves awarded at the Greek games—which were in any case competitive, a thought alien to the message of 1 Peter.

A parallel notion is found in the Dead Sea Scrolls: "All who walk in the ways of the spirit of truth [receive] eternal blessings and everlasting joy in the life everlasting, and a crown of glory and a robe of honor amid light perpetual" (1QS 4.7).

5:5a / **Young men** is lit. *younger* men (*neōteroi*). The comparative can refer to age, rank, or a recent appointment, "young in the job."

§22 The Great Virtue of Humility
(1 Pet. 5:5b–7)

5:5b / In his earlier exhortation to slaves (2:18), Peter slipped almost imperceptibly into addressing all his readers (if not in 2:21, then certainly by 2:25). So here, the apostle moves on from speaking to elders in particular to church members in general, **all of you**.

All believers are to **clothe yourselves with humility toward one another**. They are to put on, as though it were a garment, the Christlike character of humble service. By his choice of metaphor, Peter is no doubt reflecting on the scene in the Upper Room, when Jesus took up the menial task of washing the disciples' feet (John 13:4). The Greek verb Peter uses for **clothe yourselves** is a vivid one, for it is derived from a series of words implying clothing that is tightly wrapped, or rolled up, or knotted. The picture is of donning a slave's apron, tied on tightly so as to leave the body free for action. "Do not use humility as the usual loose-fitting garment, so readily put on or taken off according to whim, but as a close-fitting overall intended for work and wear." Humility is a matter not of downcast eyes, or of the mentality of a Uriah Heep ("I'm only an 'umble clerk, Mr. Copperfield"), but of active selfless service toward one another.

Once again, Peter quotes a supporting word from the OT (Prov. 3:34 LXX), **"God opposes the proud but gives grace to the humble,"** a point frequently made in the OT and memorably expressed in the Magnificat (Luke 1:51–53). God, as the Greek implies, sends his armed forces against those who consider themselves far superior to others and treat the common herd with contempt. The implication is that **the proud** are those who ridicule and despise Christian believers (2:12; 3:16; 4:4–5). Such people are oblivious of the fact that by their attitude they are foolishly pitting their puny selves against the overwhelming might of

God. By contrast, the divine favor of special blessing is bestowed upon believers who seek to follow the example of their Master in his selfless lowliness (Matt. 11:29).

5:6 / While the previous verse spoke of the expression of humility toward those who share the common faith, Peter now goes more deeply. The foundation of Christian humility is a dependent attitude toward God and his ability to rescue. That involves turning one's attention away from self and away from circumstances, however pressing and however painful. The believer's attitude must be one of taking it for granted that God's hand remains in control of events. In the OT, the expression **the mighty hand of God** almost always refers to divine deliverance. His power to deliver can still be relied upon, says Peter, provided there is trust on the believer's part. A drowning man must submit to the one who comes to his aid. If he struggles in his own strength to try to save himself—in effect in the pride of self-sufficiency—he is likely to defeat the best efforts of his would-be rescuer, who in the end may even have to disable him before getting him to safety.

Trust in divine deliverance will be rewarded **in due time**, not necessarily with the immediacy that one often craves in distress, but at the divinely right moment, as God sees the whole situation. Certainly at the end of days (1:5; 2:12), the believer's trust will be justified and the persecutor's stance exposed as one of opposition to almighty God himself.

5:7 / However trying the circumstances, therefore, believers are to look to God alone: **Cast all your anxiety on him**. Far from being an attitude of resignation, humility for the Christian has this very practical aspect. In response to humble trust, God is not only able to deliver his own, but is at all times ready and willing to do so: **he cares for you**. Without drawing attention to the fact, Peter is again quoting from the OT—this time from Psalm 55:22 LXX. Believers can safely leave all anxieties with their heavenly Father (Matt. 6:25–34). He will care about their cares. For their part, believers are to be care-free. It is one of the distinctive treasures which Christianity has inherited from Judaism that God is known to be concerned with the personal care of his people. Other religions at best see God as aloof, as one who, while good and perfect, keeps his distance from human beings.

Additional Notes §22

5:5b / **All of you** was omitted from the earlier NIV edition.

Clothe yourselves with humility: The Greek verb *enkomboomai* is rare and occurs in the NT only here. It is formed from *kombos*, a knot; cf. the noun *enkombōma*, a garment tied over other clothing, especially the apron worn by slaves (LSJ).

"When a man thinks much of the glory of heaven and little of his own glory, both the glory of heaven and his own glory are magnified. If, however, a man thinks little of the glory of heaven and much of his own glory, the glory of heaven remains unimpaired but his own glory wanes" (*Midrash Rabbah* 4.20 on Num. 4:16).

"**God opposes . . .**": The quotation, from Prov. 3:34 LXX, is also used in the same Greek form in James 4:6, with both writers replacing "Lord" with "God" to avoid suggesting to Christian readers that Jesus is meant.

Opposes (*antitassein*): A military term, used of an army drawn up ready for battle.

Proud (*hyperēphos*): One who seeks to show himself above others, haughty, disdainful.

5:6 / **Humble yourselves**: "Ever be more and more lowly in spirit, since the expectancy of man is to become the food of worms" (*Aboth* 4.4). The downcast pessimism of the rabbis contrasts with the opening Beatitude which bids the believer to look *up*: "Blessed are the poor in spirit, for theirs is the kingdom of heaven" (Matt. 5:3). See Edersheim, *Life and Times*, vol. 1, p. 531.

Under God's mighty hand: A frequent OT metaphor for divine deliverance (Exod. 3:19; 6:1; Deut. 7:8; 9:26; Neh. 1:10; Ps. 136:12; Jer. 32:21; Dan. 9:15).

That he may lift you up uses the same Greek verb as in Christ's declaration, "He who humbles himself will be *exalted*" (Luke 14:11). The Greek word suggests the bestowal of honor, position, fortune.

In due time (*en kairō*): Used also in 1:5, although there with the adjective "last" to make the eschatological note explicit.

5:7 / **Cast** is a participle in the Greek, not a separate imperative (as taken by NIV and many modern translations). The injunction therefore is closely connected with the theme of humility in v. 6. The Greek verb is an *aorist* participle, signifying a definite act of handing over the burden of anxiety. The only other NT occurrence of *epiriptein* is in Luke 19:35, where the disciples *cast* their clothes upon the animal, so letting it carry the garments.

Anxieties: The Greek implies being pulled in several different directions at once, a vivid impression of what worry means. A version of the text is found in Hermas: "Cast your cares upon the Lord, and he will set them straight" (Shepherd of Hermas, *Visions* 4.2.5).

5:8 / The exhortations to humility in verses 5b–7 are not to be taken as recommending an attitude of passive resignation, or even of stoic indifference, to painful events. Neither does the emphasis on the reality of God's care mean that Christians are to be careless—not least about spiritual perils. While the sufferings that afflict believers in the present life may come to them through the agency of other human beings, whom they can see and hear, God's people must at all times remember that behind the seen is the unseen. As part of Christ's army, they are all the time caught up in a spiritual war (Eph. 6:12).

The standing orders for Christians in this conflict include the need to **be self-controlled and alert**. As in 1 Thessalonians 5:6–8, where the same Greek terms are used, the notions of wakefulness and sobriety imply the need to avoid the opposite states of sleep and drunkenness. Drunkenness expresses the clouding of the senses, and so a lack of apprehending spiritual realities. Peter's exhortation to self-control (also in 1:13; 4:7) is always a positive one, with a view to action. Similarly, believers are to be **alert**, to be on the watch like keen sentinels, aware that the foe may attack at any time and from any quarter.

Unseen he may be, but the spiritual fact is that their **enemy the devil** is forever seeking a way to infiltrate and take advantage of any weakness among God's army of believers. The devil **prowls around like a roaring lion**, a simile chosen because of the brute's nature as a cruel and ferocious beast of prey. Believers facing distress and persecution are not to be frightened into apostasy by the fierce threats of their enemies. Only if sheep forsake the fold are they at the mercy of a prowling lion. This is not to suggest that if believers do suffer physical or material hurt, or even death, because they are Christians, they must be in some way to blame, being in sin or lacking in personal faith. Their spiritual safety is what is all-important, and provided they are loyal to God, this is beyond the reach of their enemies (1:5). Peter is addressing his readers' immediate situation and warning that the devil is constantly engaged in **looking for someone** in God's army **to devour**, any he can ruin and destroy spiritually.

5:9 / What are believers to do about the attacks of the devil? They are to **resist him**, to stand fearlessly up to him. Christians are not to fear the devil, but neither are they to underestimate him. Yet they are not to rely upon their own strength, for of themselves they are no match for the devil's capacity and skill. The devil is conquered only in Jesus Christ. So the resistance Peter urges is a **standing firm in the faith**, immovable in their steadfast reliance on the Lord and his victory. They can encourage themselves in the knowledge of two facts: (1) it is entirely *possible* for Christians to resist the devil—it is never a hopeless situation; and (2) they are not isolated and on their own in their struggles. Their Christian **brothers** and sisters **throughout the world** are also caught up in the conflict as fellow-members of the same spiritual army. They too are even now **undergoing the same kind of sufferings**, not necessarily the particular persecutions facing Peter's readers, but suffering nonetheless because they live the Christian life in a hostile, ungodly environment.

5:10 / Any suffering seems interminable at the time. But it does have an end, in both senses of that word. In terms of time, it will not go on forever: suffering will be only for **a little while**. That is not to be taken as an assurance that their suffering will be brief, which would probably be contradicted by the experience of at least some of Peter's readers, but it is temporary. Paul expresses a parallel thought: "I consider that our present sufferings are not worth comparing with the glory that will be revealed in us" (Rom. 8:18). And suffering also has an end in the sense of purpose, as Peter has been at pains many times to stress (1:7; 2:12, 15, 19; 3:9, 14, 16; 4:13–16). God is using every experience, especially perhaps the more unpleasant ones, to further his loving purpose in the lives of his people and to enable them to grow in grace and in their knowledge of him (2 Pet. 3:18).

God is **the God of all grace**, the source of all sufficiency for every demand made upon his own (2 Cor. 12:9). The goal he has in view for his people is for them to share in **his eternal glory in Christ**. That is the reason for his call. The experiences of this life are limited. What lies ahead in the purposes of God for believers is **eternal**: their coming salvation in all its fullness (1:5).

The clear object God keeps in view through all that believers face in this world should be a matter for great encouragement when days are dark and threatening. God himself is purposing to **restore you and make you strong, firm and steadfast**. Is Peter thinking of the old days, remembering how his fishing nets continually needed reinforcement and repair? The Greek he employs is reminiscent of what he used to have to do in his fishing business. The situation, spiritually speaking, is similar for all believers. After the wear and tear of daily living for God in a hostile environment, they need to be renewed, restored, fully re-equipped. Personal divine action will attend to this very need. Believers will be made **strong, firm and steadfast**—the virtual synonyms pile up as Peter strives to make the point for those who are perhaps feeling all too conscious of their present weakness and helplessness. Strength comes through *growth* and *development*, no less in the spiritual and moral field than in the physical. Experiences of whatever sort, faced in the right way and with God's help, will enable each and every Christian to grow ever stronger in and closer to the Lord.

5:11 / Having lifted his readers thoughts upward and onward, beyond present difficulties and trials to the glory that lies in the future, Peter crowns his exhortation with a doxology in praise of what will ensure that it all comes to pass: the divine power, rule, and sovereignty—for all these aspects are included in the Greek term—and closes with a resounding **Amen!** "It is so!"

Additional Notes §23

5:8 / **Be self-controlled** (lit. " be sober"): This is the third time Peter's readers have been so exhorted (1:13; 4:7), on each occasion in an eschatological context.

Both **enemy** (Matt. 5:25) and **devil** (false accuser, Rev. 12:10) are, strictly speaking, forensic terms meaning adversary (i.e., against God and his people).

According to the NT, **the devil** is allowed temporary dominion over the present world (Job 1:12; Luke 4:6; John 12:31; 14:30; 16:11; Acts 26:18;

2 Cor. 4:4; Heb. 2:14; 1 John 5:19), with his power becoming increasingly evident as the end-time approaches (Matt. 24:4–25; 2 Thess. 2:3–12; 2 Tim. 3:1–8; Rev. 20:7–8).

Like a roaring lion: The simile is also found in Ps. 91:13, but when the devil quotes this passage to Jesus during the wilderness temptations, the reference in the psalm to the overthrow of the lion is carefully omitted. In the natural world, different types of lions use different hunting methods. While one seeks to paralyze its prey by a terrifying noise, another stalks its victim silently. The devil is a master of arts. The comparison of the enemy of souls to a lion is suggested by Ps. 7:2; 10:9; 22:13. The simile refers to spiritual death, apostasy. See Horsley, *New Documents*, vol. 3, pp. 50–51. In Judaism, persecutors are often likened to lions: Jer. 4:7; Ezek. 19:6; 1QH 5.5; 4Q169 on Nah. 2:11–12.

Devour (*katapiein*): lit. "to swallow down."

5:9 / Resist here means to withstand, not to fight against, for that is beyond the ability of human beings faced by a spiritual foe like the devil. Only in Christ is there victory (Luke 10:17).

Standing firm translates one Greek word, *stereoi*, solid, firm; the corresponding verb occurs in Acts 16:5, "the churches were *strengthened* in the faith." See Eph. 6:10–18.

Brothers (*adelphotēs*, brotherhood, but including both men and women [as in 2:17]): Peter's choice of the collective term emphasizes the common bond of experience shared by all Christian believers, even those unknown to the readers.

Throughout the world is lit. the curious phrase "*in* the world." This could be a Latinism, a stock expression contrasting "in town" (i.e., in the metropolis, Rome; cf. Rom. 1:8), pointing to Rome as the place of writing for 1 Peter. See Robinson, *Redating the New Testament*, p. 160.

5:10 / Grace ("what God gives") is frequently mentioned in this letter, for everything depends upon it (1:2, 10, 13; 2:20; 3:7; 4:10; 5:5, 10, 12).

Who called you: The call of God recurs as a theme at regular intervals: 1:15; 2:9, 21; 3:9; 5:10.

Restore (*katartizein*): This word ranges in meaning from mend, furnish completely, complete, to set right (as a bone). The word is used in Mark 1:19 of James and John *mending* their nets in preparation for further service.

Make you strong (*stērizein*): to fix, set fast, establish firmly (cf. "steroids," body-building substances). It is the word used by Jesus when warning Peter about his coming denial: "When you are restored, *give strength* to your brothers" (Luke 22:32, REB).

Firm (*sthenooun*, in the NT only here): to fill with strength.

Steadfast (*themeliooun*): To lay the foundation of, settle firmly (Eph. 3:17; Col. 1:23).

5:11 / Power (*kratos*, "strength" in 4:11): often used in NT doxologies of the incomparable mighty power of God (1 Tim. 6:16; Jude 25; Rev. 1:6; 5:13).

§24 And Now, Farewell! (1 Pet. 5:12–14)

5:12 / It was common practice at the time this letter was written for the real author to take over the pen of the amanuensis and add the final words of personal greeting (Gal. 6:11). This may have happened here. Peter says he has written his letter **with the help of Silas**, an expression that, according to examples in Greek literature, can have several interpretations. Literally, the Greek is simply "through Silas." That can mean that Silas was the bearer of the letter, or that he was the writer under Peter's dictation, or that he composed the letter as a ghost-writer, embodying Peter's thoughts.

The identity of **Silas** is not altogether certain, but most assume that he is Paul's colleague Silvanus, the latter name being a Latinized form of "Silas." No other Silvanus is known. In A.D. 48 **Silas** was commissioned by the Jerusalem church, where the apostle Peter was a leading figure at the time, to tell the believers at Antioch in Syria about the settlement between Jewish and Gentile Christians (Acts 15:22, 27). Later he accompanied Paul to Asia Minor and Greece (Acts 15:40) and is named as the co-author of two Pauline letters (1 Thess. 1:1; 2 Thess. 1:1).

After these important responsibilities, it is no surprise that Silas is regarded by Peter as a **faithful brother**, a loyal fellow-believer. He is one who can be trusted not only to deliver the letter safely to distant churches scattered over a large area, but also to enlarge upon its message and answer questions as necessary, for he is one who knows the apostle's mind.

As letters go, to describe 105 verses as having **written to you briefly** may seem surprising (Heb. 13:22, where a similar comment occurs, is even more so). It was conventional politeness to proclaim one's brevity (Acts 24:4), though Peter may have in mind the vastness of the subjects he has tackled. How much more could have been said! But what he has written is intended to be **encouraging** to his readers in their tribulation, and all through the letter he has sought to draw attention to spiritual facts in order to strengthen faith and to uplift sorely tried spirits. He has been **testifying** that what he has written is his personal experience of the **true grace of God**. It is as if he were saying "I know at first hand that the grace of God, what he gives, is completely sufficient for every demand made upon a Christian life: that **grace** is **true**, 'the genuine article.' So, **stand fast in it**! Persevere to the very end along the Christian way, regardless of what happens."

5:13 / Finally, Peter conveys **greetings** from **she who is in Babylon**. The pronoun **she** almost certainly refers to a church (a feminine noun in Greek) and not to an individual, especially as the subsequent phrase **chosen together with you** more appropriately relates to a community of believers parallel to those to whom the letter is addressed. **Babylon** means Rome, although the name is not used (as in the book of Revelation) as a coded term intended to conceal the writer's whereabouts. If the letter had fallen into the hands of a Pliny (see Additional Note on 4:16), the Roman official would have applauded the exhortation to good citizenship (2:13–17). Peter's motive in using **Babylon** to mean Rome is homiletic. Babylon in the OT was notorious as the place of exile. Now all Christians, whether Jewish or Gentile, are, as it were, exiles so far as the world in which they live is concerned, as Peter pointed out in his opening greeting (1:1), and later (2:11). The Christians in Rome with Peter as he writes and the Christians in Asia Minor to whom his letter is addressed share the same status: their true home is in heaven.

Peter also includes a greeting from **my son Mark**, a term of endearment, not a reference to blood ties. But it may also imply that Peter brought Mark to faith in Christ and thus into the Christian family. The relationship clearly continued to be a close one. It is widely accepted that the second of the four Gospels in the NT was compiled by John Mark in Rome, and that it is largely based on Peter's preaching and on the apostle's memories of what Jesus said and did.

5:14 / When in conclusion Peter bids his readers to **greet one another with a kiss of love**, he is using an expression that frequently closes NT letters (Rom. 16:16; 1 Cor. 16:20; 2 Cor. 13:12; 1 Thess. 5:26). It reflects the custom of believers embracing each other during their meetings for worship, a sign of their loving relationship in the divine family. Television pictures from the Middle East have made the practice a familiar one. It corresponds to the less demonstrative handshake in the West, which is brought out by some modern translators who are also perhaps seeking to avoid romantic overtones: "Give each other a handshake all round as a sign of love" (Phillips). This scarcely conveys the emotion intended. A warm charismatic hug is nearer the mark! Whether by kiss, handshake, or hug, one implication of the action is the same for Christians: those involved are relating to one another on equal terms before God.

Peter's last word, **peace**, echoes his opening greeting (1:2). Despite their trials and tribulations, his readers are wrapped in divine peace from beginning to end. That peace is a divine gift (Phil. 4:7) and not of human generation, which is liable to be superficial, fragile, or short-lived. God's **peace** is for all who are **in Christ**, for all believers: it is their divinely bestowed privilege as members of God's family. The Father will see to it by his concern, his governing, and his power, that whatever testings of faith come to his children, they will ultimately share in the complete triumph of their risen and glorified Lord. On that their hearts can utterly rely in **peace.**

Additional Notes §24

5:12 / The name **Silas** in its Latin form is Silvanus, and in Aramaic *š^e'îlā'*, which corresponds to the Hebrew name "Saul." A Jewish Christian, he was also a Roman citizen (Acts 16:37).

Testifying (*epimartyrein*, yet another Greek word occurring in the NT only here): To declare emphatically, to speak clearly of what one knows to be true. In the OT, the word is used for the testimony of witnesses to a land-sale (Jer. 39:25 LXX = 32:10 in Hebrew text).

5:13 / The pronoun **she** is unlikely to refer to an individual (Peter's wife, for example: 1 Cor. 9:5), but means *church* (a feminine noun in Greek), as in 2 John 1, 13.

Babylon is a coded reference to Rome in the book of Revelation (Rev. 14:8, and five other verses), where other aspects of the OT city on the Euphrates are in view—its pride and godlessness—a character now taken on by Rome in the eyes of both Jews and Christians by the late first century.

Chosen together echoes the description of Peter's readers, as indeed of all Christians, as "chosen" (1:2; 2:9), i.e., by God.

Mark is John Mark (Acts 12:12), one of Paul's companions on his first missionary journey (Acts 13:5). Paul mentions him several times in his letters (Col. 4:10; 2 Tim. 4:11; Philem. 24).

5:14 / There is no verb expressed in **peace to all of you**. The expression can certainly be taken as a prayer ("*May* peace be to all of you"), but equally it may be a bold statement of fact: "Peace *is* (at all times and in all circumstances) with you." Such an interpretation is entirely appropriate to the encouraging purpose of the letter as a whole.

2 Peter

1:1 / The opening of 2 Peter is along the conventional lines of a NT letter, giving sender, addressees, greeting (see commentary on Jude 1 and Additional Notes on Jude 1–2). The sender identifies himself as **Simon Peter**. Most Greek MSS of 2 Peter transliterate the sender's first name as *Symeōn*, the Hebrew form applied to Simon Peter elsewhere in the NT only in Acts 15:14, in the appropriate Jewish-Christian setting of the Council of Jerusalem.

The author further calls himself **a servant and apostle of Jesus Christ**. The term **apostle** was used alone in the opening of 1 Peter (see Additional Note on 1 Pet. 1:1). Here, the writer adds the humbler description **servant** (*doulos*), bondslave, as do Paul (Rom. 1:1; Gal. 1:10; Titus 1:1), James (1:1), and Jude (1), i.e., one who has been bound to serve his Master.

The readers are described as those who **have received a faith as precious as ours**. The comparison **as ours** could indicate that Peter, as a Jewish Christian, is writing to Gentile Christians (but there is no other reference to any Jewish-Gentile tension in this letter), or it could point to the common faith shared by apostles and ordinary disciples alike. But the comparison need mean no more than an underlining of the community of faith shared by all believers, irrespective of class, time, or geography. It makes no difference as far as their common faith is concerned whether the readers, like Peter himself, had first-hand knowledge of the earthly Jesus. That faith had been **received**, which means not "handed down" but, as the Greek verb implies, a free gift, one bestowed upon apostles and disciples similarly, whether they were Jews or Gentiles. As a gift, it was solely the result of divine grace and not something that could be earned in any way or due to privilege.

This common faith has come to Peter's readers **through the righteousness of our God and Savior Jesus Christ**. The Greek *dikaiosynē*, righteousness, is a key term in Paul's doctrine of justi-

fication by faith, though in his teaching faith precedes righteousness. But *dikaiosynē* also regularly means justice or fair dealing,
and this rendering is more appropriate here: God has no favor-
ites when it comes to salvation through Jesus Christ (John 12:32).

1:2 / Peter's opening greeting repeats the **grace and peace
be yours in abundance** of his first letter (see Additional Note on
1 Pet. 1:2), but he now adds **through the knowledge of God and
of Jesus our Lord**. The Greek denotes exact or full **knowledge** of
God and of his ways, which follows as a consequence of conversion to Christ. A deeper personal knowledge of the Lord Jesus is
the certain safeguard against false teaching, a note on which the
letter will end (3:18). What this **knowledge** entails in practical
terms of Christian living is expounded in the following verses,
and the whole passage introduces Peter's main purpose in writing: to warn his readers against apostasizing on account of a
moral libertinism which amounts to turning away from this true
knowledge of Christ (2:2).

Additional Notes   §1

1:1 / **Simon Peter**: See Additional Note on 1 Pet. 1:1; also Cullmann, *Peter: Disciple—Apostle—Martyr*, pp. 17–21. Other NT characters
with the Hebraized name Symeon (as in the Greek here) are mentioned
in Luke 2:25, 34; Acts 13:1; Rev. 7:7).

Peter's self-description as **a servant** (*doulos*) **and apostle** (*apostolos*)
recalls the declaration of Jesus: "I tell you the truth, no servant (*doulos*) is
greater than his master, nor is a messenger (*apostolos*) greater than the one
who sent him" (John 13:16).

Righteousness (*dikaiosynē*): As used in 2 Peter (1:1, 13; 2:5, 7, 8, 21;
3:13) the term has an ethical quality. Hence in this verse "fair dealing,
without favoritism" is a fitting translation.

Our God and Savior Jesus Christ: Although the next verse (2)
distinguishes between God and Jesus Christ, the writer, in common with
other early Christian authors, is here calling Jesus Christ *theos*, God; cf.
1 John 5:20. See V. Taylor, "Does the New Testament Call Jesus God?" in
New Testament Essays (London: Geoffrey Chapman, 1968), pp. 1–38.

The title **Savior** occurs five times in 2 Peter (1:1, 11; 2:20; 3:2, 18)
out of only 24 references in the whole NT. It becomes increasingly frequent
in the early church writings, and common from the mid-second century.
See *TDNT*, vol. 7, pp. 1004–12.

Received: The Greek word is *lanchanein*, to obtain by lot; see *TDNT*, vol. 4, p. 2.

As precious as is *isotimon*, which can also be translated "of equal privilege" (as RSV, "a faith of equal standing with ours"). In secular Greek it meant equal status or rank in civic life. See *TDNT*, vol. 3, p. 349.

1:2 / **Knowledge** (*epignōsis*): a favorite word in 2 Peter (1:2, 3, 8; 2:20). It is a stronger term than the general word for knowledge (*gnōsis*). See *TDNT*, vol.1, p. 707.

§2   *God's Spiritual Provision (2 Pet. 1:3–4)*

1:3 / After the conventional opening, Peter launches straight into his message. First, he sets out the Christian truths on which he is going to base his argument. Peter picks up the theme of "the knowledge of God and of Jesus our Lord" included in his greeting (v. 2) and expounds what that means.

His divine power, i.e., the power of God shared by and active through Jesus, **has given us**, has bestowed upon us, **everything we need for life and godliness**. The last phrase is a hendiadys for "a godly life" (for hendiadys, see Additional Note on 1 Pet. 2:25). All that is needful for the believer to live the life that God intends is available in Christ (John 10:10; 2 Cor. 12:9).

The divine provision of **everything we need** for living a godly life is initially the free gift of God's unmerited grace. But we have to cooperate with God by taking it up from there and "make every effort" (v. 5). Bengel refers to the parable of the Ten Virgins (Matt. 25:1–13) and remarks: "The flame is that which is imparted to us by God and from God, without any labour on our part; but the oil is that which man ought to add by his own diligence and faithfulness, that the flame may be fed and increased. Thus the matter is set forth without a parable in this passage of Peter: in verses 3 and 4 we have the flame; but in verses 5 and 6, and those which follow, we have that which man himself ought to add [lit. *to pour upon it*], the presence of divine grace being presupposed" See Bengel, *Gnomen*, vol. 5, pp. 85–86.

This divine provision, Peter reminds his readers, comes **through our knowledge of him who called us by his own glory and goodness**. The call of Christ is initially to personal faith in him. But it is a call repeated all through the believer's life, a call to a deeper and richer understanding of the Person of Christ, and of his demands for spiritual growth and service. That first call to faith, which resulted in the conversion of the readers, came by means of Christ's **own** (*idia*, unique) **glory and goodness**. The NIV translation **goodness** for *aretē* is mild. Basically, *aretē* is that which expresses worth. Applied to human beings, it means moral goodness (as in 1:5; "virtue" in KJV). Applied to God (as here in v. 3), it means that which manifests divine miracle-working power for good.

1:4 / **Through these**, that is, on account of Christ's divine attributes of glory and excellence releasing divine power, **he has given us his very great and precious promises**. The natural reading of this passage suggests that the pledges of Jesus himself when on earth are meant. But divine promises set out in the OT are not to be excluded, since these are fulfilled in the coming of Jesus the Messiah, as proclaimed by the earliest Christian preachers (Acts 13:32–33). The promises are **very great and precious** (*timia*, highly valued, costly), the latter adjective a reminder that their fulfillment by Jesus Christ was at the great cost of his very life-blood.

The bestowal of the promises enables believers to **participate in the divine nature**. This expression, although a commonplace in contemporary Hellenistic religious literature, is found in the NT only here, although the same idea appears in Paul in terms of adoption into the divine family: "You received the Spirit of sonship. And by him we cry, '*Abba*, Father.' The Spirit himself testifies with our spirit that we are God's children . . . heirs of God and coheirs with Christ" (Rom. 8:15–17).

This sharing in the divine nature has practical implications for believers: by means of it they may **escape the corruption in the world caused by evil desires**. The Greek here for **escape** is an aorist participle and can be literally translated "having escaped." Although NIV follows the order of the Greek words, the reader can be misled into understanding that "participating in the divine nature" is prior to and the reason for "escaping the corruption in the world." The use of the aorist participle for **escape** indicates that the intended sequence of ideas is that we participate in the divine nature *after* we have escaped, turned our backs on (which brings out the decisive aorist), the corruption in a world alienated from God. Almost all the other modern translations (e.g., JB, LB, NEB, Phillips, REB, RSV) make this clear.

It will soon be evident that Peter is writing to combat antinomians, those who claim that divine grace frees them from the obligations of the moral law. Such an attitude betrays a willful intention to go on sinning. But the gift of the divine nature is offered by Jesus Christ to enable the believer to counter the fascination of **evil desires** which lead on to sin.

Peter boldly uses terms familiar in the Hellenistic thought of his day (he knew something about the art of communication), although he christianizes the ideas. Greek philosophers taught the desirability of escaping from the material world because of its corrupting influence. "Peter is careful to define the nature of the corruption he has in mind, i.e., corruption that is in (*en*) the world because of (*en*) passion. There is a deliberate avoidance of the concept that the material world is itself evil." See Guthrie, *New Testament Theology*, p. 185.

Additional Notes   §2

1:3 / **His divine power** is frequently mentioned in the NT: Matt. 24:30; Mark 5:30; Luke 4:14; 5:17; 6:19; Rom. 1:4; 1 Cor. 1:24; 5:4; 2 Cor. 12:9; Heb. 1:3.

Has given: The verb, *dōreomai*, to bestow, appears in the NT only here and in Mark 15:45 (of Pilate officially *handing over* the body of Jesus to Joseph of Arimathea). Peter's emphasis on *divine* power, as distinct from any human effort or achievement, echoes a comment in his speech at the healing of the crippled beggar in the Jerusalem temple: "Why do you stare at us as if by our own power (*dynamis*) or godliness (*eusebeia*) we had made this man to walk?" (Acts 3:12). He uses the same terms here: **His divine power** (*dynamis*) **has given us everything we need for life and godliness** (*eusebeia*).

Glory (*doxa*) is a favorite word with Peter, appearing ten times in 1 Peter and five times in 2 Peter. The transfiguration scene (Matt. 17:2; Mark 9:2–3) understandably made an unforgettable impression upon Peter. See Additional Note on 1 Pet. 1:7.

The Greek noun *aretē* is here (and in 1:5) translated in its primary sense of **goodness**, moral excellence ("virtue" in KJV). But the word (which occurs in the NT only in Phil. 4:8; 1 Pet. 2:9; 2 Pet. 1:3, 5) develops in meaning. It is treated as a synonym for *doxa* (glory) in Isa. 42:8, 12 (LXX), and renders the Hebrew *hôd* (splendor) in Hab. 3:3 and, in a messianic context, in Zech. 6:13. Finally, *aretē* comes to express the manifestation of divine power, i.e., miracle, which is probably behind the meaning here in 2 Pet. 1:3. See Deissmann, *Bible Studies*, pp. 95–97; 360–68; BAGD; Turner, p. 339.

1:4 / **He has given**, *dedōrētai*, is a Greek perfect tense, bringing out the permanence of the divine bounty. This is the same verb as in v. 3.

The Greek word used here for **promises**, *epangelmata*, occurs in the NT only in this letter (1:4; 3:13), as does the superlative adjective **very great** (*megista*), further examples of the unusual vocabulary of 2 Peter. **Precious** (*timia*) also occurs in 1 Pet. 1:19, where it is applied to the blood of Christ; the related noun *timē*, preciousness, is found in 1 Pet. 1:7 (NIV, "honor") and 2 Pet. 1:17 (NIV, "honor").

Participate in the divine nature: Parallel notions of intimate fellowship with God are variously expressed in many NT passages: e.g., Rom. 5:5; 8:14–17; Gal. 4:6; 1 John 1:3; 2:29—3:1; Heb. 3:14.

The verb used for **escape**, *apopheugein*, is confined to 2 Peter in the NT (1:4; 2:18, 20) and is found only once in the LXX (Sir. 22:22).

§3   The Need to Grow (2 Pet. 1:5–9)

1:5–7 / A more literal translation of vv. 5–7 would run: "In (*en*) your faith richly provide goodness; in (*en*) your goodness, knowledge; in (*en*) your knowledge, self-control . . . " The wording suggests organic union, a cluster of fruits on the living branch of faith (cf. John 15:1–8).

1:5 / **For this very reason**, as set out in verses 3–4, because all that we need in order to live a godly life is available in Christ, and in view of the great and precious divine promises and the prospect of sharing in the divine nature, we must grow and develop spiritually. Or, as Peter puts it, we must **make every effort** to build up and strengthen our Christian lives. The Greek verb translated **make every effort** is *pareispherein*, compiled from *pherein*, to bring, *eis*, into, and *para*, alongside: to bring in alongside, contribute. God does his part; we must cooperate and do ours (cf. Phil. 2:12). What our part is, Peter now goes on to spell out.

The Greek for **add**, *epichorēgein*, has a vivid history. In the great days of ancient Athens, the plays of dramatists like Aeschylus, Sophocles, and Euripides required large and costly choruses. But when such a play was put on, some wealthy public-spirited Athenian defrayed the vast outlay on the chorus—and consequently was known as the *chorēgos*. The noble productions were extravagantly expensive, but *chorēgoi* vied with each other in their generosity. So *epichorēgein* is far richer a term than the somewhat colorless **add** of many English translations of this verse.

Believers, Peter is saying, must be lavish in the time and effort they put into developing their Christian lives—not being satisfied with getting by on the minimum, but striving like the *chorēgos* of old to achieve the finest and most attractive production. The Christian is duty-bound, or rather love-bound, to offer the world the best possible advertisement of what God's grace can do. That is far removed from the uncomfortable observation by a cynic that in his view Christian experience was "an initial spasm followed by a chronic inertia."

The building program Peter urges upon his readers is based on **faith**, that is, on the individual's initial response to God's love as revealed in the life, death, and resurrection of Jesus Christ. Such conversion-faith is not the be-all and end-all of a Christian life (cf. James 2:20), but only the beginning—as a seed is intended to be the first stage of growth and ultimate maturity.

Peter lists seven qualities, each of which is to be supplemented by the next, culminating in the characteristic Christian virtue of **love** (1 Cor. 13). As the new life of Christ within the new believer, begun by faith at conversion, is matured, so **goodness** will be developed. The **goodness** referred to in verse 3 is a divine quality. Here in verse 5 the human situation is in view, i.e., the believer's response to Jesus Christ in quality of life. The Greek word used for **goodness** (*aretē*) is rare in early Christian literature (in the NT only in Phil. 4:8; 1 Pet. 2:9; 2 Pet. 1:3, 5). In secular Greek *aretē* denoted the proper fulfillment of anything. The *aretē* of a knife is to cut; of soil to be fertile. The *aretē* of Christians is to fulfill the purpose God has in mind for each of them, by reproducing Christlikeness in every department of life.

In turn, goodness is to be supplemented by **knowledge**. Here the context suggests that what is meant is a developing knowledge of Jesus Christ by the new believer, a growing understanding of divine principles and ways for living the Christian life (Eph. 5:17; Phil. 1:9; Heb. 5:14). It is knowledge that leads to right decisions and right actions in the sight of God.

1:6 / The growing awareness of divine standards leads to the exercise of **self-control**. Left to themselves, human beings are not strong enough to discipline their passions but are liable to give in to evil desires (as Peter will soon point out: 2:10–12; 3:3). For Christians, self-control comes about through submission to their more powerful Master, Jesus Christ.

From the practice of self-control develops **perseverance**, a patient endurance which sounds the note of trustful expectancy that God will see to it that in the end, all will be well. The corresponding Greek verb is used of Jesus who *endured* the cross for the joy that was set before him (Heb. 12:2).

1:7 / The next stage of spiritual development in Peter's list is, in the Greek, *eusebeia*, not an easy word to put into English: **godliness** is too broad. The meaning can be sensed from the use of the related term *eusebēs* as a sharp contrast with "commercial gain" in 2 Clement (19.4; 20.4). "Putting loyalty to God above all else" is a clumsy paraphrase but points in the right direction.

This expression of true piety toward God has its corresponding effect upon one believer's relationship toward another: love to God and love to neighbor are intended to go in tandem (Mark 12:30–31; John 13:34). Hence next in Peter's catalogue is **brotherly kindness**, love of other believers. And that leads straight on to the heart of Christian living for Peter and for all NT writers: the exercise of *agapē*, the expression of Christian **love** to all. The Greek word is virtually unknown before the church consecrated its use to mean God's love revealed in Jesus Christ, and the Christian's grateful response to God in moulding his or her attitude toward fellow believers.

1:8 / The development, or the lack, of **these qualities** will inevitably be shown up in the believer's life. The Greek verb *hyparchein*, which is behind the NIV translation **If you possess**, is applied in the papyri to property which the rightful owner has completely at his disposal. On the one hand, without the believer's active cooperation, all the qualities listed will stagnate and come to nothing. On the other hand, their fostering and development will prevent the Christian from being **ineffective** by being out of action, and **unproductive**, bearing no spiritual fruit. A growing **knowledge of our Lord Jesus Christ**, of his person and of his ways, is thus the climax and the prize of Christian endeavor, as it is also its source and accompaniment (vv. 3, 6; cf. John 17:3; Col. 1:10).

1:9 / But for anyone to lack these qualities means that **he is nearsighted and blind**. NIV tries to make more sense of the curious Greek order, which in fact puts **blind** before **nearsighted**, and literally reads "he is blind, being nearsighted." The Greek verb translated **nearsighted** is very rare and occurs in the NT only here. It refers to the screwing up of the eyes against the light. If we keep to the Greek order, the sense is evidently that to lack the qualities listed means that the one concerned demonstrates spiritual blindness, for what he has done is to screw up his eyes against spiritual light and to refuse to face up to what divine revelation has put before him. It is equally true to experience that Peter is meaning such an individual is blind to spiritual matters because he is nearsighted in the sense of being absorbed with worldly affairs close at hand.

Such a person **has forgotten that he has been cleansed from his past sins.** The Greek for **has forgotten** is in the aorist tense and points to a deliberate act. It suggests that the convert, by failing to make the effort to grow in grace (v. 5), has in effect willfully turned his or her back on the stand for Christ made at baptism. That was when **past sins,** that is, sins committed in the old life before conversion, were confessed. In the sacrament the believer was **cleansed,** forgiven, and so enabled to make a fresh start (1 Pet. 3:21; Rom. 6:1–14).

Additional Notes   §3

1:5 / **Add to your faith**: Lists of virtues were common in the ancient world and were frequently included in Christian writings: e.g., Rom. 5:2–5; 2 Cor. 6:6; Gal. 5:22–23; Col. 3:12–14; 1 Tim. 4:12; 6:11; 2 Tim. 2:22; Shepherd of Hermas, *Visions* 3.8.1–7; Barnabas 2.2.3; 1 Clement 62.2.

Faith (*pistis*): see Turner, pp. 153–58, 376; *TDNT*, vol. 6, pp. 174–228; *NIDNTT*, vol. 1, pp. 587–606; vol.3, pp. 1211–14.

Goodness (*aretē*): see Turner, pp. 339–40; *TDNT*, vol. 1, pp. 457–61; *NIDNTT*, vol. 3, pp. 925–27.

Knowledge (*gnōsis*): see Turner, pp. 247–49; *TDNT*, vol. 1, pp. 689–714; *NIDNTT*, vol. 2, pp. 392–408.

1:6 / **Self-control** (*enkrateia*): see *TDNT*, vol. 2, pp. 339–42; *NIDNTT*, vol. 1, pp. 494–96.

Perseverance (*hypomonē*, lit. a remaining under): see Turner, pp. 318–19; *TDNT*, vol. 4, pp. 581–88; *NIDNTT*, vol. 2, pp. 772–76.

Godliness (*eusebeia*): see Turner, pp. 111–12; *TDNT*, vol. 7, pp. 175–85; *NIDNTT*, vol. 2, pp. 91–95.

1:7 / **Brotherly kindness** (*philadelphia*): see *TDNT*, vol. 1, pp. 144–46; *NIDNTT*, vol. 1, pp. 254–60; vol. 2, pp. 547–50.

Love (*agapē*): see Turner, pp. 261–66; *TDNT*, vol. 1, pp. 21–55; *NIDNTT*, vol. 2, pp. 538–51.

1:8 / **Ineffective** (*argos*): The same Greek word is used in James 2:26, "Faith without deeds is dead (*argos*)."

Unproductive (*akarpos*, unfruitful) also occurs in the Parable of the Sower (Matt. 13:22; Mark 4:19), where it describes the fate of the good seed of God's word choked by worldly anxieties and the lure of wealth. According to Eusebius (*Eccl. Hist.* 5.1.45), the churches at Lyons and Vienne in A.D. 177 used the same expression to praise the Christian witness of the martyr Attalus: he was neither idle (*argos*) nor unfruitful (*akarpos*).

Knowledge here is *epignōsis*; see Additional Note on v. 2.

1:9 / **Nearsighted and blind**: "The whole [Greek] phrase is a trochaic tetrameter; possibly Peter culled it from some poem or ditty current at the time, as Paul sometimes did (Titus 1:12). This may account for the rather curious form of expression." (Green, p. 73). The metaphor of blindness for inability or refusal to see the truth is common in the NT: Matt. 15:14; 23:16, 24; Luke 6:39; John 9:40–41; 12:40; Rom. 2:19; 2 Cor. 4:4; 1 John 2:11; Rev. 3:17.

Sins (*hamartēma*): see Turner, p. 412.

§4 Each Believer's Objective (2 Pet. 1:10–11)

1:10 / **Therefore**, in view of all that is set out in verses 3–9, **be all the more eager to make your calling and election sure**. While **calling** and **election**, here treated virtually as synonyms, are both due to the divine initiative (John 15:16), the believer, as Peter has been stressing all along, must give a resolute and full response, and so make them **sure** (the Greek word for **sure**, *bebaios*, is a legal term in the papyri for a guaranteed security): "Show by the kind of life you lead that you have truly accepted God's call, with all its implications." Given that unhesitating co-operation with God's working in their lives, Christians **will never fall**. The word indicates that they will neither fall into misery nor come to grief.

1:11 / Furthermore, they **will receive a rich welcome** into the divine kingdom. The Greek is literally, "the entry for you will be richly abundantly supplied," using *epichorēgeoin*, as in verse 5. The writer, well aware of the limitations of words to depict spiritual truths, piles on vocabulary to try to emphasize, underline, and stress the overflowing generosity of the divine action, and the splendor of the Christian prospect. Faithful pilgrims on earth will be astonished at the lavish provision God has prepared for them when they come to enter the next world.

That entry, as Hebrews 10:19 points out, is made possible as a direct consequence of the sacrifice of Jesus Christ. So Peter here describes the **eternal kingdom** as that **of our Lord and Savior Jesus Christ**, even though the kingdom is more often specified in the NT as God's. But no distinction is intended. Peter gives a twofold description of the divine kingdom. It is **eternal**, and thus as different as can be from the transient powers and the hollow glamor of earthly realms. It is the kingdom **of our Lord and Savior Jesus Christ**. Entrance is gained only as a consequence of a living relationship with him. And once within that

kingdom, believers discover that its sphere is one of harmonious
life with him.

Additional Notes §4

1:10 / **Be all the more eager** (*dio mallon spoudasate*): The aorist
imperative *spoudasate* points to decisive action: "Determine to put in all
the more effort."
    Calling (*klēsis*): In the NT **calling** is always a divine call to salvation
(Rom. 11:29; 1 Cor. 1:26; 7:20; Eph. 1:18; 4:1, 4; Phil. 3:14; 2 Thess. 1:11;
2 Tim. 1:9; Heb. 3:1). See Turner, pp. 61–63.

1:11 / **Welcome**: cf. Dan. 7:27 LXX: "And the kingdom and the
power and the greatness of the kings that are under the whole heaven
were given to the saints of the Most High; and his kingdom is an everlasting kingdom, and all powers shall serve and obey him."
    Kingdom of . . . Jesus Christ is not a common expression in the NT,
which normally uses "kingdom of God" or "kingdom of heaven." But cf.
Matt. 13:41; 16:28; Luke 1:33; 22:29–30; 23:42; John 18:36; Col. 1:13; 2 Tim.
4:1, 18; Heb. 1:8; Rev. 11:15).
    Lord and Savior: In view of the familiarity of this double title for
Jesus since the earliest days of the church, it is surprising that it is found
in the NT only in the present letter (2 Pet. 2:20; 3:2, 18).

§5   The Need to Remember (2 Pet. 1:12–15)

1:12 / Peter now comes to the purpose of his letter. So, in view of all that I have outlined and because so much is at stake for your spiritual welfare, **I will always remind you of these things.** Here speaks the true preacher. Often a preacher is simply reminding listeners of Christian truths of faith and works they already **know**, as a spur to follow Christ more perfectly. But Peter is well aware, as have been all who have spoken in God's name down through the ages, of the fallibility of human memory, of the lure of siren voices, and of the constant necessity to be brought back to God's paths. In this, those who speak for God are following the divine example, for God himself has constantly been saying to his people "Remember!" (Num. 15:40; Isa. 46:9; Mal. 4:4; cf. Exod. 13:3; Josh. 1:13; Acts 20:35; Rom. 15:15; 1 Cor. 11:24–25; Phil. 3:1).

Peter tactfully adds **even though you know them**—again revealing the experienced preacher, ready to compliment an audience (Rom. 1:12; 1 John 2:21)—**and are firmly established in the truth** of the Christian faith. Even **firmly established** believers, mature in a faith they have practiced for some time, need to be warned against complacency and can benefit from exhortations to grow in grace. To stop is to stagnate; to stagnate is to die.

Peter's use of **firmly established** (*stērizein*), as he writes to readers he knows are in danger of wavering, is an unconscious and poignant echo of the word Jesus applied to *him* when warning the apostle of his coming denial. Peter, then so assured that he was established in his loyalty and could not possibly fail his Lord, was bidden, after the approaching drama of the arrest and crucifixion was over, to "strengthen (*stērizein*) your brothers" (Luke 22:32).

1:13 / Conscious of his apostolic responsibilities, and mindful of his own limited remaining time in which to minister,

Peter uses solemn language. **I think it is right**, I deem it my duty, **to refresh your memory** (lit. by a reminder, such as this letter) **as long as I live in the tent of this body**, i.e., while I am still here on earth. The transitoriness of the present life is a constant factor to be borne in mind, and the telling metaphor of **the tent** was often employed by early writers. A tent is a frail, temporary dwelling, up for a short period, and appropriate for a pilgrim on a journey.

1:14 / It was a memorable occasion, thirty years earlier, when **our Lord Jesus Christ** (the full title adds solemnity to Peter's words) **made** it **clear** that one day Peter would die a martyr's death (John 21:18–19; cf. John 13:36). Peter must be well into his sixties by now. Nero is the Roman emperor and Christians are becoming increasingly unpopular and suspected of disloyalty to the empire for their allegiance to "another king." The apostle is not anticipating a peaceful passing in old age. He does not elucidate, but evidently he has the feeling that his remaining time is short. He probably has in mind Christ's prophecy that his end would be a violent one.

Soon Peter will **put** the tent of his physical body **aside**, as one would a garment—and with no more effort or importance, such is the faithful believer's attitude toward the passage from this life into the next. Jesus himself once said that "if anyone keeps my word, he will *never notice* death" (John 8:51, lit.). Peter is looking forward to his own "rich welcome into the eternal kingdom" (v. 11; cf. 1 Pet. 1:4), but he is concerned for the continued well being of his readers beyond the day of his passing.

1:15 / Peter is not only writing the present letter for the benefit of his readers. He **will make every effort** to do something more. We may well assume that what Peter has in mind is a more substantial work than a brief writing such as 2 Peter, so that **after my departure you will always** (the Greek suggests "on each occasion, as you have need") **be able to remember these things**, these spiritual truths I am outlining now. The likelihood is that Peter is referring to the Gospel of Mark, widely accepted ever since the days of the early church fathers as being heavily in debt to Peter's reminiscences. The **every effort** he mentions probably means that he will do his utmost to see that Mark's Gospel is completed and that his present readers get a copy. That will provide them with a continuing source of edification even after his death.

Additional Notes §5

1:12 / The translation of the verb in **I will always remind** (*mellēsō*) **you** is a problem, as the awkward English suggests. The KJV "I will not be negligent" represents *ouk amelēsō* of later MSS, evidently an attempt by copyists to ease a difficult text. Modern renderings include: "I will not hesitate" (NEB); "I intend" (NAB, RSV). RV has "I shall be ready to," i.e., as often as necessary in the future, although **always** (*aei*) fits ill with Peter's expectation of death (v. 14). He probably means that his present letter will always be available, even after his death, as a reminder of vital Christian truths. But "always" need not cover a lengthy period of time, since the writer anticipates that the second coming of Christ is not too far away (see 1:19; 3:3, 12, 14).

Established (*stērizein*): Peter again uses the term in his final prayer in the first letter (1 Pet. 5:10) and employs a related word (*stērigmos*) in 2 Pet. 3:17.

1:13 / **Refresh**: *diegeirein* means to arouse thoroughly, as from sleepy inattention; the prefix *dia-* adds emphasis. The same phrase *diegeirein en hypomnēsei*, to stir awake by a reminder, recurs in 3:1, where NIV translates "as reminders to stimulate you."

Tent (*skēnōma*): In 2 Cor. 5:1–4 Paul uses similar language to describe the present physical body, although he employs a shorter word, *skēnos*. The Christian pilgrim can appreciate the reference to the transitoriness of earthly life by the Stoic philosopher Epictetus (A.D. 75–155): "But while God allows you to enjoy your property, use it as a thing which does not belong to you, and as a traveller uses a hostelry."

1:14 / **Made clear**: The Greek aorist *edēlōsen* points to a particular occasion: that was on the shore of the Sea of Tiberias (John 21:18–19; cf. John 13:36).

Put it aside: the same metaphor used by Paul in 2 Cor. 5:3–4.

Has made clear (*edēlōsen*) **to me**: *dēloun* can mean "to inform" (Col. 1:8), but it is also used of special revelations (1 Pet. 1:11; see *TDNT*, vol. 2, pp. 61–62).

1:15 / **I will make every effort** translates the Greek verb as a future. The oldest extant MS of 2 Peter, and one considered by scholars to be the most important textual witness (P[72]) has the present tense: "I am making every effort," which strengthens the supposition that Peter is referring to the Gospel of Mark (see commentary above).

Departure: As a euphemism for death, the Greek word *exodus* is found in the NT only here and in Luke 9:31, the transfiguration scene, where Jesus' coming *exodus* at Jerusalem is mentioned. (A third occurrence of the word, in Heb. 11:22, is to the exodus from Egypt.) "Exodus" in the sense of death is found in the Wisdom of Solomon (3:2; 7:6), a popular apocryphal work of the mid-second century B.C. Evidently it was known to Peter (cf. 1 Pet. 5:7 with Wisd. of Sol. 12:13; 2 Pet. 2:2 with Wisd. of Sol. 5:6; 2 Pet. 2:7 with Wisd. of Sol. 10:6). Wisdom of Solomon 3:2 indicates that *exodus* could mean not only death in the terminal sense, but transition to another state, as implied by Luke 9:31 and 2 Pet. 1:15.

Always, *hekastotē* (in the NT only here), is related to the adjective *hekastos*, each, every. Every time Peter's readers turn to his promised further source of edification (the Gospel of Mark is probably in mind), it will be to their spiritual benefit. That Peter refers here to the Gospel of Mark was first suggested by Irenaeus (*Against Heresies* 3.1.1; Eusebius, *Eccl. Hist.* 5.8.1–4). Peter's remarks in this passage prompted a rash of later literature, pseudonymously ascribed to him (e.g., *Apocalypse of Peter, Gospel of Peter, Preaching of Peter*).

1:16 / Whatever support Peter can hope to offer his readers in the future, there are some things that he is able to make clear to them now. Fundamental is the fact that the apostolic preaching, responsible for their faith in the first place, is firmly grounded on historical events. The apostles were not following **cleverly invented stories** for fraudulent purposes, as their opponents were alleging. Furthermore, the truth of the apostolic teaching about the second **coming of our Lord Jesus Christ** (Peter again uses the full solemn title) is guaranteed by the fact that some of the apostles, Peter included, were actual **eyewitnesses** of a singular manifestation of the **majesty** of Christ's divine glory— that which took place on the Mount of Transfiguration (Matt. 17:1–9; Mark 9:2–10; Luke 9:28–36).

1:17 / On that mountain the apostles had the unique experience of being present when Jesus **received honor and glory from God the Father**. Although the terms **honor and glory** pair naturally, the transfiguration scene can be said to refer to **honor** bestowed by the divine voice on that occasion and to **glory** received from the Shekinah cloud which enveloped the person of Jesus on the mount (Mark 9:7).

The accounts in all three Synoptic Gospels link the transfiguration of Jesus with his second coming, and Peter does the same here. The dazzling splendor on the mount was forever burned into the apostle's memory, for not even the resurrection appearances are said in the record to have had such characteristics as **honor and glory**. At all events, Peter has come to appreciate the significance of the transfiguration in terms of the relationship between the Father and the Son. It was then that Jesus **received** the divine **honor and glory**, i.e., he was invested with kingly glory as the divine Son of the Father. This will be made abundantly clear to all, not just to the apostles, when Jesus returns in power and great glory (v. 16) to carry out his appointed task of being judge over all. During his time upon earth, he walked with his divinity veiled and thus offers believers the confident hope not only that he will come again, but that men and women in the present life who acknowledge him as Savior will be able to share in his glorification in the world to come (1:4).

The voice came to him from the Majestic Glory, by which is meant the Shekinah glory cloud (cf. John 1:14): **"This is my Son, whom I love; with him I am well pleased."** The wording in the Synoptic Gospels is virtually identical and echoes that used at Jesus' baptism (Matt. 3:17; Mark 1:11; Luke 3:22; cf. Ps. 2:7; Isa. 42:1). The implication is that Jesus is the Son of God in a unique way. The repetition of the personal pronoun in **my Son** and "my beloved" (translated by NIV here as **whom I love**) intensifies the expression of intimacy and oneness.

1:18 / **We ourselves heard this voice.** The pronoun is emphatic, stressing the personal nature of the testimony of Peter and his two fellow apostles at the transfiguration. Peter does not name the **mountain**, perhaps to keep the site from becoming a place of pilgrimage. But understandably the spot was forever marked in Peter's own memory as rendered specially **sacred**. It was there that God himself had solemnly affirmed the divinity of Jesus his Son. Peter's reiteration of the apostles' eyewitness testimony in verses 16 and 18 is to underline his authority in teaching about the person of Jesus (cf. 1 John 1:1–2), since he is preparing to assail those who were spreading false doctrine (2 Pet. 2:1–3). More immediately (v. 19), he is emphasizing the solidarity between the message of the OT prophets and the teaching of the apostles. The false teachers were impugning both.

Additional Notes   §6

1:16 / **Coming** (*parousia*, appearing): In the NT *parousia* is always a reference to the second advent of Christ, not to his first coming as a babe at Bethlehem. The actual word *parousia* may not occur in 1 Peter, but the idea is present in 1 Pet. 1:7, 13; 4:13; 5:4. In the papyri *parousia* is used of the official state visit of a king. See *TDNT*, vol. 5, pp. 858–71; *NIDNTT*, vol. 2, pp. 898–935; Turner, pp. 404–8.

Cleverly invented (*sesophismenois*): This was a term applied to the claims of quack doctors.

Stories: The Greek word is *mythois*, fables, myths in the popular sense of stories of gods descending to earth, which reports of the transfiguration might have suggested.

Told (*gnōrizein*): to make known, often used in the NT for revealing a divine mystery (Luke 2:15; John 15:15; 17:26; Rom. 16:26; Eph. 6:19; Col. 1:27).

Eyewitnesses (*epoptai*): This expression, found in the NT only here, was a technical term in classical Greek for those who reached the highest degree in the Eleusian mystery religions (see *TDNT*, vol. 5, p. 374.).

Majesty (*megaleiotēs*): This word occurs elsewhere in the NT only in Luke 9:43, of the people's amazement at God's action as revealed in the healing of the demoniac boy, an incident immediately following the transfiguration; and in Acts 19:27, where it is used of the "magnificence" of the Ephesian goddess Artemis. The word often appears in the papyri as a ceremonial title.

1:17 / **For he received** (*labōn gar*): lit. "for having received." The sentence is anacoluthic, containing two participles and no main verb. The writer's excitement has played havoc with his grammar. The use of the aorist *labōn* indicates a particular action at a certain definite moment.

The two terms **honor and glory** pair naturally, as in Rom. 2:7, 10; 1 Tim. 1:17; Heb. 2:7, 9, quoting Ps. 8:5; Rev. 4:9, 11; 5:12. Here Peter's use of the expression may allude to Ps. 8:5 ("you . . . crowned him with glory and honor") or to Dan. 7:14 ("he was given authority, glory and sovereign power").

The voice: The presence of Moses and Elijah at the scene of the transfiguration, as recorded in the Synoptic Gospels, affirmed the prophetic role of Jesus, already foretold by Moses: "The Lord your God will raise up for you a prophet like me from among your own brothers. You must listen to him" (Deut. 18:15).

Came: Instead of the usual word for "come," Peter here has the verb *pherein*, to bear (as appears also in Acts 2:2, for the coming of the Pentecostal wind). Peter makes use of the same verb in 1 Pet. 2:24, 2 Pet. 1:18 (in connection with the gift of prophecy), and in 2:11).

Majestic Glory is a rare expression, but a typical Hebrew periphrasis for God. It occurs also in 1 Clement 9.2, and in later Greek liturgies. The Greek for **majestic** is *megaloprepēs*, formed from *megas*, great, and *prepei*, it is becoming: "that which befits greatness." The word appears in Deut. 33:26 LXX as an epithet for God. **Glory** (*doxa*) is used in the Third Gospel to describe first the transfiguration (Luke 9:32) and then the second coming (Luke 21:27).

From (*para*) **God . . . from** (*hypo*) **the Majestic Glory**: The different Greek prepositions suggest intimate personal action: *para*, from the side of; *hypo*, by (agent).

The words of **the voice**, as recorded here by Peter, are almost the same as those in Matt. 17:5. Peter omits Matthew's "Listen to him!" but in v. 19 he inserts a similar notion with his "pay attention" to the word of prophecy. Mark and Luke do not read **with him I am well pleased**. It is likely that, had 2 Peter been the work not of the apostle but of a later pseudonymous writer, the divine words would have been reported in a version copied from one of the Gospel accounts. As it is, assuming apostolic authorship of this letter, the record in 2 Peter is an early testimony to the Gospel narratives, preceding them in time by some years.

This is my Son, whom I love translates a text preserved in P[72], the earliest extant MS (3rd or 4th cent.) of 2 Peter and in B (Codex Vaticanus, 4th cent.). The words **my Son** at the transfiguration were seen early on as an allusion to the messianic Psalm 2:7; and Peter evidently has this in mind, for he refers to the "sacred mount" in the next verse (18). The Greek translated by NIV as **whom I love** (*ho agapētos mou*) is lit. "my beloved" and is a very early messianic title, according to J. Armitage Robinson, *St Paul's Epistle to the Ephesians* (London: Macmillan, 1903), pp. 229–33. The phrase is used by God of Abraham's "beloved son" when he commands the patriarch to offer Isaac as a sacrifice (Gen. 22:2).

§7   Scriptural Evidence (2 Pet. 1:19–21)

The authority for the apostolic teaching on eschatology is twofold. Peter has just been speaking of the apostles' testimony to the transfiguration of Jesus (vv. 16–18). They were eyewitnesses of what happened on that momentous occasion. As a consequence, their teaching is not a collection of dreamed up myths. That is the first factor. Peter now turns to the second: the evidence of the divinely inspired OT Scriptures (vv. 19–21).

1:19 / **The word of the prophets** is too narrow a translation of what is literally "the prophetic word," for all the known instances of the Greek phrase *ton prophētikon logon* point to its being synonymous with the term "Scriptures" (Bauckham, p. 224). That prophetic word is now said, according to NIV, to be that which the apostles **have . . . made more certain** (*echomen bebaioteron*). The Greek expression usually means "to have firm hold on something." The word *bebaioteron* is grammatically a comparative, but in Koine Greek it often has the superlative meaning ("very firm"). So here, Peter is not making a *comparison* with the transfiguration, or with anything else, but is expressing complete confidence: "we possess the prophetic word as altogether something reliable" (NAB). Peter's readers must take the same attitude: **pay attention** to the inspired Scriptures, for they act as **a light** (*lychnos*, lamp) **shining in a dark place**. **Dark** renders the Greek *auchmēros*, dry, squalid, dismal: the term subtly associates the idea of darkness with dirt, thirst, and general neglect, conditions which are exposed when divine illumination blazes forth.

The inspired authority of Scripture is totally sufficient for this present life, until the Parousia, when **the day** of the Lord **dawns** (3:10) **and the morning star** (Christ, Rev. 22:16) **rises in your hearts**. Prophecy's function for this life is to illuminate the darkness of ignorance. But at the Parousia prophecy will be superseded (1 Cor. 13:8–10) as the full light of God's glorious revelation in Christ floods the hearts of his people. A lamp is no longer required once the sun is up.

1:20–21 / When Peter's readers obey his behest and study the OT, they must keep clearly in mind as they do so that **no prophecy of Scripture came about by the prophet's own interpretation**. The words they read are not what a prophet has thought up for himself. True prophecy never came about as a result of some individual's personal ideas: it **never had its origin in the will of man.** The impulse came from the Holy Spirit of God. When the OT prophets spoke, they were not passing on some understanding or view of their own. They were revealing a message from the Spirit: they **spoke from God.** It was for this reason that their words must be closely heeded.

It follows, therefore, that readers of the Scriptures must look to the same divine Spirit to inspire their understanding of the text (Ps. 119:18). It is the Spirit who must interpret and apply his own message in his own way. The translators of KJV were very conscious of this fact, as is shown by their frequent prayer during their work: "More light, Lord!"

But one other point must be borne in mind. If a student of Scripture finds that some personal interpretation is at variance with that which has been generally accepted down the long centuries by the church, then the student should be prepared to humbly reconsider his or her view. Is a supposed insight truly the outcome of fresh light from the Holy Spirit, or is it in fact only a personal opinion? It has always been easy enough for a reader to be **carried along** by preconceived ideas about some aspect of Christian doctrine, rather than **by the Holy Spirit**, who is operating in the church, the body of believers as a whole, as well as in individuals. At the end of his letter (3:16), Peter refers to false teachers who are going fatally astray because they are expressing their own wishes due to a wrong interpretation of Scripture. But Peter is far from warning off his readers from studying the word of God for themselves—just in case they get it wrong! He has just reminded them that the Scriptures are a "shining light" (v. 19). Light is given to be *used.*

Additional Notes §7

1:19 / **The word of the prophets** is the NIV rendering of *ton prophētikon logon*, lit. the prophetic word. The expression has been variously understood as referring to one or more OT messianic prophecies or to the transfiguration itself as a prophecy of the Parousia. But the Greek phrase in contemporary literature embraced the whole OT, not just the prophets (Philo, *On Noah's Work as a Planter* 117; 2 Clement 11.2; Justin, *Dialogue with Trypho* 56.6).

You will do well is the usual phrase for "please" in the papyri (and in James 2:3, RSV).

A light shining: The same expression is applied by Jesus to John the Baptist (John 5:35) as the last of the prophets of the old covenant.

The **morning star** is Venus (*TDNT*, vol. 9, p. 312), which in fact rises *before* dawn, not after, as the wording here implies. But the sun may be meant: the expression is symbolic for the dawn. The reference, of course, is to Christ (Rev. 22:16). There is probably an allusion also to Num. 24:17 LXX, "a star shall rise out of Jacob," a verse interpreted messianically in Judaism.

1:20 / **Above all** (*touto prōton ginōskontes*): lit. "knowing this first" (as KJV), taking this as your basic principle. The phrase recurs in 3:3.

By the prophet's own interpretation: NIV gives the more likely understanding of **own** (*idias*) by inserting the words **the prophet's** (not in the Greek). Others take *idias* to indicate that the text means "No interpretation of Scripture is a matter of one's own interpretation" (cf. KJV, RSV, JB), which at its face value rules out any individual freedom to interpret the Bible, implying that it must be left to some hierarchical pronouncement.

Interpretation (*epilysis*): solution, explanation (lit. an unravelling), found only here in the NT, although the corresponding Greek verb *epilyein* occurs in Mark 4:34 (of the *understanding* of parables) and in Acts 19:39 (of a case being *settled* in court).

1:21 / **Were carried along** (*pheromenoi*): as a ship by the wind (Acts 27:15, 17). Here the Holy Spirit is the wind (Acts 2:2; John 3:8). "The prophets raised their sails, so to speak (they were obedient and receptive), and the Holy Spirit filled them and carried their craft along in the direction he wished" (Green, p. 91).

By the Holy Spirit: The only direct reference to the Holy Spirit in this letter; cf. 1 Cor. 2:9–16.

Peter began this letter by speaking of the divine provision for a godly life (1:1–11). He went on to stress the divine inspiration of Scripture truths (1:12–21). Now he warns against those who are threatening the church's spiritual well being by the way they falsely treat these matters (2:1–22).

2:1 / In some respects times do not change. All prophecy, whoever gives it and in whatever circumstances, needs to be interpreted. Furthermore, just as in the period of the OT there were **false prophets**, such as Balaam (2:15), whose activities threatened to poison spiritual life **among the people** of God, so Peter cautions his readers that in their own day **there will be false teachers** operating among them. Their teaching is invidious: **they will secretly introduce destructive heresies**. Their method is suggested by the Greek verb Peter uses, which is literally "bring in alongside"; that is, they deviously smuggle false doctrine into true and thereby pervert the way of truth. The result is **destructive heresies**, the intrusion of unorthodox opinions which lead to the ruin of spiritual life, the doom of the people involved, and their loss of all that is eternally worthwhile.

Peter does not shrink from using language that recalls his own cowardly failure (Matt. 26:69–75), although his fall was swiftly followed by repentance and restoration. The attitude of the false teachers is, by contrast, both persistent and malignant. They are **denying the sovereign Lord**, that is, the Lord Jesus Christ who owns their allegiance through dying for them on the cross.

The precise nature of the false teachers' denial is not spelled out by Peter here (or in Jude 4). It could be the practical denial exhibited by ungodly lives, or the blatant rejection of Jesus Christ as Son of God (1 John 2:22–23). At all events, their denial amounts to a repudiation of the fundamental doctrine that the

Lord Jesus Christ died for their sins. By that sacrifice on the cross he **bought them** with his own life-blood (1 Pet. 1:18–19). By his death Jesus ransomed men and women from the slavery of sin.

The false teachers are rejecting all this. Yet in so doing they are not merely expressing a human opinion but deliberately refusing to accept divine truth as revealed in the inspired Scriptures and in the person and work of the Lord Jesus Christ. These men are not simply misguided, but heretics who have refused divine light, preferring their own views on spiritual matters. As an inevitable consequence they are **bringing swift destruction on themselves.** Peter's warning is in line with the general expectation of early Christians that the period preceding Christ's Parousia would be marked by false teaching, blasphemy, and immorality, leading to apostasy (Mark 13:22; 2 Thess. 2:3, 11–12; 1 Tim. 4:1–3; 2 Tim. 3:1–5).

The next two verses set out four factors about the false teachers and their activity and influence.

2:2–3 / The *motive* of the false teachers is **greed**, an unlawful desire to grasp more than one's due. The Greek word can involve coveting other people's money or goods, engaging in illicit sexual indulgence, or lusting for power, all of which speak of going after selfish gain at the expense of others and of a reckless disregard of the moral order. These men have become "experts in greed" (2:14).

The *method* of the false teachers is to **exploit you with stories they have made up**. To be effective, any evil propaganda must be a mixing of truth with falsehood. This is exactly what these men are doing. They are guilty of having fabricated fictitious arguments. Furthermore, the use of the term **exploit** implies that these false teachers are financially making a good living out of their dupes (cf. Jude 11, 12, 16).

The *effect* of the false teaching is to lure others into similar paths of immorality and so to bring discredit upon Christ. **Many will follow**, for the attraction of this sort of conduct will be hard to resist, appealing as it does to the worst side of human nature. It issues in **shameful ways**, in acts of unbridled lust and brazen excess, which **will bring the way of truth**, Christ's program for the believer's manner of life, **into disrepute**, and with it malign Jesus himself. Some of those whom the public views as his followers are perniciously misrepresenting the way of life he has prescribed. Scandalous behavior is giving Christianity a bad name among outsiders.

The *end result* of false teaching is the proponents' inevitable **condemnation** and **destruction**. The OT had long ago foretold this (Deut. 13:1-5; Jude 4), and although the carrying out of the sentence may seem to have been shelved, or even somehow rendered invalid, judgment **has not been sleeping**, whatever the appearance to the contrary (3:9). Judgment at the last was certain to be carried out, as true believers knew (1:19). As far as the false teachers were concerned, "perdition waits for them with unsleeping eyes" (NEB).

Additional Notes   §8

2:1 / From this point (2:1-3:3) there are many resemblances between the present letter and Jude 4-18, but few exact verbal coincidences, suggesting that the two writers did not copy one from the other but drew upon common material (see Introduction, pp. 13-14).

There were (*egenonto*, arose, came into being) **false prophets**: The use of this particular verb hints at self-appointment. **False prophets**, who appear all through the OT (Deut. 18:20; 1 Kings 22:12; 2 Kings 18:19; Isa. 9:15; Jer. 14:14; Ezek. 13:3; Zech. 13:4), are treated as parallel with **false teachers** in Peter's day, since their harmful influences were much the same. Technically, false prophets differed from false teachers in claiming direct inspiration from God, rather than from the result of studying Scripture; but the deleterious effect of both groups upon God's people in general was similar. There are many and frequent NT warnings against false teachers (see, for example, Matt. 24:4-5; Acts 20:29-30; Gal. 1:6-9; Phil. 3:2; Col. 2:4; 2 Thess. 2:1-3; 1 Tim. 1:3-7; 2 Tim. 3:1-8; 1 John 2:18-19; 2 John 7-11; Jude 3-4).

There will be false teachers: Peter uses the future tense since he anticipates a worsening of the situation (cf. Matt. 24:11). But this is not to exclude current antagonists, whom he goes on to mention in vv. 10, 17-18. The letter of Jude has much subject matter in common with 2 Peter 2. In referring to false teachers, Jude 4 speaks of them as already present, which could have something to say about the relative dates of the two letters. The "falseness" of these men applies both to their message and to their implicit claim to be authoritative guides.

Destructive (*apōleia*) **heresies** (lit. heresies of destruction, a Hebraism) . . . **swift destruction** (*apōleia*): The Greek *apōleia* (doom) is repeated in v. 3 and in 3:7, 16. The repetition is nicely brought out by the shades of meaning listed by BAGD: "the *destruction* that one experiences, *annihilation* both complete and in process, *ruin*."

Heresies: The Greek *hairesis* originally meant a school or sect of philosophy, the word implying primarily a choice of belief or opinion (as *party* in Acts 5:17; 15:5; *sect* in Acts 24:5, 14). The coming of Jesus as the "truth" (John 1:14, 17; 8:32; 14:6; 16:13) set the God-given standard, which ruled out mere human opinion of truth. Now people must accept or reject God's truth as proclaimed by Jesus, the one sent down from heaven (John 1:9). In Christian writings the term *hairesis* henceforth acquired a negative sense: an opinion contrary to orthodox Christian doctrine. To follow a *heresy* results in *schism* (1 Cor. 11:18–19). Those who teach heresy are to be strictly warned, and then disowned (Titus 3:10). See *TDNT*, vol. 1, pp. 180–84; *NIDNTT*, vol. 1, pp. 533–35; Turner, p. 211.

Denying the ... Lord: cf. 1 John 2:22.

Sovereign Lord translates one Greek word, *despotēs*, which unlike the similar sounding modern English word "despot" can have a neutral sense: one with absolute ownership and in complete control; *despotēs* is used in the LXX as a title for God.

The verb **bought** is *agorazein*, one of three words in the NT translated "redeem." In classical use it meant "to purchase in the market place" and was frequently applied to the purchase of slaves. Those who were thus purchased became the property of their master. The terminology is applied in the NT to Christians. They have become, by the payment of a price (Mark 10:45; 1 Pet. 1:18–19; Rev. 5:9), slaves of their Master (*despotēs*) Christ; cf. 1 Cor. 6:20; 7:23; Gal. 3:13. See I. H. Marshall, "The Development of the Concept of Redemption in the New Testament," in R. Banks, ed., *Reconciliation and Hope: New Testament Essays on Atonement and Eschatology* (Exeter: Paternoster/Grand Rapids: Eerdmans, 1974), pp. 153–69; *NIDNTT*, vol. 3, pp. 177–221.

2:2 / **Many will follow**: The verb is *exakolouthein*, to follow out to the end, used in the NT only in this letter (1:16; 2:2, 15).

Shameful ways is one word in the Greek, *aselgeia*, licentiousness, wantonness, unbridled lust, excess; also used by Peter in 1 Pet. 4:3; 2 Pet. 2:7, 18.

The way of truth, the path of truth; or as a Hebraism, the true path (cf. Ps. 119:30). The metaphor of "way" for conduct, ethical behavior, is common in the OT, in intertestamental literature, and in Philo. See Didache 1:1–2; see also *TDNT*, vol. 5, pp. 42–96; *NIDNTT*, vol. 3, pp. 888, 933–47.

Bring ... into disrepute renders one word, *blasphēmein*, to revile, defame (2 Kings 19:4; Isa. 52:5; charged against Jesus, Matt. 9:3; 26:65; and against Stephen, Acts 6:11; confessed by Paul, 1 Tim. 1:13). Blasphemy will be characteristic of the last days (2 Tim. 3:2; Rev. 13:1; 17:3). See Turner, pp. 46–48; *TDNT*, vol. 1, pp. 621–25; *NIDNTT*, vol. 3, pp. 340–47.

2:3 / **Greed** was a notorious mark of itinerant sophists in the Greek world, a failing repudiated by Paul in his apostolic work (1 Thess. 2:5; cf. 1 Tim. 6:5).

Exploit (*emporeuesthai*): to traffic in (cf. "emporium").

Made up is Greek *plastos*, from the verb *plassein*, to mould, as in wax or clay; cf. 1:16, "cleverly invented stories."

Has long been hanging over them: lit. "for whom the judgment from long ago is not idle." Although the sentence was pronounced in the distant past and has not been executed, it has not been set aside or overlooked.

Their destruction has not been sleeping, lit. "their destruction (doom) is not asleep," but is being actively planned. "Destruction" is personified, although we are not told who the divine agent will be.

§9 Examples of Judgment and Deliverance (2 Pet. 2:4–10a)

To underline the certainty of retribution by the eventual carrying out of the divine sentence, however much apparently delayed in the case of the false teachers, Peter quotes three notorious examples from the book of Genesis which tell of God's destroying the wicked.

The first illustration is of fallen angels (v. 4), the second, of the Flood (v. 5), and the third, of the cities of the plain (vv. 6–8). Nevertheless, Peter's main thrust is positive, for he stresses the fact that the godly caught up in these situations were kept safe by God—Noah (v. 5) and Lot (v. 7)—and so concludes on the reassuring note that "the Lord knows how to rescue godly men" (v. 9). This is a point absent from the parallel passage in Jude 5–7, but a theme which recurs in the present letter (1:4, 11, 19; 3:9, 11–14).

2:4 / The **angels** that **sinned** is an allusion to Genesis 6:1–4, although Peter does not define their wrongdoing. Lust is mentioned in the Genesis account, but rebellion against God was the main motive, as is brought out by the other references to the episode in Jude 6 and Revelation 12:7. Even exalted orders of beings such as angels were not exempt from the consequences of disobeying God, so the implication for nefarious human beings who had led God's people astray is inescapable.

The mutinous angels were **sent . . . to hell**, committed to Tartarus, as the Greek has it, the prison in the nether region for the worst of the wicked. The notion of Tartarus was taken over by Jewish apocalyptic from Greek mythology. The rebels were confined in **gloomy dungeons**, pits of densest darkness, the furthest imaginable extremity from the fullness of dazzling light that such angels had once enjoyed in the presence of God.

There the fallen angels were **to be held**, kept under guard **for judgment**. The **judgment** is defined as the "great Day" of the

great white throne judgment (Rev. 20:11) in the parallel passage
in Jude 6. But, unlike Jude, Peter here gives no hint of alluding to
the details in the tradition of the fall of the Watchers in 1 Enoch.
This was a highly popular work among Jews of the time and
Peter's reference to Tartarus, which in the book of Enoch was the
place of punishment of fallen angels, suggests that he may well
have known the work. But Peter is not so much endorsing the
tradition as employing popular Homeric imagery with which his
readers were familiar.

2:5 / Peter continues his *a fortiori* argument by turning
for his second illustration to the story of the Flood (Gen. 7:1–7).
That event can be viewed as the fearful consequence of the angels' sin (Gen. 6:1–7) in leading on to the ruin of the world at that
time. Peter's wording highlights the contrast between one man's
being kept safe on account of his righteousness, as against (lit.) "a
world of ungodly ones" being destroyed because of their sin.

It is an example of divine judgment that Peter can recall
being used in Jesus' teaching about his Parousia (Matt. 24:37–39),
and one that the apostle has already included in his first letter
(1 Pet. 3:20). The parallelism extends even to the reference to the
number of those saved from destruction, **Noah . . . and seven
others**, i.e., only his immediate family, his wife, with their three
sons Shem, Ham, and Japheth, and their wives.

Peter describes Noah as **a preacher of righteousness**. Despite the absence of any direct reference in the Genesis account
to Noah's preaching, there was a widespread Jewish tradition to
this effect. It is likely that he did preach—even if results were
minimal—during the 120 years the ark was being built (Gen. 6:3).
But in any case, Noah's godly life would in itself be a powerful
and continuous sermon to the godless world around him. Words
are not essential for one to be **a preacher of righteousness**.

But here Peter simply draws attention to the destruction of
the earth by the deluge, giving as the reason for the catastrophe
the wickedness of the population. He then focuses attention
upon the fact that amidst it all God **protected Noah** and his
family.

Peter thus maintains his pastoral purpose of encouraging
his readers to keep faith with God in their own situation. Such a
loyal stand will neither go unnoticed nor fail to attract a similar
divine protection from the consequences of the sin of the godless

who have no time for God. The false teachers of Peter's day face certain retribution. Yet, as God kept Noah and his family from perishing in the Flood which carried off the wicked of those times, so the same God will protect believers who remain faithful to him in later generations. Whichever course people choose, loyalty to God or following the ways of a world that leaves God out of account, the consequences are guaranteed by the word of the Lord.

2:6 / Peter's third illustration alludes, without elaborating, to the destruction of **the cities of Sodom and Gomorrah** (Gen. 19:25). On the one hand, this example of divine judgment also occurs in Jude 7, although again Jude does not mention the rescue of the righteous, as Peter does when he goes on to speak about the deliverance of Lot (v. 7). On the other hand, Jude specifies the sins of the cities of the plain, but Peter does not refer directly to the reason for their overthrow, except to call their inhabitants **ungodly**, with no time for God (as in v. 5).

The destruction of the cities was brought about **by burning them to ashes**. As in the case of his previous example, that of the Flood and the preservation of righteous Noah, so with his next reference to the destruction of Sodom and Gomorrah and the rescue of righteous Lot, Peter uses the same illustrations as Jesus did in his teaching about the Parousia (Luke 17:26–29).

The disaster which befell Sodom and Gomorrah **made them an example**. The Greek word means a pattern (as in James 5:10; Heb. 4:11). In other words, there is an inevitable pattern of events: sin, unconfessed and unforsaken, will lead to judgment and destruction. This, says Peter, is **what is going to happen to the ungodly**, any who live in such a manner that they leave God out of their calculations. And this, more immediately for Peter's purpose, includes the false teachers whose activities are a threat to his readers.

By employing successive examples of divine judgment by water and by fire, Peter is preparing the way for his summarizing climax in 3:6–7.

2:7–8 / In these two verses, Peter three times describes **Lot** as **righteous**, a term not applied to him in the Genesis account. There Lot appears as self-centered, an opportunist (Gen. 13:10–14) who had strayed from the God of his fathers. True, he offers hospitality (Gen. 19:1–3), but he is so depraved (Gen. 19:8) that he has lost the power of moral choice (Gen. 19:14). He is weak-willed (Gen. 19:16) and preyed upon by drink (Gen. 19:33). He has so settled down into the life of Sodom that force has to be used to drag him to safety (Gen. 19:16). Nevertheless, God **rescued Lot**, which only serves to underline the sheer unmerited grace of God's merciful action. Lot's character-sketch in Genesis is hardly to his credit. It might be thought that Peter calls him **righteous** in contrast to the depraved inhabitants of Sodom. But it is to be noted that in his intercession for any "righteous" in Sodom, Abraham obviously had his nephew very much in mind (Gen. 18:22–32). At all events, Lot's heart was clearly still somewhat responsive to God, even after having his permanent home in such an environment. The inner struggle Lot suffered **day after day** meant that he **was distressed by the filthy lives of lawless men**. He was worn down by being exposed day in, day out, to the vile manner of life of those who scorned the moral code and the law of God.

Lot was repeatedly **tormented in his righteous soul**. The verb is active, not passive, and implies that Lot put himself on the rack. That he is feeling pain, so to speak, is heightened by the fact that the verb is put last in the Greek sentence and so in a position of strong emphasis. **Tormented** is not too strong a term, therefore, to describe his spiritual suffering at what was going on around him. The **lawless deeds**, the unrestrained behavior that defies established codes, human and divine, were expressed in the sights and sounds **he saw and heard** every single day of his life. They were a continuous scourge to his soul. That feeling of intense distress proved to be Lot's lifeline, for the believer's greatest peril is when conscience becomes so dulled that it is no longer disturbed by evil happenings. Or, as Cardinal Newman is said to have once remarked: "Our great security against sin lies in being shocked at it."

2:9 / Despite the sheer intensity of the divine judgment, whether by water (as in the case of the Flood) or by fire (as in the case of Sodom and Gomorrah), the Lord still preserved godly Noah in the former instance and righteous Lot in the latter. Since the biblical record makes it abundantly clear that **this is so**, then it follows as certainly as dawn follows dark that **the Lord** has demonstrated to believing hearts that he **knows how to rescue godly** people of any generation and in any situation **from trials,**

testings, and afflictions arising from their living among unbelievers or from evil in the present world. No doubt some of Peter's
readers, galled by the pernicious workings of the false teachers,
must often have asked how long God would allow the situation
to persist. In his role as pastor, Peter reassures them. Divine deliverance may seem to be uncertain, or at least long in coming.
But come it will, for God is in control all along —as is illustrated
in the experiences of Noah and Lot.

Furthermore, since God is Lord of heaven as well as earth,
it also follows that his saving and keeping power, on the one
hand, and his power to inflict judgment, on the other hand, extend beyond the present world. The physical destruction wrought
by the divine action is not the end of the story. God will **hold the
unrighteous for the day of judgment.** The consequences of unrighteousness, in other words, do not come to an end with those
concerned being annihilated, reduced to nothingness, which
was the fate of their physical bodies. **Their punishment** carries
on (cf. 2:4). This is not vindictiveness on the part of a God who
has been scorned, but the inevitable outworking of divine principles built into the created order. Life and peace come from and
are dependent upon the living God. Any who willfully choose to
reject God thereby cut themselves off from the source of life and
peace (2 Thess. 1:9). Logically, therefore, it follows that for them
these qualities must be absent. In other words, they can know
only an eternal state of death and restlessness.

The NIV translation **continuing their punishment** seeks to
catch the sense of what is one word in the Greek, *kolazomenous,* a
present participle. The ungodly are represented as already suffering some sort of penal process. The Greek ethical writers on
punishment (e.g., Aristotle, *Rhetoric* 1:10) distinguished between
kolasis, inflicted for the good of the sufferer, and *timōria* (Heb.
10:29), imposed for the satisfaction of justice. Since Peter's term
is reflected in the former, he may be hinting at the notion of the
penalty being corrective (cf. 1 Pet. 3:19; 4:6).

2:10a / To turn from examples of OT history to the situation being faced by Peter's readers: **all this is especially true** of
the false teachers. Like those unrighteous people of earlier generations which Scripture describes, they also are guilty of similar
practices which they are insidiously carrying on in the Christian
community—those of immorality and the defiance of authority.

But it is also true that, whatever they may be thinking, God is still sovereign and will execute judgment.

In the first place, they are **those who follow the corrupt desires of the sinful nature**. Peter's charge of sexual malpractice is frequently alluded to in this letter, and in 2:19 he will point to the fact that these false teachers are assuming that Christian liberty exempts them from the ordinary rules of morality applying to less enlightened people.

The phrase **corrupt desire** is literally "in lust of defilement." If the genitive **of defilement** is objective, the sense is "in hankering after lust;" but if subjective, as is more probable, "in lust which defiles." These men cannot avoid the consequential effect of immoral practices: they defile, they stain—as though with a dye.

In the second place, the false teachers **despise authority**. Peter may be bringing a general charge: these men are independent free-thinkers, bowing to nobody's authority—certainly, it may imply, not to that of church leaders. As in 2:1, what the indictment refers to specifically is not clear to us today. But apparently these men were deprecating the divine authority of the Lord Jesus Christ in some way, for the following verse (2:11) refers to angels standing before the Lord: *they* never forget the awesome restraint of that divine presence. Yet these false teachers, whether they realize it or not, also speak in fact "before the Lord," in the sight and hearing of God, yet think nothing of what that means.

Additional Notes §9

2:4 / Of the three illustrations from Genesis which Peter uses in 2:4–8, two are quoted by Jude: the rebellious angels (Jude 6; 2 Pet. 2:4) and the cities of the plain (Jude 7; 2 Pet. 2:6–8). Jude's other example, of the Israelites who grumbled in the wilderness (Jude 5), is replaced by Peter with a reference to the Flood (2 Pet. 2:5). Unlike Jude, Peter places the events in chronological order. All of 2 Pet. 2:4–10a constitutes a single sentence in the Greek, peppered with repeated *if*-clauses in vv. 4, 5, 6, 7, and 9, as Peter builds up to the climax of vv. 9–10a.

Angels when they sinned: In Gen. 6:1–4, to which Peter here alludes, the **angels** are termed "the sons of God," a common expression for them in the OT (Job 1:6; 2:1; 38:7; Ps. 89:6). The Genesis story is further developed in 1 Enoch (dating from 170 B.C.), where these angels were subject to chains, fire, and darkness (1 Enoch 6:2; 10:4, 12–13; 54:4–5).

Sent . . . to hell (*tartarōsas*): The only occurrence in the NT of the verb *tartarein*, formed from *Tartarus*, in Greek mythology the place of punishment for the departed spirits of the worst of the wicked. In Jewish apocalyptic, which adopted the idea, Tartarus was said to be in the charge of the archangel Uriel (1 Enoch 20:2). In Homer, Hades is the place of confinement for dead human beings, and Tartarus is the name applied to a murky abyss below Hades in which the sins of fallen mortals are punished. See Turner, pp. 210–11.

Dungeons translates the plural of Greek *siros*, also spelled *seiros* in some MSS (meaning cave, pit; cf. RSV). Other MSS have *sira* or *seira*, chain. Neither *siros* nor *sira* is common, and the MS evidence is equally balanced. But "pits of darkness" makes better sense than "chains of darkness"(KJV).

Held for judgment: Unlike Jude in the parallel passage (Jude 6), Peter gives no hint of alluding to details in the tradition of the fall of the Watchers in 1 Enoch, even though he probably knew this popular work of the time. Cf. Isa. 24:21–22; 1 Cor. 6:3; 1 Pet. 3:19–20. The judgment of angels is a theme in the Dead Sea Scrolls (1QH 10.34).

2:5 /   The **ancient world** is the antediluvian epoch, the first period in a threefold division of history which Peter seems to envisage. The present post-Noachian age will be followed by the new world-order ushered in by the "day of God" (3:12–13).

When he brought the flood (lit.) "upon a world of ungodly people" echoes Gen. 6:18 LXX, "I bring a flood of water upon the earth."

Its ungodly people (*asebēs*): the impious, those with no time for God.

Protected (*ephylaxen*): stood guard over. The choice of language indicates God's personal concern.

A preacher (*kēryx*): herald; cf. 1 Tim. 2:7; 2 Tim. 1:11, the only other NT occurrences of the noun). Although Genesis says nothing about Noah preaching, there was a well-established tradition that he did so: "Many angels of God now consorted with women and begat sons, who were overbearing and disdainful of every virtue. . . . But Noah, indignant at their conduct . . . urged them to come to a better frame of mind and amend their ways" (Josephus, *Ant.* 1.73–74). "Noah preached repentance, and those that obeyed were saved" (1 Clement 7.6).

And seven others (*ogdoon*): lit. the eighth, a common Greek idiom for "seven others." But there are more possibilities Peter may have in mind. He could mean that Noah was the eighth from Adam along the line of faith represented by the genealogy of Seth and Enoch (Jude 14; cf. Heb. 11:5). Or Peter may be alluding to the eschatological symbolism of the number eight. Early Christians referred to Sunday, the resurrection day, as the "eighth day" (Barnabas 15.9). Justin indeed associates the Sunday symbolism with the eight souls saved in the ark (*Dialogue with Trypho* 138.1).

2:6 /   **Condemned** (*katakrinen*) is augmented in some MSS by *katastrophē*, by an overthrow, i.e., condemned to extinction. It has been suggested that the alliteration *katastrophē katakrinen* is original, since it was intended by the writer to reinforce the parallelism with the preceding example of destructive judgment, *kataklysmon kosmō*, the deluge of the world. See J. H. Neyrey, "The Form and Background of the Polemic in 2 Peter," *JBL* 99 (1980), pp. 407–31.

Sodom and Gomorrah: Only these two places are mentioned by Peter. According to Gen. 14:2, the other cities of the plain involved were Admah, Zeboiim, and Bela, also known as Zoar. The event made an indelible impression upon the Jews, and throughout their history the warning example was used by biblical writers: Deut. 29:23; Isa. 1:9–10; 13:19; Jer. 49:18; 50:40; Lam. 4:6; Amos 4:11; Zeph. 2:9; Matt. 10:15; 11:23–24; Luke 17:29.

Burning them to ashes (*tephrōsas*): Burning or turning to, or covering with, ashes, occurs only here in the NT. But it is used by Dio Cassius (66) in his account of the eruption of Vesuvius in A.D. 79, which buried Pompeii and Herculaneum in lava. Strabo (*Geography* 16.2.44) describes the Dead Sea area as "a land of ashes." The means used by God to destroy Sodom and Gomorrah was the rain of brimstone and fire, probably brought about by the igniting during an earthquake of the concentrated chemical deposits in the region (salt, potash, magnesium, calcium chloride, bromide) that give the Dead Sea its extraordinary buoyancy but fatally affect fish (Gen. 19:15–28). See *IBD* vol. 1, p. 372.

2:7 / **Lot, a righteous man**: He is also so called in Wisd. of Sol. 10:6; 19:17.

Distressed (*kataponein*): to wear down with toil or evil. The only other occurrence of the word in the NT is in Acts 7:24, of Moses seeing a fellow Israelite being *mistreated* by an Egyptian.

Filthy (*aselgeia*): unbridled lust, excess, shamelessness.

Lives renders *anastrophē*, manner of life, a favorite word with Peter (1 Pet. 1:15, 18; 2:12; 3:1, 2, 16; 2 Pet. 3:11).

Lawless men translates the plural of *athesmos*, used of one who bursts through the restraints of moral law to gratify lust. The term occurs in the NT only here and in 3:17. See Turner, pp. 254–55.

2:8 / **Tormented**: *Ebasanizen* is a Greek imperfect, indicating constant action. The verb *basanizein* basically means to rub on the touchstone, or to put on the rack. It describes the *terrible suffering* of the centurion's servant (Matt. 8:6), the eventual *torture* anticipated by demons at the judgment (Matt. 8:29), and the disciples *straining* at the oars against the gale (Mark 6:48).

Lawless (*anomos*) **deeds**: The practice of those who completely flout the law (*nomos*) of God.

2:9 / The conclusion regarding the contrasting destiny of **godly men** and the fate of **the unrighteous** forms the apodosis of the extended conditional clause which began at v. 4. This twin conclusion of deliverance and punishment (only the latter appears in the corresponding passage in Jude 6–8) is also found in 1 Clement 11.1 and Philo, *Moses* 2.57, both of which use the examples of the Flood and Sodom.

To rescue (*rhyesthai,* to draw to oneself, hence to deliver) echoes the same Greek verb used of Lot's deliverance in v. 7.

From trials, not necessarily from temptation to sin (as in the case of the devil's onslaught on Jesus, Luke 4:13), but from the consequent antagonism suffered by the righteous for reacting against the evil around them, as in the cases of Noah and Lot. Believers are never said to avoid tribulation at the hands of the ungodly, but to be rescued out of such trials. Meanwhile, those who trust God will be given strength to stand up to these testings (1 Cor. 10:13). In any event, the experience can be used to develop spiritual and moral strength (James 1:2, 12). There may be an echo here of the last two petitions of the Lord's Prayer (Matt. 6:13).

The words *tērein* (**hold,** keep) and *hēmera kriseōs* (**day of judgment**) recur together in 3:7, one of several little links between the two chapters. In 2 Peter **the day of judgment** is the final judgment at the Parousia. Even in the interim, the wicked dead are in a state of suffering (*kolazomenous,* here translated **punishment**), as are the fallen angels in Tartarus (2:4); cf. the story of the rich man and the beggar Lazarus (Luke 16:24).

While continuing their punishment is one Greek word, the present passive participle of *kolazein,* which ranges in meaning from curtail or prune to restrain or chastise, and is used in the NT only here and in Acts 4:21. The present sense of the participle cannot be pressed, since a future passive participle is extremely rare in the Greek of the period. In 3:11 Peter uses a present participle *lyomenōn* (lit. being dissolved) in a future sense; see J. H. Moulton & N. Turner, *A Grammar of New Testament Greek* (Edinburgh: T. & T. Clark, 1963), vol. 3, pp. 86–87.

2:10a / **Those who follow** (*poreuomenous*): lit. travelling: often used metaphorically, as here, for going along on a certain course of conduct. The Greek verb is similarly employed in Jude 11, 16.

The corrupt desire (*en epithymia*): lit. "in lust of defilement," is a Hebraism for "defiling lust"; cf. 2:1, where "destructive heresies" is lit. "heresies of destruction."

The phrase **of the sinful nature,** *opisō sarkos* ("after the flesh," KJV), is used in Jude 7. Other similarities to Jude's vocabulary in this verse of 2 Peter are: *miasmou,* lit. defilement (cf. *miainousin,* they defile; Jude 8); *kyriotētos kataphronountas,* lit. despising authority (cf. *kyriotēta athetousin,* they reject authority; Jude 8); *en epithymia poreuomenous,* lit. following desire, i.e., travelling along the road of lust (cf. *kata tas epithymias poreuomenoi,* following evil desires; Jude 16). The resemblances are close enough to suggest the use of a common source, but not sufficiently exact to indicate that Peter copied Jude, or vice versa.

Authority (*kyriotēs*): Paul employs the Greek word to describe a class in the angelic hierarchy (Eph. 1:21; Col. 1:16), but it is improbable that the false teachers were being scornful about certain ranks of angels. On the contrary, these men appear to be extremely materialistic and not to take the spiritual world seriously at all. More likely Peter alludes to the lordship of Christ, for *kyriotēs* is used in this sense in Didache 4.1, and by the Shepherd of Hermas, *Similitudes* 5.6.1.

§10 The False Teachers' Effrontery (2 Pet. 2:10b–12)

2:10b / Peter now launches into a direct tirade against the false teachers, using some of the most colorful invective in the NT. These men are **bold and arrogant**, presumptuous and conceited in self-gratification, characteristics which are exhibited in their brazen behavior. One who is **bold** (*tolmētēs*, wildly irresponsible in reckless daring) rides roughshod over the rights, opinions, and interests of others, human or divine. One who is **arrogant** (*authadēs*, obstinately self-seeking) will not be deterred by the challenge of any appeal to logic, common sense, responsibility, or feeling of decency, from doing exactly as he pleases. The false teachers are willfully blind to the consequences of their attitude and conduct.

These men are not afraid to slander even **celestial beings** (*doxai*). In what manner these men were engaged in slander is not specified, nor is it certain what is meant by *doxai* (lit. glories), although the NIV translation **celestial beings** is probably correct. The general sense of Peter's charge is that these men are making light of the unseen spiritual world and ignoring (and thus flouting) divine authority over matters of human ethical behavior.

2:11 / **Yet even angels**, notwithstanding their lofty position and superior powers, do not take advantage of their status and capabilities when facing something of a comparable situation. And this is despite the fact that they are **stronger and more powerful** than **such beings** (*kat' autōn*). The identity of the latter is unclear, since *kat' autōn* is literally a vague "against *them*," which could refer to beings human (the false teachers) or supernatural (the fallen angels; cf. v. 4). The parallel passage in Jude 8–10 applies the reluctance of the angels to bring **slanderous accusations against such beings** to the tradition of the archangel Michael disputing with the devil about the body of Moses. Michael, however, refused to usurp the divine prerogative, but left it to the Lord to administer the rebuke. Although Peter makes no direct reference to the story, it seems likely that he has it in mind. He could reasonably expect his original readers to appreciate the allusion, since the tradition about Michael confronting Satan was well known at the time. If it be objected that fallen angels can hardly be described as "glories," (*doxai*, translated as **celestial beings** in v. 10), this is to attach too positive and unsullied a character to "glories," which in today's colloquial terms might be called "leading lights" without any necessary implication of their moral standing. The fallen angels were still of an order different from human beings.

2:12 / **But these men**, by stark contrast with the angels who displayed such humble restraint, only betray their abysmal ignorance of spiritual concerns when they **blaspheme in matters they do not understand**. For all their pretensions to a plane of higher spirituality, they are in reality completely out of their depth. They are no better than unreasoning **brute beasts** that live simply according to the dictates of their natural instinct and that have no notion of moral issues. The destiny of such creatures is to come to a violent end, for they are **born only to be caught and destroyed** by man or beast (Ps. 49:12). In like manner, these evil men are slaves to their animal instincts, and in the end they too **will perish**.

Additional Notes §10

2:10b / **Bold** (*tolmētai*): lit. darers (a noun, not an adjective); the word occurs in the NT only here. Jude 9 uses the corresponding verb *tolman*.

Celestial beings is an interpretation of *doxai* (lit. glories). Perhaps instead of pointing to angels, the reference may be to local "luminaries," church leaders (Bigg, pp. 279–80). They might well chide the false teachers and be abused in return for their trouble. In the LXX *doxa* can be used to mean leader or nobleman (Mic. 1:15). But NIV is probably right to interpret *doxai* as angels. The Dead Sea Scrolls indicate that angels were thought of as present at meetings of the congregation (1QSa 2.8) and in the camp of the "sons of light" (1QM 7.6). The slander of the false teachers would be the decrying of such a notion. See also Additional Note on Jude 8 regarding *doxai*.

2:11 / **Stronger and more powerful**—than what or whom? The reference is unclear, but the comparison may be with the false teachers (GNB) or "other celestial beings" (Barclay), thus implying that "the glories" (*doxai*) of the previous verse are fallen angels, deserving condemnation. Other translations leave the matter open. Contempt for angelic powers was found early on among heretics (1 Cor. 11:10).

The NIV **yet** corresponds to the Greek *hopou*, lit. "where," i.e., "in a situation in which."

Slanderous accusations: The tradition about Michael and Satan was in the now lost ending of the *Assumption of Moses*. See Additional Note on Jude 9. For the Greek term (*blasphēmos*), see Turner, p. 46.

2:12 / For **blaspheme**, see Turner, pp. 46–48; *TDNT*, vol. 1, pp. 621–25; *NIDNTT*, vol. 3, pp. 340–45. When Jesus spoke of the unforgivable sin as one which was blasphemy against the Holy Spirit (Matt. 12:31; Mark 3:29; Luke 12:10), the context suggests that it was a denial that the new dispensation of the kingdom of God had already broken into history, a rejection of the signs of divine intervention against the powers of evil. The false teachers in Peter's sights are similarly guilty of arrogantly and ignorantly dismissing spiritual activity. See A. Richardson, *Introduction to the Theology of the New Testament* (London: S.C.M., 1958), p. 108.

§11 The False Teachers' Love of Evil (2 Pet. 2:13–16)

2:13 / **They will be paid back with harm for the harm they have done**. Peter is making a point valid for all generations. Quite apart from their effect upon other people, those who give themselves up to the pursuit of materialistic and fleshly pleasures will ultimately so corrupt their own body, mind, and spirit that they lose even the ability to enjoy such pleasures. Sensuality is self-destructive (Gal. 6:8).

The self-indulgent striving after pleasure yields diminishing returns, and so ever more extreme efforts have to be made to obtain satisfaction. These men no longer confine their ill-doing under the cover of darkness, but are now prepared to **carouse in broad daylight**, a practice that has long been recognized as a sign of degeneration (Isa. 5:11).

They are blots (*spiloi*) **and blemishes** (*mōmoi*), precisely the opposite of what believers are called to be in Christ, "spotless" (*aspiloi*) and "blameless" (*amōmoi*), as Peter so describes them in 3:14 (cf. 1 Pet. 1:19).

Even **while they feast with you** these men are **reveling**, luxuriating, **in their pleasures** (*agapais*). The latter word appears as the very similar *apatais*, deceptions, in some important MSS, in which case the punning meaning is "reveling in *deceits* while sharing *eats* with you." NIV, however, prefers the reading *agapais*, the regular term for the Christian love-feasts. Paul too knew of the problem of immorality and selfish greed during the love-feasts in the church at Corinth (1 Cor. 11:20–22).

2:14 / **With eyes full of adultery** is literally "of an adulteress," and so can be loosely rendered: "they all have lustful eyes for a madam." **They never stop sinning**, because they are constantly carried along by the powerful current of their own lusts. And, not satisfied with their own immoral practices, **they seduce**

the unstable, those who are insufficiently grounded in the faith, in contrast to Peter's readers, whom he has earlier generously described as "firmly established in the truth" (1:12). Furthermore, the immoral practitioners are **experts in greed** (literally having covetousness, the desire for advantage), an echo of Peter's earlier charge (2:3). These men are out for what they can get. Instead of displaying true Christian generosity in giving to others, they are only taking advantage. They are concerned with lining their own pockets by means of their pernicious practices. Peter explodes: **an accursed brood!** "God's curse is on them!" (NEB).

2:15 / The character and activities of these men suggest comparison with the life of Balaam (Num. 22–24). Like him, for the sake of gain **they have left the straight way**, the path of obedience to God, and are endeavoring to induce believers to join them on the slippery road. In his day, Balaam tried to seduce the people of Israel to follow immoral practices (Num. 25:1–9; 31:16; Rev. 2:14). More than that, Balaam was out for personal honor and material gain at the expense of God's people, and Balaam might have been the means of cursing, not blessing, the Israelites, if Balak king of Moab had had his way. Similarly, the false teachers of Peter's day are seeking to lure believers into immoral revelry, into "having a good time." They are advancing destructive heresies, aimed at making believers deviate from the way of truth. And, as in the case of Balaam of old, **who loved the wages of wickedness**, they too are carrying on their pernicious teaching for financial reward, presumably by charging for it.

2:16 / Balaam was recognized in early times as a notorious example of one who was privileged to be a prophet of God, and yet went off the rails because he harbored the desire for financial gain. All this was despite God's efforts to pull him up. Those efforts included even getting **a beast without speech**, a dumb animal, to give Balaam a verbal warning. The animal's speaking **with a man's voice** would have been just as unlikely to a person in antiquity as to a modern person today. Whether or not the donkey really spoke is immaterial. Balaam certainly thought it had, and in modern parlance he "got the message."

Peter's mention of the incident (Num. 22:21–35) may be seen as an oblique reference to his description of the false teachers as being "like brute beasts" (2:12). In fact, Balaam's **donkey**, an animal proverbial for its dullness and obstinacy, proved to be more sensitive than its master who, though a prophet, was himself mastered by a material love for "the wages of unrighteousness" (v. 15). The false teachers likewise have convinced themselves that they can get away with their disregard of God's commands and prosper in their wrongdoing. They too in due course will be paid their "wages"—they will get their just recompense.

Additional Notes   §11

2:13 / **They will be paid back with harm for the harm they have done**, just three words in the Greek: *adikoumenoi misthon adikias*, which can also be translated "being cheated of the profits of their wrongdoing" (Cranfield, p. 184). KJV follows another MS reading: "shall receive the reward of unrighteousness."

Blots (*spiloi*): In the corresponding passage Jude has *spilades*, reefs; see Additional Note on Jude 12.

Reveling (*entryphōntes*) occurs in the NT only here and in the LXX of Isa. 55:2; 57:4; Hab. 1:10. The verb means "to luxuriate" (in a good or a bad sense).

While they feast with you (*syneuōchoumenoi*): Found in the parallel passage in Jude 12, but nowhere else in the NT.

Pleasures translates *agapais*, the reading in several good MSS. In others, including P⁷², important for the Petrine letters, the word appears as *apatais*, deceptions. NIV chooses the former, although it may well be a later scribal "correction" of an original *apatais* to match the corresponding text in Jude 12.

2:14 / **With eyes full of adultery**: A contemporary saying was that the shameless man "has harlots, not virgins [*korai*, a pun; for the word also means the pupil of the eye] in his eyes" (Plutarch, *Morals* 528e; cf. Matt. 5:28).

They never stop sinning (*akatapaustos hamartias*): lit. "restless in respect to sins."

Seduce (*deleazein*): to lure with bait (a fisherman's term), is used by Philo (*On Rewards and Punishments* 25) of the impostor who takes in the young and inexperienced.

Unstable (*astēriktos*): The word occurs in the NT only here and in 3:16. Peter himself had known what it was to be unstable, and he remembered Christ's word to him: "When you have turned back, strengthen (*stērison*, make firm) your brothers" (Luke 22:32). See Turner, p. 484.

Experts (*kardian gegymnasmenēn*, lit. a heart having been exercised) **in greed**; i.e., when it comes to covetousness, men with, so to speak, the heart of an athlete well trained in the gymnasium. The perfect participle *gegymnasmenēn* indicates a past action with continuing effect: these men are set in their practices. The contrast is with **the unstable,** *psychas astēriktous*, unsteady souls.

An accursed brood! (*kataras tekna*): a Hebraism, lit. "children of a curse!" i.e., people thus marked out by God (cf. Matt. 23:15; Eph. 2:2–3; 2 Thess. 2:3; 1 Pet. 1:14).

2:15 / **They have left** (*kataleipontes*): They have forsaken, abandoned, deserted.

The straight (*eutheian*) **way** (*hodon*): The adjective *eucheia* can be used literally (as in Straight Street, Damascus; Acts 9:11), or metaphorically, as here, in the moral sense. Peter again in this verse alludes to the "Two Ways" (see Additional Note on 2:2). The metaphorical use of the expression *hodos eutheia* for the path of obedience to God was common (see Bauckham, p. 267).

Wandered off (*eplanēthēsan*): have gone astray. In the corresponding passage, Jude 11 uses a related noun: *tē planē ton Balaam*, the error of Balaam.

The Greek verb for **follow** is the compound *exakolouthein*, lit. to follow out (*ek*), i.e., to the end. These men have left the straight, divinely appointed path of life, and have taken to the way of Balaam—and they are determined to keep on it. Balaam was a hireling prophet who commercialized his gift (Num. 22–24). So, too, these false prophets practice their profession for what they can get out of it. It is possible that they are related to the heretics of Rev. 2:14, since both groups are described as copying Balaam. **Balaam** figures prominently as a biblical warning: Deut. 23:4–5; Josh. 13:22; 24:9–10; Neh. 13:1–2; Mic. 6:5; Jude 11; Rev. 2:14.

Son of Beor. Some MSS read "son of *Bosor*." If *Bosor* is original, Peter may be alluding to the false teachers' sins, by paronomasia with the Hebrew word *basar*, flesh. Others suggest that *Bosor* represents a Galilean dialect mispronunciation of the Hebrew; if so, that could be a pointer to Petrine authorship (cf. Matt. 26:73).

The wages of iniquity (*misthon adikias*) reproduces the expression Peter used of Judas Iscariot (Acts 1:18).

2:16 / **He was rebuked** (*elenxin eschen*): lit. "he had a rebuke." The noun, which occurs in the NT only here, is related to *elenchein*, a verb ranging in shades of meaning from "treat with contempt" to "convict," "reprove," "expose." The synonym *epitiman* expresses a simple rebuke, undeserved (Matt. 16:22), or ineffectual (Luke 23:40); *elenchein* implies to "rebuke and so engender conviction." The noun *elenxis* occurs in the LXX of Job 21:4; 23:2.

His wrongdoing (*idias paranomias*): lit. "his own transgression" (*para*, contrary to; *nomos*, law). The possessive *idias* emphasizes the personal responsibility for the wrongdoing.

Donkey (*hypozygion*): lit. "one under a yoke," is used in the LXX specifically for an ass; also in Matt. 21:5, and in the papyri.

A beast without speech renders *aphōnon*, "dumb" (KJV). In the ancient world animals were termed mute, not because they were silent, but on account of their inability to use human language; cf. 1 Cor. 1:27–29.

Spoke translates the Greek verb *phthengesthai*, to give out a noise or cry, used of any sound or voice, whether human, animal, or inanimate, including thunder and musical instruments. But the verb is especially employed of portentous prophetic utterance, as by Philo, *On the Confusion of Tongues* 14 (1.414).

Madness translates *paraphronia*, found only here in extant Greek literature. Peter probably chose this unusual word for its assonance with *paranomia*, **wrongdoing**. Paul employs the corresponding verb *paraphronein* in 2 Cor. 11:23 ("I am out of my mind"). Peter's use of *paranomia* and *paraphronia* in the same sentence is appropriate, bearing in mind the meaning of the prefix *para-*, beside, over against. Balaam's action was not firmly *on* the path of God's law (*nomos*), but off to one side of it; consequently, his mind and thinking were of the same order, *para*, off to the side of, *phrēn*, the mind; i.e., he was "out of his mind," "mad."

2:17 / Following the Balaam lesson, Peter resumes his direct attack on the false teachers with two colorful metaphors, both suggesting **these men** promise much, only to deceive and disappoint. First, as teachers without true knowledge, they are **springs without water**. The green vegetation that attracts the weary traveller turns out to be the site of a spring that has failed. There is no cool water there to refresh a thirsty throat. Unlike these false teachers, it is only one who is truly in Christ who is in a position to offer others living water, the recreative water of life-satisfaction (John 4:13–14; 7:38).

Second, these men are **mists driven by a storm**, gone before any useful amount of moisture can fall to revitalize the earth, serving merely to make the sky depressingly overcast. The temporary darkness these men cause will result in their suffering themselves something far worse, which is stored up and awaiting them: **blackest darkness is reserved for them**. Significantly, Peter uses the same verb for **reserved** (*tērein*) as he does to describe the exactly opposite prospect in 1 Peter 1:4, when speaking of the heavenly inheritance held safely in store for faithful believers. The destiny of believers and unbelievers alike is under the controlling hand of God, and no power on earth can change that.

2:18 / Why Peter describes the false teachers as waterless springs and storm-driven mists is now explained. New converts from paganism, **people who are just escaping from those who live in error**, are a soft target for the false teachers. Not yet strong in the Lord or able to exercise his mighty power (Eph. 6:10), and not firmly grounded in the faith, they are an easy prey to the impressive but worthless talk of the false teachers. As yet, the converts lack Christian understanding for resisting their specious arguments, when **they mouth empty, boastful words**, full of high-sounding verbosity without substance.

Even more perilous to converts who have only recently broken with their old life is the method used by these false teachers. They seek to **entice**—the Greek word means to lure with bait—by **appealing to the lustful desires of sinful human nature**. "There is great passion in the words. Grandiose sophistry is the hook, filthy lust is the bait, with which these men catch those whom the Lord had delivered or was delivering" (Bigg, p. 258).

2:19 / Their boastful claim is to **promise** the new converts **freedom** in the moral sphere—in plain terms, sexual license—on the pretended grounds that it is the particular privilege of Christians to be free to do what they like, an antinomian heresy Paul also had to combat (Gal. 5:13; cf. 2 Pet. 3:16). True Christian liberty, on the contrary, involves moral restraint (Acts 15:29; 1 Pet. 2:16). The liberty these men vaunt is not true liberty at all. In their mouths "liberty" can be said to be a catchword in a quite literal sense, and **they themselves** are the living proof, since they **are slaves of depravity** in their own lives, slaves of their own passions—**for a man is a slave to whatever has mastered him** (John 8:34; Rom. 6:16). True liberty from the death grip of **depravity** (*phthora*) comes through divine power, the result of knowing God in Jesus Christ. That alone provides the way to escape corruption (*phthora*) in the world caused by evil desires, as Peter has pointed out at the beginning of his letter (1:3–4).

2:20 / The false teachers had once known true freedom from **the corruption of the world**, that is, from the sphere of life which leaves God out of account. That liberty had come to them through **knowing our Lord Jesus Christ** (cf. 1:3–4). But evidently this had been head knowledge rather than heart knowledge (Matt. 13:20–21). Now these men **are again entangled** in the corrupting influence of the world, having slipped back into their old pattern of life. As a result, they are **worse off at the end than they were at the beginning**. These words echo the warning of Jesus himself about a man whose evil spirit was reinforced by seven others worse still (Matt. 12:45; Luke 11:26). These men are **worse off** because they have rejected the forgiveness of their past sins and so they continue to bear them personally. Indeed they have incurred even greater culpability by flouting that gospel after once having known it, and thus they have rejected the only source of salvation. Furthermore, their future ability to resist sin has been fatally weakened by their returning to embrace it.

2:21 / Someone who has never known the right way cannot be blamed for not following it. But this is not the case with the false teachers. Once **to have known the way of righteousness**, i.e., the Christian way (Acts 9:2), and then to have rejected it, means that these men are sinning against the light. They have turned **their backs on the sacred command**, the body of teaching contained in the Christian gospel. That gospel, together with all its implications, had been entrusted to them. But these men have broken the golden chain of receiving and passing on the gospel. They not only have rejected its teachings for themselves, but have perverted its content and thus criminally misled others by their own twisted version (cf. 2:1–3). The greater the knowledge one has in any field, the greater is one's duty to accept and to respond to it. To reject the true knowledge of God which Christ has revealed is to commit the most heinous of offenses, for it is tantamount to denouncing light as darkness, to repudiating **the sacred command** as something evil.

2:22 / The spiritually deplorable condition of these men is an illustration of the truth of some proverbial sayings. The nature of **a dog** (Prov. 26:11) or of **a sow** remains unaffected by any occasional cleansing action of their own. Both slip back into their familiar old habits, even after liberal applications of pure water. Similarly, these men, whatever temporary outward changes in life-style there may have been, are not demonstrating the transformation of the inner person, which is the hallmark of a true Christian.

Peter clinches his earlier comparison of the false teachers to unreasoning animals ("brute beasts," 2:12), by likening them to dogs and pigs. Both animals were unclean to the Jews and symbols of pagan immorality (cf. Matt. 7:6; Rev. 22:15).

In both pictures, there had been a change at one point for the better. The dog had ejected something unpleasant. The sow had been washed clean. But natural habits prevailed. The dog was lured back by its instinct, the pig by its pleasures, because in neither case had inner nature been changed by outer action.

Additional Notes §12

2:17 / **Mists**: The rare Greek word *homichlai* is used by Aristotle (*On Meteorology* 1.346b) for the haze heralding dry weather. The term occurs in the NT only here. Some MSS have altered it to *nephalai* (clouds), as in the corresponding passage, Jude 12. Peter may have chosen **mists** also to suggest the confusing haziness of thought and dryness of spirit resulting from the speculations of the false teachers.

Driven: The Greek verb *elaunein* describes the activity of demons in Luke 8:29.

Storm (*lailaps*): hurricane, whirlwind; found elsewhere in the NT only in Mark 4:37; Luke 8:23.

2:18 / The Greek verb for **they mouth** is *phthengesthai*, a term employed for portentous prophetic speech. The flowery and imposing oratory of the false teachers was tailored to impress the hearers.

Empty, boastful words renders *hyperonka mataiotētos* (**words** is not in the Greek, but is rightly supplied by NIV). The term *hyperonkos* means "of excessive bulk," "swollen beyond natural size"; it also appears in the corresponding passage in Jude 16. The noun *mataiotēs* means vanity, emptiness, purposelessness. See Turner, p. 502.

Error (*planē*) in the NT usually refers to paganism (Rom. 1:27; Titus 3:3); see *TDNT*, vol. 6, pp. 230–54. The new converts who are in danger are evidently Gentiles.

2:19 / **Depravity** is the correct NIV interpretation of *phthora*, which is generally translated "destruction" (as in 2:12), "corruption" (as in 1:4), or "decay"; moral degeneracy is plainly meant here.

Mastered (*hēttētai*): The verb *hēttan* means to make inferior (2 Cor. 12:13); in the passive, to be overcome (so translated in 2:20), to be worsted by. "To be enslaved to oneself is the heaviest of all servitudes" (Seneca). The imagery derives from the ancient practice of turning prisoners of war into slaves.

2:20 / **If they have escaped the corruption** (*ta miasmata*, lit. the defilements, pollutions) **of the world** unfortunately too closely echoes the NIV translation of 1:4, "escape the corruption (*phthora*) in the world," since different Greek words are used for "corruption." Only here in 2:20 is *miasmata* found in the NT. It occurs in the *Apocalypse of Peter* 9 as a description of adultery, and in view of Peter's frequent allusions in this letter to immoral practices, his use of *miasmata* probably has sexual overtones.

Entangled nicely translates *emplekein*, lit. to in-weave. The term suggests a gradual process of intertwining, which implies that the false teachers were bit by bit enmeshed again in their previous way of life. The verb is used in 2 Tim. 2:4, but nowhere else in the NT.

The phrase **worse off at the end** echoes the virtually identical warning by Jesus concerning the consequences that will follow an evil spirit's return (Matt. 12:43–45; Luke 11:24–26).

2:21 / From the earliest days of the church, **the way** was a term that described Christianity (see Additional Note on 2:2). Peter several times employs a similar expression: the way of truth (2:2); the straight way (2:15). The expression **the way of righteousness** occurs in the LXX of Job 24:13 and Prov. 21:16, 21; also in Matt. 21:32.

Righteousness is here a reference to right living (in Tudor English "righteous" was "right-wise") in accordance with the Christian gospel, rather than to the spiritual grace-gift credited by God to believers, as usually in Paul (Rom. 1:17).

Turn their backs on the sacred command: Apostasy from Christ, with its awesome consequences, is a real possibility for any who deliberately reject the gospel message they once professed to accept (cf. 1 Cor. 10:1–12; Heb. 3:12–18; 6:6; 10:26–39; Jude 4–6). **The sacred command** is an omnibus term for the whole Christian gospel.

Passed on: delivered, handed on to (cf. Jude 3). The gospel of Christ was authoritatively entrusted by the apostles to new converts, who were in turn to hand it on unadulterated to others.

2:22 / The NIV plural **proverbs** is in fact a singular in the Greek (*paroimia*), and only one actual proverb is quoted. Peter cites Prov. 26:11 from the Hebrew (not LXX): in full this reads: "As a dog returns to its vomit, so a fool repeats his folly." Peter quoted only the first clause, but evidently expects his readers to know the whole proverb and to appreciate its appropriateness to describe the false teachers. No proverbial saying about **a sow** occurs in the Bible, although the picture of a sow enjoying a bath but then as happily returning to roll in the mud is true enough to life! The basis of Peter's saying is close to a tale in the Egyptian *Story of Ahikar* (*APOT* vol. 2, p. 772): "My son, you were to me like a pig which had been in a hot bath with people of quality, and when it came out and saw a filthy pool went down and wallowed in it. And it called to its kindred, 'Come, bathe!' " See *TDNT*, vol. 3, pp. 1100–1103.

In the mud: The Greek *borboros* is rare and occurs elsewhere in the Bible only in the description of the miry pit into which Jeremiah the prophet was dumped (Jer. 45:6 LXX [NIV Jer. 38:7]).

The Greek here for **dog** is *kyōn*, the wild scavenger of the streets and rubbish tips, not a pet house-dog (*kynarion*, Matt. 15:26–27; Mark 7:27–28).

On *paroimia*, proverb, see Turner, p. 306.

§13 The Writer's Purpose Restated (2 Pet. 3:1–2)

3:1 / After his lengthy tirade against the false teachers and their perverted life-style so dangerous to the well being of his readers, Peter turns—one senses, with warm relief—to address his **dear friends** directly. He now reverts to his opening exhortation to them to foster their spiritual life (1:5–8).

This is now my second letter to you, he declares, although whether he means 1 Peter or some other letter, now lost, is uncertain. Since Peter is evidently not able to visit his friends in person, his pastoral concern impels him to do the next best thing and commit his message to writing. That in any case has the advantage of greater permanence, and the **reminders** it contains (1:12, 13, 15) will continue to be on hand to do their work. Moreover, a letter can be copied and distributed, and its message thus accurately conveyed to others. Teaching passed on by word of mouth might not achieve this so well.

Peter is writing a second time—reiteration is the mark of a good teacher (Phil 3:1)—**to stimulate you to wholesome thinking** (Phil. 4:8). The NIV translation obscures the fact that Peter is, again like an experienced tutor, paying his readers a compliment, for the latter words are literally "your pure minds," i.e., your spiritual discernment, uncontaminated by the heretical efforts of the false teachers. It is as if he is saying: "Keep on reminding yourselves what great souls you really are because of Christ's grace. Don't let the enemy drag you down into the mud."

3:2 / To that end, Peter bids them **recall the words spoken** by God's messengers **in the past**, and in particular, as the following verses indicate, on the subject of the return of Christ in glory and its implications for the moral requirements of the gospel. He bases his appeal (as he did in 1:16–21) on the twin authorities of OT **prophets** and NT **apostles**. Both convey the divine message. Peter is thus already at this early date viewing both the Hebrew Scriptures and the apostolic writings as a unity, with **our Lord and Savior** as their basis and focus.

The use of the expression **your apostles**, which 3:15 implies included Paul, has been taken by some to betray the fact that the author is not Peter but someone pretending to write in his name. But **your apostles** can equally mean either that Peter speaks as a representative of the apostolic band, or that he refers to "the particular apostles who evangelized your area, and who are therefore held especially in esteem by you." At all events, Peter's emphasis is on apostolic reliability in matters of faith, by contrast with the false teachers.

Additional Notes   §13

3:1 / **Dear friends** translates *agapētoi*, beloved ones, i.e., beloved by God (see Additional Note on 1 Pet. 2:11). The term also occurs in 2 Pet. 3:8, 14, 17.

My second letter most naturally refers to 1 Peter. But this is uncertain, especially since the contents of 1 Peter are not readily described as a "reminder," nor does that letter deal pointedly with false teaching, as does 2 Peter. Furthermore, 1 Peter addresses readers across five Roman provinces, without suggesting that the writer knows them well—which is certainly the case in 2 Peter. The previous letter that Peter mentions here may well not have survived, as happened with some of Paul's letters to the Corinthian church (1 Cor. 5:9).

Reminders: "It is not sufficiently considered that men more frequently require to be reminded than informed" (Dr. Samuel Johnson).

Stimulate (*diegeirein; dia*, thoroughly; *egeirein*, rouse up): as in 1:13 ("*refresh* your memory"). Here in 3:1 the wording lit. runs: "I rouse your pure mind by a reminder" (cf. Jude 5).

To wholesome thinking (*tēn eilikrinē dianoian*): The adjective *eilikrinēs* (pure, unalloyed, unadulterated) means that which is flawless even when held up to the sunlight (*heilē*, heat of the sun; *krinein*, to examine); see Turner, pp. 416–17; *TDNT*, vol. 2, pp. 397–98. Paul employs *eilikrinēs* in Phil. 1:10 to describe the purity required of believers on the day of Christ (the corresponding noun appears in 1 Cor. 5:8; 2 Cor. 1:12; 2:17). The precisely opposite notion occurs in Eph. 4:18, "darkened in their understanding (*dianoia*)." Plato uses Peter's phrase to mean *pure reason*, i.e., thinking unaffected by the senses. But in Christian writings *dianoia* usually does not refer to the mind in the intellectual sense but to the faculty of spiritual discernment (Eph. 4:18; Col. 1:21; 1 John 5:20).

3:2 / This verse has a succession of genitives in the Greek, making translation difficult. The problem is often eased in English versions by the addition of **through** (NIV, RSV; not in the Greek). But the general sense is clear. Possibly a word has dropped out of an early MS, or the expression *tou kyriou sōtēros*, **of the Lord and Savior**, may have been added by the writer as an afterthought: "the command of your apostles, or, rather, I should say, of the Lord" (Bigg, p. 290).

Holy prophets . . . apostles: The way Peter here associates the OT with the apostolic writings is reminiscent of 1 Pet. 1:10–12; 2 Pet. 1:19–21. The phrase **holy prophets** occurs elsewhere in the NT only in Luke 1:70 and, perhaps significantly for the question of authorship, in a speech of Peter's in Acts 3:21.

3:3 / One of the signals of the nearness of the **last days** before the return of Christ in power and great glory will be the appearance of those who jeer at the very idea of a second coming. From NT times right up to the present day, there have always been those who scoffed at this subject. So how can this be a sign of the impending Parousia? The scoffing that Peter warns about goes beyond the utterance of mere words, for the Greek terms imply physical persecution. This antagonism is the result of such scoffers **following their own evil desires**, an expression which suggests that Peter particularly has in mind the false teachers of his own time. But the principle holds for all generations. Other scoffers **will come**. If derisive words alone fail to have their intended effect in discouraging believers, then those who scoff will not hesitate to go further in their hostility, for they too are **following their own evil desires**, that is, they are driven by what Judaism called "the evil inclination." To deny the fact of Christ's return, and so the judgment that goes with it, is to weaken moral incentive and to invite careless conduct.

The scoffing of religious truths and practices can easily lead to despondency among believers, especially if it is uttered by those (the false teachers in this case) who know something of the Scriptures but imply that they are superior in understanding. So Peter seeks to forestall the adverse effects of such derision upon his readers. So, far from discouraging believers, the arrival of these scoffers is itself a fulfillment of prophecy and proof of the approaching end, when the faith of Christians will thus be justified.

3:4 / The scoffing specifically denies the reality of the return of Christ. **"Where is this 'coming' he promised?"** But it also challenges the veracity of Christ's own word by scorning the truth of a clear promise he made on a specific subject (Matt. 10:23;

24:3). Such an attitude to his word will not be confined to one doctrine. It inevitably promotes doubts and disbelief of other aspects of Christ's teaching, to the point that an individual feels free to pick and choose what suits and fits in with personal desires. In the case of the second coming of Christ, the argument of the false teachers is that **ever since our fathers died** things have continued as they always were. The years have gone by and nothing dramatic has happened. In any case, common sense surely indicates that some cataclysmic end to history is unthinkable. The unhindered daily round **since the beginning of creation** "proves" it. Such naive comments can be made, of course, only by those who have never been caught up in some terrifying (even if local) natural upheaval—earthquake, hurricane, volcanic eruption, tidal wave.

3:5 / Their reasoning is fallacious. Such people, says Peter, **deliberately forget** what is recorded in the Scriptures. They choose to shut their minds to what did indeed once happen— even if it was **long ago**. The book of Genesis narrates the story of the original creation. Peter paraphrases that account: **long ago by God's word the heavens existed and the earth was formed out of water and by water**. According to Genesis, there was originally a kind of watery waste (Gen. 1:2). Then by divine fiat ("Let there be . . . "), the world **was formed** by the separation of land from water (Gen. 1:6–10). Furthermore, life in that world was *sustained* by water (Gen. 2:6).

3:6 / But that was not the end of the story. Because of the wickedness of those who then inhabited the earth, God intervened in judgment. And he did so by using the same element: **by . . . waters also the world of that time was deluged and destroyed** (Gen. 6:17; 7:23). The moral of the event is that God is not only creator but also judge, for the sins of the occupants of his world will not continue to go unpunished. Jesus himself used the incident to point out that lesson, and at the same time linked it with his own future return (Matt. 24:37–39), a possibility that the false teachers were ridiculing.

3:7 / However regular and unchanging conditions may appear, however solid and immovable the world itself may seem, especially to those who willfully ignore what has happened in the past, God does from time to time decisively intervene, as he sees fit. Having created the world, he destroyed that world by water. **By the same word**, just as the Scriptures told of the Flood judgment, so they foretell another judgment, still to come. **The present heavens and earth** will be destroyed too—this time by **fire**. The "coming" that Christ promised (v. 4) is no less certain, whatever the false teachers may assume to the contrary. And all these events of divine intervention are bound up with the **judgment and destruction of ungodly men**, such as the false teachers. God has, in effect, said, "Thus far, and no further," as those who leave him out of their calculations will one day suddenly and fatally discover. The whole scenario is **being kept**, as if in an impregnable prison under secure guard, **for the day of judgment**.

Additional Notes §14

3:3 / **In the last days scoffers will come**: Matt. 24:3–5, 11, 23–26; 2 Tim. 3:1–5; James 5:3; Jude 18.

Scoffers . . . scoffing (*empaigmonē empaiktai*, lit. the Hebraism "scoffers with scoffing"): The vocabulary used implies that more than the mere expression of words is involved. The Hebrew equivalents of the Greek terms indicate that **scoffers** (*empaiktai*) engage in violent persecution of believers. The noun *empaigmos*, scoffing, is used for the *force* with which Egyptians tyrannized the Israelites (Exod. 1:13) and for the *ruthlessness* forbidden to a master overworking fellow Israelites who were his slaves (Lev. 25:43, 46). In the NT, *empaigmos* refers to the suffering of the Maccabees (Heb. 11:36). See Turner, pp. 141–42.

Evil desires (*epithymias*): as in 1 Pet. 1:14; 2:11; 4:2, 3; 2 Pet. 1:4; 2:10, 18; also in the parallel passages, Jude 16, 18. The Greek term sometimes translates the Hebrew *yēṣer hā-rāʼ*, "the evil inclination."

3:4 / **"Where . . . ?"** The scoffers pour scornful doubt upon the truthfulness of the divine word, written or spoken. They are not the first: see Ps. 42:3; 79:10; Isa. 5:19; 28:14; Jer. 17:15; Ezek. 12:22; Mal. 2:17.

'Coming' (*parousia*): the technical term for the return of Christ in power and glory. See Additional Note on 1:16.

Our fathers could mean the first Christian leaders, such as Stephen, James son of Zebedee, and James the Just, all of whom had died by the date of this letter. But more probably the reference is to OT figures, as with all other passages mentioning "the fathers" in the NT (Acts 3:13; Rom. 9:5; Heb. 1:1) and especially in view of the words **since the beginning of creation**.

Died prosaically translates *ekoimēthēsan*, lit. and more strikingly "have fallen asleep," the usual biblical expression for the passing on of believers (Mark 5:39; John 11:11; 1 Thess. 4:13–14), even in the case of their violent death (Acts 7:60).

3:5 / Creation **by God's word** is a frequent theme (Gen. 1:3; Ps. 33:6–9; 148:5; Wisd. of Sol. 9:1; John 1:3; Heb. 11:3; 1 Clement 27.4; Shepherd of Hermas, *Visions* 1.3.4).

The earth was formed out of (*ex hydatos*) **and with water** (*dia hydatos*) is a problem in the Greek. The preposition *dia* with the genitive, as here, basically means *extension through* (Mark 9:30, "*through* Galilee"). So here Peter may be meaning "continuous land, rising out of and extending through water" (Moule, *Idiom-Book*, p. 55).

3:6 / **The world** (*kosmos*) **of that time** was destroyed by the Flood. The Greek *kosmos* here means its human inhabitants (as in 2:5).

Deluged translates *kataklyzein* (cf. Eng. cataclysm), to inundate, overwhelm; the Greek verb occurs in the NT only here.

3:7 / **Reserved** (*tethēsaurismenoi*) **for fire**: The verb *thēsaurizein*, to lay up in store, is behind the Eng. word "thesaurus," a storehouse (of information). See *TDNT*, vol. 6, pp. 928–52. The association of **fire** with divine activity is a frequent biblical theme (Exod. 3:2; Ps. 50:3; Isa. 29:6; 30:30; 66:15–16; Nah. 1:6; Mal. 4:1). The future destruction of the world by fire is mentioned in the Bible only in this verse. Our contemporary world with its atomic bombs is the first generation to see one way in which the fiery destruction of **heavens and earth** could be feasible on such a scale.

Being kept, as under guard (1 Pet. 1:4; 2 Pet. 2:4, 9, 17). The expression emphasizes the absolute certainty of judgment to come, since no power in heaven or earth or hell can possibly interfere with what is divinely ordained.

Toward the end of the second century A.D., Melito of Sardis may well have 2 Peter in mind when he writes: "There was a flood of water. . . . There will be a flood of fire, and the earth will be burned up together with its mountains . . . and the just will be delivered from its fury as their fellows in the ark were saved from the waters of the Flood." A similar idea also appears in the Dead Sea Scrolls (1QH 3.28), though not, of course, with reference to 2 Peter.

§15 The Certainty of the Second Coming
(2 Pet. 3:8–10)

3:8 / We can readily appreciate that the false teachers' denial of the veracity of the promised return of Christ could expect to gain a certain amount of credence among church members, for it was true enough that some time had gone by since the resurrection of Jesus, a number of Christians had died, and there was still no sign that the Parousia was about to take place. But Peter seeks to encourage his readers by drawing attention to a fundamental distinction between divine and human viewpoints. People's outlook is limited by time. Not so God's perspective. Prompted by the wording of Psalm 90:4, Peter reminds believers that **with the Lord a day is like a thousand years**. But there is an interesting difference in the application of those words. The Psalmist is contrasting the insignificance of time, the brevity of human life, with the eternity of God. Peter uses the OT words to highlight the impatience of human expectations, compared with the infinite and purposeful patience of God. Peter then repeats the saying, but reverses the terms (**a thousand years are like a day**), in order to underline the fact that in the purposes of God, a delay of even a millennium is, from his standpoint, like no more than the passage of a single day. Therefore believers should not be disturbed, if nothing seems to be happening in fulfillment of divine promises. God's word is his bond. The timing of its being carried out must be left to him.

3:9 / The explanation of divine delay? **The Lord is not slow** (the Greek word means to loiter, be slack, be late) as some charge. He is indeed able to fulfill his word and is not indifferent about doing so. The reason for the delay is that he wants to give every possible opportunity to all to **come to repentance** (1 Tim. 2:4). The Lord has no pleasure in **wanting anyone to perish**. Some are going to perish (v. 7), but it is certainly not God's will that they should do so.

3:10 / The day of the Lord, when Christ returns in glory, to judge or to bless, is not only certain to take place, whatever may be the professed view of the false teachers. Its arrival will also be without warning and totally unexpected (Matt. 24:42–44), **like a thief** breaking into a house. Believers, therefore, should watch and be alert at all times (Matt. 25:13; 1 Thess. 5:6). As for those who disbelieve Christ's word on the subject, such as the false teachers of Peter's day, there will be no second chance then for a change of heart.

That day will be marked by a cosmic catastrophe on a cataclysmic scale, involving **the heavens** and **the elements** and **the earth**. But Peter's thought is not limited to the notions of destruction and annihilation. He is looking beyond all this to the renovation of heaven and earth (v. 13; cf. Rev. 20:11; 21:1).

In making a distinction between the heavens, the elements (*stoicheia*), and the earth, Peter is apparently not using the term *stoicheia* in its sense of the four elements (fire, air, water, earth), which were considered in antiquity to be the basis of all known phenomena. The Greek word can also refer to the heavenly bodies (sun, moon, stars; as in Justin, *Apology* 2.5). Judaism (1 Enoch 60:12; Jubilees 2:2) and Paul (Gal. 4:3, 9; Col. 2:8, 20) both imply that hostile cosmic forces are behind these bodies, and this is probably Peter's meaning here. The sequence of terms (**heavens . . . elements . . . earth**) forms a trio in descending order, none of which will be excluded from the consequences of the advent of the day of the Lord.

The whole passage is a ringing declaration of the sovereignty of the Lord Jesus Christ and of his redemptive purpose, which is not limited to justified human beings, but extends to the whole of creation (Rom. 8:19–21).

Additional Notes §15

3:8 / Do not forget: lit. "do not let [this] be hidden from you"— as was happening in the case of the scoffing false teachers. They were deliberately allowing the fact of the difference in divine and human viewpoints not to enter their calculations. It was culpable ignorance on their part, as in the matter of the second coming (v. 4).

With the Lord a day is like a thousand years was evidently a saying that registered with the apostolic age, for it is quoted in Barnabas 15.4–7. Peter's words gave rise to Millenarianism (or Chiliasm), the belief that at the end of the present age Christ will reign on earth for one thousand years (Rev. 20:1–10); see *NIDNTT*, vol. 1, pp. 52–53.

3:9 / **The Lord is not slow in keeping his promise** about the second coming. The delay in the Parousia worried Paul's friends at Thessalonica (1 Thess. 4:13–15; 2 Thess. 2:1–2), but it did not disturb Peter. He had been warned that he himself would not live to see the Parousia (2 Pet. 1:14; John 21:18–19).

He is patient (*makrothymein*: see Turner, pp. 315–18; *TDNT*, vol. 4, pp. 374–87). The corresponding noun (*makrothymia*) is used in 1 Pet. 3:20 in connection with God's delaying the Flood in the days of Noah.

A respite to give opportunity for **repentance** is often associated with the divine patience: Joel 2:12–13; Jon. 4:2; Rom. 2:4; Shepherd of Hermas, *Similitudes* 8.11.1; *Clementine Homilies* 11.7.2.

3:10 / **The day of the Lord**: Similar expressions in this letter are: day of judgment (2:9; 3:7); day of God (3:12); cf. day of visitation, 1 Pet. 2:12.

Like a thief: The simile of "the thief in the night," to illustrate an unwelcome surprise, derives from the teaching Peter heard from Jesus (Matt. 24:43–44; Luke 12:39; cf. 1 Thess. 5:2, 4; Rev. 3:3; 16:15).

The heavens will disappear is language reminiscent of Isa. 13:10–13; 34:4; cf. Rev. 20:11.

With a roar translates the onomatopoeic Greek adverb *rhoizēdon*, which occurs in the NT only here. This is a vivid term, as are the corresponding noun *rhoizos* and verb *rhoizein*, used by Greek writers to express shrill rushing sounds, such as the hissing of a snake, the whir of a bird's wings, the whistle of an arrow or a spear through the air, or the crackling of flames in a forest fire.

The elements (*stoicheia*): In *T. Levi* 4.4, invisible spirits are said to "dissolve" on the day of judgment. In modern Greek *stoicheia* still denotes spirits, angels, or demons. See also *NIDNTT*, vol. 2, pp. 451–53; *TDNT*, vol. 7, pp. 670–87; Turner, pp. 88–91, 392.

The earth and everything in it includes all that is involved in the human occupation of this globe—people, buildings, institutions, systems, deeds.

Laid bare (*heurethēsetai*, lit. "will be found," i.e., discovered, exposed) is one textual possibility among many variations in the MSS and is probably the most likely. Among numerous suggested emendations are "will be burned up" (KJV, RV, RSV, JB); "will vanish" (GNB); and "will not be found" (Wand, Moffatt), which assumes that a negative *ouk* fell out of the text at a very early date and consequently bequeathed a translation problem to those who copied MSS in later times.

3:11 / In view of the fact that the present world, with all its human and spiritual depravity, is to be totally replaced, it follows that God's people ought to prepare themselves for the new order. This they can do by living **holy and godly lives**, thus fitting themselves for the righteous environment that the new world will provide. In other words, Peter is using the certainty of the second coming, not to terrify believers, but to spur them to righteous living. If the false teachers had been correct in their denial of the Lord's return to set up a new order, then life in the present world would be without real purpose. The pagan slogan, "eat, drink, and be merry" (Luke 12:19), for extinction is all that lies ahead, would be depressingly true; there would be in reality nothing to live for. Peter knows better. His Master had taught him to pray for the coming of God's kingdom (Matt. 6:10) and to evangelize the nations: "then the end will come" (Matt. 24:14).

3:12 / Such prayer and evangelism by Christ's followers, backed by their godly lives, will be the means by which they give expression to the way they **look forward to the day of God**, and so help to **speed its coming**. Peter is not propounding a novel doctrine. The rabbis declared that "if Israel kept the law perfectly for one day, Messiah would come." The more profound point behind Peter's words is that the material world is transient and can be no sure foundation for life. By contrast, a life based on the truths of holy living and trust in a loving God concerned for his people's welfare here and hereafter is the one eternal reality. The principle is like that of the parable about building on sand or on rock (Matt. 7:24–27).

3:13 / The dramatic events associated with the second coming have long been foretold. But they are not an end in themselves, however desirable the destruction of all that is evil may be. God has a much more positive and constructive end in view. **In keeping with his** (God's) **promise** (Isa. 65:17; 66:22), Peter reminds his readers that as God's people **we are looking forward** (*prosdokan*, as in vv. 12 and 14) to what is to replace all that will have been destroyed. By divine act, God will create **a new heaven and a new earth** (Rev. 21:1), fitting spheres for his redeemed people, for there **righteousness** will be permanently at home, i.e., perfect relationships with God and with others will be the norm, unspoiled by sin or the machinations of evil.

3:14 / The consequence of knowing that God is preparing for his people a new heaven and a new earth as their abode, the characteristic of which is righteousness, is that they should even now be fitting themselves for such a prospect. Their priority must be to **make every effort** in their individual spiritual lives **to be found** by the returning Lord Jesus Christ to be **spotless** and **blameless**. Thus they will be fit to present themselves to God through Christ as a perfect offering (1 Pet. 1:19), in stark contrast to the characteristics of the false teachers (2 Pet. 3:3), and thereby be **at peace with him**, with nothing to fear (1 John 2:28). Peter began his letter by alluding to the fact that a right relationship with God sets a person on the Christian path (1:3). Now he reminds his readers that they must give their constant attention to maintaining that relationship throughout life, right up to its end—whether that be at death (1:14) or at the second advent (1 Thess. 4:17).

Additional Notes §16

3:11 / **Destroyed** (*lyonmenōn*, lit. "being loosed, dissolved"): The present tense suggests that disintegrating forces are already at work.

What kind of (*potapous*) **people ought you to be?** The use of *potapos* in such contexts as Matt. 8:27 ("What kind of man is this?" [when Jesus stilled the storm]) and Mark 13:1 ("What massive stones! What magnificent buildings!") implies that God's people, in Peter's view, should be outstanding in the quality of their lives.

Holy and godly lives translates *en hagiais anastrophais kai eusebeiais*, lit. "in holy forms of behavior and godly deeds," the plurals implying that there are many ways in which these can be practiced. On *eusebeia*, see Turner, p. 111.

The doctrine of the second coming was used as an argument for godly living in the teaching of Jesus (Luke 12:35–40), Paul (Rom. 13:11–14; 1 Thess. 5:4–11), and Peter in his first letter (1 Pet. 1:13; 4:7–17).

3:12 / **The elements** (*stoicheia*) **will melt in the heat** repeats the gist of v. 10; see Additional Note there.

Will melt translates the prophetic present tense *tēketai*. The verb, used in the NT only here, occurs in Isa. 64:1 LXX, referring to the melting of the mountains at the eschatological coming of God, when also fire burns up his enemies.

3:13 / **A new** (*kainos*) **heaven and a new** (*kainos*) **earth**: Of the two regular Greek adjectives for "new," *neos* means new in relation to time (young, recent). But *kainos* means new in relation to type (novel, fresh, unused). The NT almost always uses *kainos*: it is applied to the new commandment (Luke 22:20), Jesus' new teaching (Mark 1:27), new tongues as a sign of the activity of the Holy Spirit (Mark 16:17 [longer ending]), Jesus' new commandment (John 13:34), the new creation at conversion (2 Cor. 5:17), a new name and a new song in heaven (Rev. 2:17; 5:9).

The home of righteousness translates *en hois dikaiosynē katoikei*, lit. "in which righteousness dwells." Righteousness is virtually personified, as in the messianic passage Isa. 32:16 LXX: "righteousness will dwell in Carmel." Righteousness as a mark of the new age is frequently mentioned: Isa. 9:7; 11:4–5; *Psalms of Solomon* 17:40; 1 Enoch 5:8–9; Rom. 14:17. Satan may have control over the present world (John 12:31; 14:30; 2 Cor. 4:4; Eph. 2:2; 1 John 4:4; 5:19), but his rule is doomed to be brought to an end (John 16:11). Peter's phrase finds an echo in 1 Enoch 46:3, "the Son of Man, who has righteousness, with whom righteousness dwells."

3:14 / **Dear friends** (*agapētoi*): beloved (by God), as in 1 Pet. 2:11; 4:12; 2 Pet. 3:1, 8, 15, 17. This is friendship based not on a social relationship but on a common faith in God through Jesus Christ. See Additional Note on 1 Pet. 2:11.

Make every effort: *Spoudazein* means "be zealous, be eager, give diligence, make haste" (also used at 1:10, 15). The need is to concentrate urgently on developing one's Christian manner of life by following the example of Jesus (1 Pet. 2:21).

Spotless (*aspilos*): Metaphorically "free from censure, irreproachable" (as in 1 Tim. 6:14; James 1:27); and **blameless**, (*amōmētos*), without fault; the word is used of sacrificial animals (Num. 28:3 LXX). Neither characteristic can be acquired by self-effort. Both come only through reliance on the finished work of Christ (1 Pet. 1:19, where both adjectives are used of Jesus; cf. Jude 24; Rev. 14:5). On *aspilos*, see Turner, p. 483.

At peace with him: cf. Ps. 85:10; also Isa. 32:17–18, "The fruit of righteousness will be peace; the effect of righteousness will be quietness and confidence forever. My people will live in peaceful dwelling places, in secure homes, in undisturbed places of rest."

3:15 /   The delay in the second advent is due to two factors. The first has already been implied in Peter's reference to the
need for believers to live godly lives (v. 11), for this will speed the
coming of Christ. Now he mentions the second reason for the
delay, one he earlier spelled out in verse 9. The delay is due to the
merciful goodness of the **Lord's patience** in holding back the day
of judgment, which gives every possible opportunity for unbelievers to come to a knowledge of salvation before it is too late.

That explanation of the delay in the Parousia harmonizes
with the one put forward by **our dear brother Paul** (as, for
example, in Rom. 2:4). Paul, and by implication Peter himself, was
enabled to express such sentiments because they were made
known to him from on high, rather than being a matter of personal guesswork: the apostle **wrote you with the wisdom that
God gave him**. That, as Peter delicately hints, is his own authority too.

3:16 /   Paul is consistent in the message he gives on this
point: **he writes the same way in all his letters**. Peter's readers
will have had the opportunity to check up on the truth of this
from firsthand knowledge of at least some of Paul's correspondence, for at an early stage copies of letters in the NT were shared
by churches other than those to whom they were first addressed.

Peter cheerfully admits that even as an apostle himself, and
one who indeed for three years had the inestimable privilege of
hearing Jesus firsthand, he finds that Paul's **letters contain some
things that are hard to understand**. (Not all Peter's transmitted
words are easy to understand, for that matter.) But it is one thing
to come across fish bones on the plate. It is quite another to try to
swallow them. Yet such commonsense wisdom is not shared by
all. Some **ignorant and unstable people distort** the teaching of
Paul's writings, twisting it for their own purposes, **as they do the**

other Scriptures. (Peter clearly has the false teachers' treatment of his own letters in mind.) And what happens? Such distortions of true doctrine lead to the **destruction** of the perpetrators, for they themselves are thereby led astray from the right road to God. It is noteworthy that Peter puts Paul's letters on a par with **the other Scriptures**, i.e., the Old Testament. It was the practice in the early church from the beginning to carry on the Jewish synagogue custom of reading two passages, one from the Pentateuch and one from the Prophets, but then to add a reading from an apostolic writing (Col. 4:16). Although at first sight this may seem surprising to the modern reader, the explanation is not hard to find. The first Christians recognized that the same Holy Spirit who inspired the OT prophets was still at work. Indeed, he was carrying forward his earlier revelations of divine purposes now that Jesus the Messiah had come. There was nothing incongruous in setting apostolic words on a level with the Old Testament (1 Cor. 12:8; 2 Cor. 13:3; 1 Thess. 2:13).

Additional Notes   §17

3:15 / **Bear in mind** (*hēgeisthe*) **that our Lord's patience means salvation** pointedly balances the use of the same verb in v. 9: "The Lord is not slow in keeping his promise, as some understand (*hēgountai*) slowness."

Peter's reference to **our dear** (*agapētos*, beloved by God) **brother Paul** employs the regular Christian vocabulary to express the warm, harmonious apostleship that Peter and Paul share; the disagreement between the two men over Peter's inconsistent attitude toward Gentile Christians (Gal. 2:14) was brief. For his part, Paul mentions Peter in two of his letters (1 Cor. 1:12; 3:22; 9:5; 15:5; Gal. 1:18; 2:7–9; cf. Acts 15:7, 12).

Paul also wrote you. Copies of Pauline letters were sent early on to other churches, quite apart from occasions when the apostle himself gave instructions to that end (Col. 4:16). Peter could be referring to our letter to the Romans (2:4), 1 Thessalonians (chs. 4 and 5), 2 Thessalonians (ch. 2), Ephesians (1:14; 2:7; 3:9–11), Colossians (1:20), or possibly to some other correspondence that has not survived.

3:16 / **Ignorant** (*amathēs*): In the NT only here, *amathēs* means uninstructed, unlearned, unscholarly. Such men were probably making their calamitous errors by tearing proof-texts out of context to fit their own ideas.

Unstable (*astēriktos*): again, in the NT, only in 2 Pet.; lit. "without a staff, unsupported." This rare term is used by Peter to describe the un-qualified teachers who disastrously misinterpret Paul's writings. Earlier Peter applied the word to the Christian beginner who falls an easy prey to false teaching (2:14). See Turner, p. 484.

Distort (*strebloun*): Occurring in the NT only here, *strebloun* means "to twist, torture, dislocate the limbs on the rack," a singularly vivid term to describe their perversion of Scripture.

To their own destruction (*apōleia*, as in 2:1, 3; 3:7, referring to the last judgment): "they rush headlong into ruin" (Calvin) by misinterpret-ing, perhaps even deliberately, what was intended to be for their eternal benefit in salvation.

§18 Summary (2 Pet. 3:17–18)

3:17 / Forewarned is forearmed. **Since you already know this**—that false teaching is threatening your spiritual well being—**be on your guard**, stand as an alert sentinel over your understanding and grasp of true doctrine, especially that which concerns the return of the Lord Jesus Christ. Thus Peter's readers will be kept from being **carried away** by the powerful current of nefarious **error** propagated by **lawless men**, those who preach a false libertinism that claims freedom from all moral constraint by adopting a perverted view of Christian liberty. To be deceived by that ruinous teaching, Peter warns, would mean that you would face spiritual disaster, nothing less than a fatal **fall from your secure position** in Christ. To guard against such spiritual poison threatened from without, there is one sure antidote: to go on making healthy progress in the Christian life that is within (cf. Ps. 1:1–3).

3:18 / **But grow**—or rather, "Keep on growing"—is Peter's concluding word to his readers, as he harks back to his opening theme (1:3–8). There must always be constant growth in the believer's spiritual life, for stagnation spells disintegration. As in the natural world, so in the spiritual sphere, growth is not a matter of a leaf or twig making some strenuous individualistic effort. Growth comes from maintaining a healthy relationship with the parent vine (John 15:1–8). Accordingly, the way to grow spiritually is to maintain a healthy relationship with the source of all spiritual life, God himself through Jesus Christ. The believer will then develop and mature, as surely as sunrise follows the night, by continuously drawing on the free unearned and unearnable **grace** of Christ, and so increase in the personal **knowledge** of the Savior (Col. 1:10).

With such a certain and inexhaustible supply of spiritual life to draw upon through the finished and perfect work of

Christ, there can be only the response of the glad doxology: **To him be glory both now**, utterly sufficient for the demands of the present life, **and forever** (*eis hēmeran aiōnos*, lit. "unto the eternal day"), i.e., right up to the day of the Lord (3:7, 10, 12) which ushers in eternity.

Amen may well be a later stereotyped addition to the earlier MSS. But its appropriateness ("So it is!") at the close of Peter's exhortation finds a ready echo in the believer's heart.

Additional Notes   §18

3:17 /   **Dear friends** (*agapētoi*): Beloved by God, as in 3:1, 8, 14; 1 Pet. 2:11; 4:12; Jude 3, 17, 20. Even the way Peter addresses his readers is a reminder of their relationship with God in Jesus Christ, and with other believers, for they share in the same love. See Additional Note on 1 Pet. 2:11.

You already know this (*proginōskein*): see Turner, pp. 178–79.

Be on your guard: The verb is *phylassein*, a military term. The Christian life is a spiritual warfare against the hosts of evil; cf. 1 Cor. 10:12; Eph. 6:10–18.

Carried away translates *synapachthentes*, the passive form of a compound verb, *syn* (together with), *apo* (away from), *agein* (to lead or drive). The sense of the danger that Peter warns against is that of "being swept along with the crowd" away from the true Christian way of life. The same verb is used of the defection of Barnabas in Gal. 2:13.

Error (*planē*): erroneous teaching or, more aggressively, a deliberate leading astray.

Lawless (*athesmos*): one who breaks the law of nature and conscience in order to gratify lust. The term appears in the NT only here and in 2:7 (regarding the Sodomites). See Turner, pp. 254–55.

Fall (*ekpiptein*): The verb is used of shipwreck in Acts 27:26, 29.

Secure position (*stērigmos*): a rare word (only here in the NT, although the corresponding verb occurs in 1:12 and in 1 Pet. 5:10). But the term contrasts nicely with the character of the false teachers and their dupes, whom Peter calls *astēriktos*, unstable (2:14; 3:16). The verb *stērizein* is applied to Peter himself in Luke 22:32, "When you have turned back, strengthen (*stērixon*) your brothers."

3:18 /   **Grow** (*auxanete*, present imperative: "keep on growing"): "Not only do not fall from your own steadfastness, but be so firmly rooted as to throw out branches and yield increase" (Alford); cf. Ps. 1:2–3.

To him be glory is the only NT doxology (other than 2 Tim. 4:18; Rev. 1:6) indubitably ascribed to Jesus Christ alone. If the letter had been written later than Peter's lifetime, a more stereotyped liturgical doxology would have been expected. As it is, the expression is almost unique. Furthermore, the Greek behind the translation of the following phrase, **and forever** (*eis hēmeran aiōnos*, lit. "unto the eternal day"), is found in the NT only here. Before the end of the first century, stereotyped formulas to round off doxologies were commonplace, so Peter's unusual expressions imply an early rather than a late date for this letter and offer evidence for its authenticity.

Jude

§1   Writer and Readers (Jude 1)

1 /   By custom, Hellenistic letters began with a threefold formula: (a) the name of the sender; (b) the name of the recipient; and (c) an opening salutation. Greek writers followed the pattern "(a) to (b): greetings." A NT example is the letter of Claudius Lysias to Felix (Acts 23:26). Jewish letters were introduced slightly differently. The opening sentence gave the names of writer and recipient. A second sentence invoked a blessing upon the reader.

The three elements of (a) author, (b) addressee, (c) greeting are clearly seen at the beginning of most of the NT letters—as here: (a) **Jude**; (b) **to those who have been called**; (c) **mercy, peace and love be yours in abundance** (Jude 1–2).

The writer introduces himself by name (**Jude**), by status (**a servant of Jesus Christ**), and by relationship (**a brother of James**).

Jude is evidently not an apostle, for unlike Paul and Peter in their letters, he makes no claim to have apostolic authority to lend weight to his words. Indeed he distinguishes himself from the apostles by writing "Remember what the apostles of our Lord Jesus Christ foretold" (Jude 17).

No doubt it was out of humble reverence that neither Jude nor James in writing their letters makes any reference to being a blood relation of the Lord. Each calls himself simply **a servant** (lit. bondslave) **of Jesus Christ**. Even leading apostles like Paul (Rom. 1:1) and Peter (2 Pet. 1:1) were content to own the same title, a remarkable state of affairs in view of the way slaves were so often maltreated in NT times. But the early Christians discovered that to be the slave of Christ is to be the Lord's freedman (1 Cor. 7:22). Complete and loyal submission to the service of Jesus Christ is, paradoxically, the pathway to perfect liberty. Jude has come to realize that the greatest distinction that anyone can achieve in life comes about through always being at the complete disposal of the Lord Jesus Christ.

For Jude to call himself "a *brother* of James" was not the customary practice. Normally a person was identified by the name of the father. Jude's describing himself as "a brother of James" suggests that this James was well known. The readers would be in no doubt as to the man meant. Jude seems content to be distinguished simply as a sibling of the more celebrated figure, just as Andrew seemed happy to be in the shadow of his prominent brother Peter. Both Jude and Andrew had the priceless and rare enough gift of being prepared to play second fiddle.

The outstanding James in the early church was the brother of Jesus who was converted after the resurrection (1 Cor. 15:7) and became the leader of the Jerusalem church (Acts 12:17; 15:13).

So the sense of the opening words of this letter is: "Jude, the bondslave, I dare not say brother, of Jesus Christ, but certainly James's brother."

Jude addresses his readers as **called . . . loved . . . kept**. The writer's fondness for triple expressions constantly surfaces throughout his brief letter (see Introduction, p. 19). "Called" is one of the great biblical terms to describe believers. The verb "to call" (*kalein*) is regularly used in four main senses.

1. It means to call a person or a place by name, as in Luke 10:39 ("a sister called Mary") or Luke 7:11 ("a town called Nain").

2. It means to call someone to take up a task or responsibility. Paul is "called to be an apostle" (Rom. 1:1). Certain servants are "called" to take charge in their master's absence (Luke 19:13).

3. It is used to summon someone to a law court to give an account of his actions (Acts 4:18; 24:2).

4. It is the regular word for calling friends to a meal, inviting them to a pleasant social occasion, as in the parable about the wedding guests (Matt. 22:3). It is the word used for those who are "called" to the wedding supper of the Lamb (Rev. 19:9). In short, it is the term for a hospitable invitation. "The called" (*ho klētos*), the corresponding noun from the verb *kalein*, was in fact a technical term for "guest."

So, in describing his readers as "called," Jude is in effect reminding them of their high privileges. As believers, they have been called out of darkness into God's wonderful light (1 Pet. 2:9). They have responded to the divine call to faith in Jesus Christ. They are called by the name of Christ, that is, "Christians." One day they will be summoned to the judgment seat of Christ to report on their Christian life and witness (2 Cor. 5:10). Meanwhile they can rejoice in the satisfying service to which they have been invited, as to a festive occasion, one constantly shared with their ever-present divine Host.

Who are loved by God the Father. The Greek is, literally, "in" (*en*) God the Father. Paul often refers to believers as being "in Christ" or "in the Lord," but nowhere else in the NT are Christians said to be loved "in" (*en*) God the Father. It is possible that originally Jude left a gap after the "in" for a place-name to be inserted, when his messenger took the letter to various towns where the incipient heresy he writes about had begun to spread. (Something like this may have happened with the "in Ephesus" of Eph. 1:1.) So we could translate: "to those resident in [—], who are loved by God the Father."

Kept by Jesus Christ is, rather, **kept** *for* (dative of advantage) **Jesus Christ** (as RSV); that is, kept safely, by the one born of the Father, from the evil one (1 John 5:18), for Christ's second coming (John 6:39, 44, 54; 1 Cor. 1:8; 1 Thess. 5:23), and for the kingdom he will establish. God does not intend to lose any of those whom he has called to be his own. Jude appropriately stresses this theme as he begins a letter warning his readers of their need to be kept safe from the influence of false teachers.

Both *ēgapēmenais* (**loved**) and *tetērēmenois* (**kept**) are perfect participles. The Greek perfect tense speaks of a past complete act having continuing effects. The divine love and keeping power are constantly holding believers with safe arms (Deut. 33:27). As Christians, Jude's readers not only were the objects of God's personal care and love in the past, but they still are and always will be.

Additional Notes §1

1 / **Jude** or Judas (the same word in Gk.), was a common name in biblical times. It was borne by: (1) the son of Jacob who became head of the tribe of Judah (Matt. 1:2–3); (2) one of the brothers of Jesus (Mark 6:3); (3) one of the Twelve (Luke 6:16; Acts 1:13), and also known as Thaddaeus (compare Matt. 10:3; Mark 3:18; John 14:22); (4) a Christian prophet, one of the leading men appointed by the Jerusalem church, Judas Barsabbas (Acts 15:22); (5) a freedom fighter, Judas the Galilean (Acts 5:37); (6) a

citizen of Damascus, in whose house on Straight Street Paul stayed after his conversion (Acts 9:11); and, of course, (7) the traitor, Judas Iscariot (Matt. 10:4).

Loved: A number of later MSS modify *ēgapēmenois*, "loved," to read *hēgiasmenois*, "sanctified" (KJV), on the model of 1 Cor. 1:2. NEB's "who live in the love of God the Father" is an unlikely paraphrase. Westcott and Hort suggested that the "in" is misplaced and should be before "Jesus Christ." We could then translate: "beloved by God the Father and kept safe in Jesus Christ." J. B. Mayor's proposal to read "beloved [by us] in the Father" is ruled out because all three participles, **called . . . loved . . . kept**, have the same divine agent as subject.

Some confirmation that **James** here is the brother of Jesus comes from a report by a second-century Jewish-Christian historian. Hegesippus describes how grandsons of Jude ("who is said to have been the brother, according to the flesh, of the Savior") were summoned before the Roman emperor Domitian. This would be about A.D. 96. But, when the emperor observed their labor-hardened hands and realized how poor they were, he contemptuously dismissed them as being no danger to his empire (Eusebius, *Eccl. Hist.* 3.19.1; 3.20.6; Josephus, *Ant.* 20.200).

Kept: Christians belong to Jesus Christ and are kept safe for him until he comes to claim his property (cf. 1 Pet. 1:4, where the inheritance of Christians is declared to be kept safe in heaven until they are able to claim it, at the Parousia). **Kept** is a key-word of the letter; it occurs five times, in verses 1, 6 (twice), 13, and 21.

§2   Greeting (Jude 2)

2 / Jude's opening greeting is another example of his fondness for a trio of expressions. He prays that his readers may know **mercy, peace and love**. These are virtues which cannot be acquired by self-effort. Neither can they be expected as just deserts. They are gifts of divine grace, and Jude prays that his readers may receive them **in abundance** (*plēthyntheiē*, filled to capacity). The faith of Jude's readers is threatened by dangerous infiltrators, and so Jude prays that they may receive divine **mercy**, the pity that comes to aid, in total sufficiency. The readers' fellowship with God through Jesus Christ is being disturbed; consequently they must have their divine **peace** reinforced, the peace that follows from an unsullied relationship with God. Supremely, the readers need God's all-comprehending **love** (*agapē*) in overflowing measure. This will bind them to God and to one another in their Christian community.

Jude's prayer is of permanent value, for "the called," that is, believers in every generation, constantly need divine mercy, peace, and love. That prayer can be prayed in all confidence, since God delights to show mercy (Mic. 7:18). Christ himself is our peace (Eph. 2:14), and the Holy Spirit is the agent of love (Rom. 5:5).

Additional Notes   §2

2 / A prayer for **mercy** is unusual in an opening NT greeting, although examples do occur (1 Tim. 1:2; 2 Tim. 1:2; 2 John 3). Paul's prayer is more likely to be for "grace and peace from the Lord Jesus Christ," as in 1 Cor. 1:3.

The same Greek term *plēthyntheiē*, be multiplied (RSV), occurs in the opening greeting of Peter's two letters. See Additional Note on 1 Pet. 1:2.

Jude's three terms, **mercy, peace, love**, occur together in the letter to the church at Smyrna on the martyrdom of Polycarp (A.D. 155).

Peace (*eirēnē*, the verbal form of *eirein*, to join): Peace is the result of joining together that which has been separated.

3 / **Dear friends** is a free translation of *agapētoi*, lit. "beloved ones," that is, "beloved by God, and beloved by me, because we share in divine love." Although *agapētoi* was an expression in general use, Christians gave the Greek term a new depth of meaning, for it described the quality of the Father's feeling for Jesus: "This is my beloved (*agapētos*) Son" (Matt. 3:17; KJV, RSV).

Jude did not set out to compose this particular letter. He had wanted **to write** (*graphein*: present infinitive, which could suggest "in a leisurely manner") on the general subject of **the salvation we share.** That "common salvation" (KJV, RSV) was one that belonged to all believers equally. It included sharing the same Christ (Acts 4:12), the same grace (Eph. 2:8), the same justification with God (Rom. 3:22), and the same entrance by faith (2 Pet.1:1). But Jude's intention to enlarge on such themes to edify his readers was overtaken by events. News suddenly reached him that his Christian friends were threatened by a dangerous heresy. The report made him snatch up his pen there and then **to write** (*grapsai*, aorist infinitive) a very different letter from the one he had originally proposed.

I had to write (*anankēn eschon grapsai*): The compulsion (*anankēn*) to write at once was as clear as if he had been given a verbal order to do so. In obedience to that inner constraint, and out of love for his Christian friends, he writes without delay to **urge** them **to contend for the faith.** The Greek word for **urge** is *parakalōn*, from *parakalein*, to call (*kalein*) alongside (*para*). Jude would prefer to be alongside his friends in their peril, but since he is unable to be with them in person, he does the next best thing by sending a letter.

He bids them **contend**—an athletics metaphor. Believers are expected to be spiritually fit, prepared at any time to meet spiritual challenges, which may arise suddenly and from an unexpected quarter.

Jude's readers are exhorted to engage in a determined and costly struggle to maintain **the faith** (*pistis*). Here *pistis* is a reference not to the personal faith of the individual, its usual sense in the NT, but to the body of Christian truth. This body of belief, Jude says, was **once for all entrusted** (*paradidōmai*, to commit, hand over) **to the saints**, to the people of God as a whole, not just to apostles or to later leaders. **The faith** is not something we discover for ourselves, still less is it something constructed from our own ideas. It is the truth about God in Christ that has been handed down from believer to believer in an unbroken chain, stretching back to the teaching of Jesus himself as recorded in the NT. Each individual Christian has the dual responsibility of maintaining that truth unadulterated and of carefully handing it on to others.

4 / The reason Jude's readers must contend for the pure faith of true Christianity is that **certain men**, itinerant false teachers, have infiltrated the church. Their subsequent **condemnation** (*krima*, judgment), Jude declares, **was written about long ago**. He may be referring to a prediction of Enoch (who is mentioned in v. 14). But Jude is more likely alluding to some tradition, then current, that described such a judgment in more detail.

In the present case, as Jude explains, the peril has arisen more subtly, for **certain men . . . have secretly slipped in** (*pareisedysan*) **among you**. The Greek word, which occurs in the NT only here, is most expressive: *pareisdyein* is used of the clever pleading of a lawyer, gradually insinuating his version of the evidence into the minds of judge and jury. It describes the action of a spy stealthily getting into the country, or of someone sneaking in by a side door.

False teachers have managed to get into the church. Jude describes the troublemakers in three ways, each term leading on to the next. The men are **godless** (*asebeis*, with no reverence for God): they leave God out of account (Ps. 14:1). And because of that, they are antinomians, they despise God's laws (cf. 1 Cor. 6:12; 10:23). They substitute blatant **immorality** (*aselgeia*, lasciviousness, wantonness) for **the grace of our God**. And because of *that*, they are self-assertive: they **deny** (*arnesthai*, to disown) that **Jesus Christ** is their **only Sovereign and Lord**. The Greek is literally: "They deny both (*kai*) the only Sovereign (*despotēs*) and also (*kai*) our Lord (*kyrios*) Jesus Christ." The word *despotēs* (absolute owner, one who has complete power over another), when used in the NT of God, always refers to the Father (apart from 2 Pet. 2:1). So Jude appears to have in mind both God the Father and the Son of God: the intruders disown both.

Additional Notes §3

---

3 / The affectionate *agapētoi*, "beloved ones," which appears again in vv. 17 and 20, derives from the verb *agapan* ("to love with God's love"), used in v. 1. The Greek for **I had to** (*anankēn eschon*) with an infinitive refers to orders received, as in Luke 14:18; 23:17; 1 Cor. 7:37; 9:16; 2 Cor. 9:7; Heb. 7:27; see Horsley, *New Documents*, vol. 1, p. 45.

The Greek verb for **urge** gives us the noun *paraklētos*, Paraclete, Counselor, "one called alongside to help," a title for the Holy Spirit in John 14:16, 26.

Contend: The Greek verb *epagōnizomai* occurs in the NT only here. But Paul uses a similar athletics metaphor in Phil. 1:27, "contending as one man (*synathleō*), as athletes with true team spirit, for the faith of the gospel"; and in Phil. 4:3, "women who have contended at my side (*synathleō*), women who were spiritual athletes, in the cause of the gospel."

Faith has the same meaning of "the body of Christian truth" in v. 20. (See also 1 Pet. 3:15.) This usage is found as early as Gal. 1:23.

The Greek verb here translated **entrusted** gives rise to the noun *paradosis*, that which is handed down, tradition. On the Christian *paradosis*, as distinct from human traditions, see O. Cullmann, "The Tradition," in *The Early Church* (London: SCM Press, 1956), pp. 59–99. See also 1 Cor. 15:1–3; 2 Thess. 3:6.

4 / The expression **certain men** (*tines*) is often used in the NT to denote a particular group of people: "You know who I mean!"

Long ago (*palai*) can equally well refer to the recent past, as in Mark 15:44 and 2 Pet. 1:9. Itinerant preachers and teachers frequently caused trouble in the early church (Matt. 7:15; 2 Cor. 10–11; 1 John 4:1; 2 John 10; Didache 11–12; Ignatius, *To the Ephesians* 9:1). A similar passage found among the Dead Sea Scrolls (1QS 4.9–14) rebukes the "spirits of iniquity" in terms reminiscent of Jude's accusations, so the problem was not new; various religious leaders spoke and wrote about it. If both Jude and 2 Pet. 2:1–3 have independently drawn upon such a tradition, this would readily explain the differences and the similarities between the two writings. But in any case, the peril to the early church of such false teachers was clearly predicted (1 Tim. 4:1–2).

Jude's verb *pareidyein*, to slip in secretly, is similar to the *pareisagein*, to smuggle in, of 2 Pet. 2:1.

Who change the grace of our God into a license for immorality agrees with 2 Pet. 2:18–19 in pointing to a group who, under the pretense of magnifying the grace of God (Rom. 6:1) and of asserting their Christian liberty, were leading base and licentious lives. The practice was not uncommon, for it was condemned alike by Paul (1 Cor. 6:9–18), Peter (1 Pet. 2:16; 2 Pet. 2:19), and John (1 John 3:7–10; Rev. 2:24).

And deny Jesus Christ: A similar thought is in 1 Enoch 48:10: "they have denied the Lord of Spirits and his Anointed."

The term **godless** (*asebeis*) "may be almost said to give the keynote to the Epistle (cf. vv. 15, 18) as it does to the Book of Enoch" (Mayor). "Because, for the Jew, God's commandments regulate the whole of man's conduct, the irreverent attitude to God is manifested in unrighteous conduct" (Bauckham, p. 38).

Sovereign (*despotēs*): The modern meaning of "despot" is entirely negative and implies oppression and even slavery. But the Greek *despotes* is morally neutral: one in absolute control can be good or bad.

5 / Sooner or later divine justice will catch up with those ungodly men, just as it did in OT times. To illustrate his point, Jude quotes three examples of divine judgment that his readers will recall (**you already know all this**). Although the men who were corrupting the church are described by Jude as "godless" (v. 4), they would not have regarded themselves in that light. Neither would they have viewed themselves as the enemies of the Christian church. Rather, they were proud of being free thinkers, a spiritual elite, unencumbered by owning lordship to anyone.

The first two examples Jude chooses make it clear that even if someone has received the greatest of spiritual privileges from God, that person must constantly watch and pray to avoid falling into disastrous error.

At one point in their history, **the Lord delivered his people out of Egypt** and bondage in spectacular and miraculous fashion (Exod. 14:26–31). Yet even that extraordinary blessing did not mean that subsequently **those who did not believe** escaped the dire consequences of turning their backs on God, but they were **destroyed**. When they were on the verge of entering the promised land, the people of Israel took fright at the majority report of the spies Moses had sent ahead to reconnoiter, and they refused point-blank to go on. They did not believe that God would enable them to conquer the land in front of them (Num. 13:26–33). As a consequence, apart from faithful Joshua and Caleb, that entire generation was condemned to spend the rest of their lives in a physical and spiritual desert. Thus they never enjoyed the land of milk and honey God had promised to give them (Num. 14:34–38). The continuous blessing of God depends on continuous reliance on God. The fate of those disbelieving Israelites haunted the minds of the NT writers (1 Cor. 10:5–11; Heb. 3:1–4:2).

6 / The second warning example from the OT concerns the sin and fate of fallen **angels**. They became disgruntled with their **positions of authority**, Their lofty station, Jude says, the angels **did not keep** (*tērein*, to watch over). They failed to do their duty in guarding something of great value. They were not single-minded in maintaining the exclusive position for which God had purposely created them. They chose to look elsewhere and **abandoned their own home**. They deserted in order to further their own ends.

According to Isaiah 14:12; 24:21–22, pride drives some to rebel (Isa. 14:13). Certain angels were expelled from heaven and sentenced to eternal doom (Isa. 24:21–22; see also Matt. 25:41; Luke 10:18).

The book of Enoch has much to relate about the angels that "have deserted the lofty sky and their holy everlasting station (1 Enoch 12:4). Those rebels are to be chained until judgment day (1 Enoch 10:15–16). Their ringleader Azazel is sentenced: "Cover him with darkness, and let him dwell there forever" (1 Enoch 10:5). So *pride* was one cause of the angels' fall. But there was another cause. This comes out in the story of the angels who left heaven and seduced mortal women (Gen. 6:1–4), and so fell through *lust*.

Jude combines the two ideas. First, the angels deserted their appointed place of authority to go after a position not intended for them. Second, they abandoned their proper domain to cohabit with beautiful women on earth. Such notions may sound bizarre to modern ears, but their implication is plain. *Pride* and *lust* ruined the angels that fell. The evil interlopers Jude warns his readers against are equally guilty of pride and lust. Their judgment is as certain as that which befell those angels, despite their exalted status.

The angels who defected have been sentenced to be **kept in darkness, bound with everlasting chains.** We are not intended to imagine a literal dungeon in which fallen angels are fettered. Rather, Jude is vividly depicting the misery of their conditions. Free spirits and celestial powers, as once they were, are now shackled and impotent. Shining ones, once enjoying the marvelous light of God's glorious presence, are now plunged in profound darkness. There is grim irony in Jude's repetition of the same verb. The wicked angels proved too proud to *keep* (*tērein*) their exalted positions, so God has *kept* (*tērein*) them in deepest detention—a hint that the punishment fits the crime (1 Cor. 3:17;

Rev. 16:6). A note in 2 Peter 2:4 adds that they have been sent to Tartarus (NIV, "hell"), regarded in the ancient Greek world as the abyss of punishment. There these angels are secured until the **judgment on the great Day** when the final settlement takes place.

7 / Jude's third warning example is the fate that befell **Sodom and Gomorrah and the surrounding towns** (Gen. 19:1–25). The **surrounding towns** included Admah and Zeboiim, according to Deut. 29:23 and Hos. 11:8. A fifth town, Zoar, was spared after Lot's intercession (Gen. 19:20–22). The spectacular and utter destruction of these places, and of Sodom in particular, made such an indelible impression that among later generations the event became a warning byword for divine judgment.

These places were condemned because their inhabitants engaged in flagrant immorality. They **gave themselves up to . . . perversion** is lit. "going off after different (*heteros*, different in kind) flesh" ("strange flesh," KJV; "unnatural lust," RSV). Both the fallen angels and the men of Sodom had aggravated their sexual sins by lusting after "different" flesh. The angels of Genesis 6, although spiritual beings, had desired mortal women. The converse also was virtually true, for Jude ignores the fact that the Sodomites were unaware that Lot's two visitors were angelic beings, not men (Gen. 19:1, 5). In Jude's view the Sodomites' intended homosexual practice was likewise a **perversion**, that is, unnatural sexual conduct, and not of God's appointment.

George Adam Smith vividly describes what probably happened in the valley near the southern end of the Dead Sea when "burning sulphur rained down" (Gen. 19:24): "In this bituminous soil took place one of those terrible explosions which have broken out in the similar geology of the oil districts of North America. In such soil reservoirs of oil and gas are formed, and suddenly discharged by their own pressure or through an earthquake. The gas explodes, carrying high into the air masses of oil, which fall back in fiery rain, and are so inextinguishable that they float afire on water." (G. A. Smith, *Historical Geography*, p. 508). In such a manner **Sodom and Gomorrah and the surrounding towns . . . serve as an example of those who suffer the punishment of eternal fire.** What happened to Sodom and Gomorrah may have taken place a long time ago as far as Jude's readers were concerned. But the event remains as a permanent warning for all generations.

The godless intruders among Jude's Christian friends betray a decadence that pervades their whole lives, which these OT examples illustrate. Physically, these men have become immoral. Intellectually, they have grown arrogant. Spiritually, they defy God by their disobedience. Sooner or later, they will bring God's judgment down upon themselves. The sins may differ, whether a matter of unbelief (v. 5), rebellious discontent (v. 6), or gross fornication (v. 7). The sinners may differ, whether Israelites, privileged to have the divine promises (v. 5), or angels, appointed to a splendid domain in heavenly glory (v. 6), or Gentiles (v. 7) dwelling in pleasant places, "well watered, like the garden of the Lord" (Gen. 13:10).

The punishment of eternal fire implies a destruction as final and total as is portrayed by the utter desolation of the area where the towns once stood. Nothing lives there. The towns themselves are believed to lie buried beneath what are now the southern waters of the Dead Sea. Sir George Adam Smith comments: "In this awful hollow, this bit of the infernal regions come up to the surface, this hell with the sun shining into it, primitive man laid the scene of God's most terrible judgment on human sin." (*Historical Geography*, p. 504)

Additional Notes   §4

---

5 / **I want to remind you**: a frequent admonition in the NT (1 Cor. 4:17; 15:1; 2 Tim. 1:6; 2:14; Titus 3:1; 2 Pet. 1:12–13; 3:1; Jude 17), although of value only if readers have at some time known the story. Present-day preachers can take much less for granted.

Those who did not believe (Num. 14:1–35): Other NT writers make use of the incident of the unbelieving Israelites in the wilderness (Acts 7:39; 1 Cor. 10:1–11; Heb. 3:12–19). While Jude and 2 Peter often cover much the same ground, and both refer to this event, only Jude mentions the deliverance from Egypt, and only Peter speaks of Lot and his rescue. This suggests that it is unlikely that one writer copied from the other.

6 / The wicked angels did not **keep** (*tērēsantas*: aorist, denoting a past action over and done with), so God for his part has **kept** (*tetērēken*: perfect, denoting a past action with continuing consequences).

Positions of authority (*tēn heautōn archēn*; the Greek word *archē* means beginning, and then sovereignty, rule): "Their original dignity and high position." Wycliffe translates as "princehood." *Archē* is used in 1 Enoch 12:4 of the Watchers (angels) who "abandoned the high heaven and the holy eternal place and defiled themselves with women" (Gen. 6:1–4, where "sons of God" was universally understood not as men but as angels, or "Watchers," in Judaism until the middle of the second century, and in Christianity until the fifth century (Bauckham, p. 51). The earliest extant account of the fall of the Watchers (1 Enoch 6–19, early 2nd cent. B.C.) tells how in the days of Jared (Gen. 5:18) two hundred angels descended on Mount Hermon, lusting for human wives. Their giant offspring were taught forbidden knowledge by the angels. That led to the total corruption of the world, which God then had to destroy by the Flood. The Watchers were sentenced to be left bound under the earth until the Day of Judgment, when they will be cast into Gehenna (Bauckham, p. 51).

Abandoned (*apolipontas*): The aorist tense indicates a once-for-all action. The angels deserted their post. They left forever **their own home** (*to idion oikētērion*), their own dwelling place, that is, heaven, their own special abode. See "Heaven" in *IBD*, vol. 2, p. 466; *NIDNTT*, vol. 2, pp. 184–96; *ZPEB*, vol. 3, pp. 60–64; *ISBE*, vol. 2, pp. 654–55. "Heaven was made for angels, not for man. It is the temporary abode of the departed saints until the new heavens and the new earth are brought into being, but men's eternal dwelling place will be on the perfect earth." (Wuest, *In These Last Days*, p. 240).

The fallen angels once enjoyed God's marvelous light (1 Pet. 2:9); now they are plunged **in darkness** (*hypo zophon*, lit. *under* darkness). The phrase is commonly used in Greek poetry for the intense blackness of the underworld (Homer, *Iliad* 21.56; *Odyssey* 11.57; Hesiod, *Theogony* 729; Aeschylus, *Sibyline Oracles* 4.43).

The Greek translated **chains** by NIV is *desmoi*, bonds, that is, anything used for tying. In the healing of the deaf man with an impediment in his speech, it is said that "the *string* (*desmos*) of his tongue was loosed" (Mark 7:35 KJV). The angels' **chains** are described as **everlasting** (*aidios*). The Greek word excludes any notion of interruption, but rather lays stress on permanence and unchangeableness. Elsewhere in the NT, *aidios* occurs only in Rom. 1:20, where it is used of God's *eternal* power.

The expression **judgment on the great Day** is unique in the NT, although similar phrases occur in the book of Enoch: "the Great Day of Judgment" (1 Enoch 10:9); "the Day of the Great Judgment" (93:8; 97:15; 104:3); "the Great Day" (16:2); "the Great Judgment" (22:5).

7 / How deep an impression the utter destruction of **Sodom and Gomorrah** made is reflected in the frequency of references to that event: Deut. 29:23; Isa. 1:9; 13:19; Jer. 23:14; 49:18; 50:40; Lam. 4:6; Ezek. 16:48–50; Hos. 11:8; Zeph. 2:9; Wis. 10:7; Sir. 16:8; 3 Macc. 2:5; *Jub.* 16:6, 9; 20:5; 22:22; 36:10; *T. Naph.* 3:4; 4:1; *T. Ash.* 7:1; Philo, *Questions and Answers on Genesis* 4:51; *On Abraham* 140; Josephus, *War* 4.483–485; 5.566. In the NT: Matt. 10:15; 11:24; Luke 10:12; 17:29. See J. P. Harland, "Sodom and Gomorrah," in *Biblical Archaeologist* 5 (2, 1942), pp. 17–32; 6 (3, 1943), pp.41–52.

They serve (*prokeintai*): are set forth, exposed to public gaze. The Greek verb is used of food laid out on the table ready for guests, or (by contrast) of a corpse laid out before mourners, prior to burial. **Example** is *deigma*, sample, pattern, though in this context, something certainly *not* to be copied.

Eternal fire: Matt. 5:22; 13:42, 50; 18:8; 25:41; Rev. 20:14–15. "And Michael and Gabriel and Raphael and Phanuel [four of the seven archangels, according to 1 Enoch 20:1–7; Tobit 12:15] shall take hold of them on the great day and cast them into the burning furnace" (1 Enoch 54:6).

The paradoxical combination of **darkness** and **fire** occurs also in 1QS 2.8, "the gloom of eternal fire." The language conveys the impression of a state of intense heat and intense darkness, and so of intense isolation.

§5   Brazen Ignorance (Jude 8–10)

8 / The NIV translation **In the very same way** (*homoiōs mentoi*) disregards the Greek *mentoi* ("but yet"). The sense is: "Though these men have such dreadful examples set clearly before them, *yet* they persist in their sin."

Jude describes such men as **dreamers** (*enypniazomenoi*), and says that they **pollute their own bodies**. The expression could be taken to mean that the godless intruders beguile themselves with erotic fantasies (KJV, "filthy dreamers"). But **dreamers** applies to all three following clauses. The Greek word occurs elsewhere in the NT only in Acts 2:17, and there refers to prophetic dreams. The Septuagint employs the same verb to describe false prophets (Deut. 13:2, 5, 6; Isa. 56:10; Jer. 23:25; 34:9; 36:8). Jude is therefore referring to men who falsely claim to have visionary revelations to justify their teaching and actions. In verse 11 Jude implies that they even expect a fee for divulging their esoteric knowledge. Jude's recognition that such men would be troubling the people of God is not a novelty. Another writer speaks of the sinners in the last days who "will sink into impiety because of the folly of their hearts, and their eyes will be blinded through the fear of their hearts and through the visions of their dreams" (1 Enoch 99:8).

By **pollute their own bodies**, Jude means by sexual excesses, comparable to the practices of Sodom and Gomorrah (cf. 2 Pet. 2:2, 10, 18). Presumably these men justified their actions by claiming enlightenment through their alleged revelatory dreams. According to one early Christian writer, some later Gnostics, such as the followers of Simon Magus, could refer to promiscuous intercourse as "perfect love" (Hippolytus, *Refutation of All Heresies* 6.14). Sexual license was a problem in the church from its earliest days, as St. Paul knew only too well (1 Cor. 5:1; 6:9; 2 Cor. 12:21).

Such men also **reject authority** (*kyriotēta*, lordship; abstract noun from *kyrios*, lord). There are three possible interpretations.

The Greek *kyriotēs* could refer to (1) ecclesiastical or civil authority. Calvin and Luther took it in this way, understandably in view of the turbulent days of the Reformation in which they lived. But nothing else in Jude's letter is concerned with that topic. Or (2) a class of angels known as *kyriotētes* ("authorities" in Col. 1:16). But Jude's use of the singular seems to rule this out. Or (3) the lordship of God (as in Didache 4:1), or the lordship of Christ (as in Shepherd of Hermas, *Similitudes* 5.6.1). The last is the most probable explanation and corresponds to the earlier "deny Jesus Christ our only Sovereign and Lord" (v. 4).

Again, these men **slander celestial beings**. It is not clear in what way the false teachers were disparaging angels. Usually the NT writers are warning believers against giving undue deference to angels (1 Cor. 6:3; Col. 2:18; Heb. 1:4–5). Perhaps the men deemed themselves to be superior to mere angels, or they may have scorned the very idea of their existence, claiming to be free from such superstitious nonsense. But as the regular Greek word for "angel" (*angelos*) can simply mean "messenger," Jude may be intimating that the false teachers consider themselves to be far above mere messenger boys. The implication of the passage for the readers is plain enough. Jude is warning that what the false teachers may have regarded as advanced morality and advanced thought on their part can easily lead to advancing deafness to God's voice.

9 / The opening words, **But even** (*de*) **the archangel Michael**, imply a close link with what has gone before. All three accusations in verse 8 concern the rejection of the moral order, so the "slander" probably relates to the angels' function as mediators of the law of Moses (Acts 7:38, 53; Gal. 3:19; Heb. 2:2; Jubilees 1:27–29; Josephus, *Ant.* 15.136) and as guardians of creation (1 Cor. 11:10; Shepherd of Hermas, *Similitudes* 8.3.3), a responsibility which some angels had abdicated (Jude 6).

The OT makes no reference to Michael **disputing with the devil** and simply states that God buried his servant Moses "in Moab, in the valley opposite Beth Peor, but to this day no one knows where his grave is" (Deut. 34:6), a secret no doubt designed to prevent the Israelites from turning the spot into an idolatrous sanctuary.

The dispute referred to by Jude was recorded in the now lost ending of an apocryphal Jewish work called the *Assumption of Moses*. But the tradition can be reconstructed from references to that account in a number of early Christian writings (see Bauckham, pp. 65–76). Satan laid claim to the corpse of Moses for his kingdom of darkness because Moses had killed an Egyptian (Exod. 2:12). He was therefore a murderer, however virtuous his subsequent achievements, and so was unworthy of honorable burial. Satan, in his ancient role of accuser of God's people (Rev. 12:10), was seeking to prove Moses' guilt.

In response to the charge, **Michael did not dare to bring a slanderous accusation against** Satan. Barclay (DSB, p. 188) expresses the opinion of most commentators that Jude means: "If the greatest of the good angels refused to speak evil of the greatest of the evil angels, even in circumstances like that, surely no human being may speak evil of any angel." This interpretation takes **accusation** (*blasphēmias*) as a genitive of quality (Moule, *Idiom-Book*, p. 175), and as such it suits the context both in Jude and in the parallel passage in 2 Peter 2:11 (*blasphēmon krisin*, "slanderous accusations"). The terms used in this passage are forensic, the language of the courtroom. Bauckham (p. 43) considers that Jude's meaning must be determined by his source, the *Assumption of Moses*, and according to that it was Satan who had "slandered" (*eblasphēmsei kata*) Moses by accusing him of murder. Michael, in his capacity as a legal advocate, refuted the slander (*blasphēmia*) and appealed to God for judgment against Satan: **"The Lord rebuke thee!"** Michael refused to take it upon himself to pronounce judgment, for that was God's prerogative.

10 / **These men**, the false teachers, betray by their attitude that **they do not understand** spiritual matters in general, or the role of angels in the divine scheme of things in particular (cf. 2 Pet. 2:12). All that **they do understand** is the result of natural instincts, on a par with **unreasoning animals**, brute beasts. In other words, they are simply giving rein to their sensual nature. They are devoid of spiritual discernment and are therefore living on no higher plane than the animal creation, despite any ecstatic claims they may make for themselves. But such a sensual motive in life will ultimately **destroy them**; it will lead to their eternal ruin. This is not a prophecy about the medical peril of AIDS but a reference to the inevitable judgment of God, as evidenced by Israel in the wilderness (v. 5) and by the cities of the plain (v. 7).

Additional Notes   §5

8 / **Slander celestial beings** (*doxas*, lit. "glories"): a term used for angels in the Dead Sea Scrolls (1QH 10.8) and in other early literature (2 Enoch 22:7, 10; *Ascension of Isaiah* 9:32; probably also Exod. 15:11 LXX, "Who among the gods (*doxais*) is like you, O Lord?" The term "glories" is used of angels because they share or reflect the glory of God.

9 / **"The Lord rebuke you!"** According to the account in the *Assumption of Moses*, the devil was silenced and fled. Michael was left in peace to bury Moses' body. A forensic plea similar to Michael's appears in v. 2 of Zech. 3, a chapter quoted again later by Jude (vv. 22–23). The Greek verb for **rebuke** (*epitimēsai*) is in the optative mood, used to express a desire.

The term **archangel** (*archangelos*) occurs in the NT only here and in 1 Thess. 4:16. Elsewhere *archangelos* is used of the most senior angels, numbering four (1 Enoch 40:9) or seven (1 Enoch 20:7; cf. Rev. 8:2) and also called "the angel of the [divine] Presence." **Michael** is their leader, "the chief of the holy angels" (*Asc. Isa.* 3:16), and especially acts as the guardian angel of the Jews against their godless enemies in Greece and Persia (Dan. 10:13, 21; 12:1; 1 Enoch 20:5; 89:76; 1QM 17). Michael is therefore the main adversary of Satan.

10 / **Speak abusively against** (*blasphēmousin*): The Greek word echoes "slander (*blasphēmousin*) celestial beings" (v. 8), and "a slanderous (*blasphēmias*) accusation" (v. 9).

They do not understand: cf. 1 Cor. 2:7–16. *T. Asher* 7.1 refers to "Sodom, which did not recognize the angels of the Lord, and perished forever."

Unreasoning animals is not a disparaging description but translates the regular Greek formula *aloga zōa* for the animal creation, brute beasts (Wisd. of Sol. 11:15; 4 Macc. 14:14, 18; Josephus, *Ag. Ap.* 1.224; 2.213; *Ant.* 10.262; *War* 4.170; Philo, *On the Virtues* 117; *On the Contemplative Life* 8; see *TDNT*, vol. 4, p. 141).

§6 Three Examples of Wickedness (Jude 11)

11 / **Woe** (*ouai*) **to them!** is a phrase typical of OT prophets, but it is not necessarily threatening language. The onomatapoeic *ouai* can indicate either a denunciation or a lament (the latter most clearly in Matt. 24:19). So Jude may be as much expressing Christian grief at the spiritual blindness of the false teachers as invoking their condemnation, for they themselves are heading for destruction.

In verses 5–7 Jude quoted three OT passages to portray the infiltrators as sinners in quite general terms. Now he uses three more OT illustrations to take his charge a step further. **Cain, Balaam,** and **Korah** were three notorious individuals who led others astray by their example. In other words they, like the infiltrators now, were by their actions false teachers.

The infiltrators **have taken the way of Cain**, that is, their attitude and conduct are like his. **Cain** murdered his own brother (Gen. 4:1–15), so Jude may be implying that the false teachers in his sights are Cain's spiritual descendants and nothing better than the destroyers of souls. Jewish tradition enlarged upon the biblical account and considered Cain to be the type of selfish, cynical, and materialistic individual who neither takes God into account nor in practice believes in a moral order. The Jerusalem Targum on Genesis 4:8 portrays Cain as saying: "There is no judgment, no judge, no world to come; no reward will be given to the righteous, and no destruction meted out to the wicked." So one who takes the attitude of a Cain feels free to do as he or she likes, and Cain's example misleads others: Cain is the archetypal false teacher.

According to the OT account, **Balaam** first refused fees or bribes to curse Israel (Num. 22:7–18), but eventually the monetary lure proved too strong to be resisted (Deut. 23:4), and he fell into **error** (*planē*, a wandering off from the right way). As a consequence, he led others astray. In the OT account, Balaam's advice to Balak is never spelled out. But comparing Numbers 25:1–2 with Numbers 31:16 suggests that Balaam was guilty of inciting Israel to lie with Moabite women, who in turn seduced Israel into worshiping Baal. That broke the first of the Ten Commandments, "You shall have no other gods before me" (Exod. 20:3). By the first century A.D., Balaam was considered a notorious character in Jewish tradition. So Jude's readers would readily pick up the meaning of the allusion. At the time Jude was writing, the name of Balaam was a byword for antinomianism (Rev. 2:14).

Grammatically, **Balaam's error** can be taken in a passive sense (they too are victims of the weakness that seduced Balaam) or an active sense (they seduce others in the way he did). In either case the false prophets are motivated by greed: the prophets are out for **profit** (also v. 16), a vice not unknown among teachers in NT times (1 Tim. 6:5; Titus 1:11; Didache 11.5–6).

The end of such men is inevitable. **They have been destroyed in Korah's rebellion**: they are as good as dead. As in the case of Korah and his confederates, the false teachers of Jude's day may well have been sowing unrest and promoting discontent against the authority of church leaders. Korah, with Reubenites Dothan and his brother Abiram, and On, and two hundred and fifty other agitators, had rebelled against the divinely appointed authority of Moses and Aaron (Num. 16). The mutineers' punishment was swift and dramatic—the earth gave way beneath their feet and swallowed them alive. Some sort of fearful fate for the false teachers is as certain.

Additional Notes   §6

---

11 / **Way** (*hodos*): "road"; metaphorically, "a course of conduct." **Taken** translates *eporeuthēsan*, "travelled"; metaphorically, "followed in the footsteps, copied the example." Jude again uses the verb *poreuesthai* in vv. 16 and 18 ("they *follow* their own evil/ungodly desires").

Cain is also mentioned in Heb. 11:4, where he is contrasted with his brother Abel who held nothing back from God. In 1 John 3:12, he is mentioned again; this time it concerns the murderous hostility of the wicked against the godly. Irenaeus (*Against Heresies* 1.31.1) mentions a second-century Gnostic sect who called themselves Cainites (cf. Epiphanius (*Panarion* 38.1.1–3). They regarded the God of the OT as responsible for the evil in the world, and so hailed those who resisted him as heroes, e.g., Cain, Esau, Korah.

They have rushed for profit into Balaam's error (*misthou exechythēsan*): "They went headlong for a reward," genitive of quality (Moule, *Idiom-Book*, p. 39). The verb is the passive aorist of *ekchein*, to pour out: "they were poured out," i.e., "they plunged." Bengel suggests "streamed forth like a torrent without a dam" (*Gnomen*, vol. 5, p. 166).

Balaam's error: In the NT *planē* (**error**) always refers to deceit in morals or religion (Matt. 27:64; Rom. 1:27; Eph. 4:14; 1 Thess. 2:3; James 5:20; 2 Pet. 2:18; 3:17). Cain and Korah are not mentioned in the parallel passage (2 Pet. 2:15).

Destroyed is a Greek aorist (*apōlonto*) and equivalent to a prophetic perfect: their frightful fate is settled.

Korah's rebellion: In a similar context regarding false teachers endangering the faith of others, 2 Tim. 2:19 ("The Lord knows those who are his") is also probably alluding to the Korah tradition; cf. Num. 16:5: "The Lord will show who belongs to him."

From comparing the libertines with notorious OT sinners, Jude goes on to portray the objects of his invective in a series of colorful and barbed metaphors. His word-pictures correspond to the four regions of the physical world: clouds in the air, trees on the earth, waves of the sea, stars in the heavens.

12 / In saying that **These men are blemishes** (*spilades*) **at your love feasts**, Jude uses a word that occurs nowhere else in the NT and has two meanings. Both fit the context. The commentators are equally divided between "rocks washed by the sea, reefs" (ASV, Weymouth, NASB) and "spots, blots, blemishes, stains" (KJV, NEB, Phillips, RSV). Jude is warning, either that the false teachers are like treacherous reefs and can shipwreck one's faith (1 Tim. 1:19), or that these immoral men pollute the fellowship meals by their very presence.

These men pose a dangerous threat **at your love feasts**. This is the earliest mention of the love feast (*agapē*). In the early days the *agapē* was a meal of fellowship in the house-churches on the Lord's Day. The meal was shared by all the members, of whatever class of society, with each one bringing a contribution of food, according to ability. In practice, it sometimes fell short of the ideal (cf. what happens at the Lord's Supper in 1 Cor. 11:17–22). Jude warns that the infiltrators are seeking to take advantage of what was intended to be a fellowship of Christian love, and threatening to wreck it by their perfidious teaching. Yet they are acting quite shamelessly, **eating with you without the slightest qualm—shepherds who feed only themselves**, lit. "shepherding themselves." Evidently these men were making sure that they looked after their own greedy self-interests at the gatherings (1 Cor. 11:20–22), not unlike the scene painted in Ezek. 34:2, 8, 10. The sort of thing that could go on is indicated by Didache 11.9, which declares that no prophet who (supposedly "in the spirit") orders a meal is to eat of it, or else he is not a true prophet.

Such men are like **clouds without rain**, which disappoint the farmer's hopes. They promise much, but fail to provide. All they do is to obscure the light. Just as clouds are **blown along by the wind**, so these men are carried along by their own verbosity, and their words supply no life-giving refreshment. These men are spiritually dead, for they exhibit no spiritual fruit in their lives. They are like **autumn trees**, which, after having had the opportunities of a full season of growth, ought to be laden. But they are **without fruit**, barren. They have failed to fulfill their purpose. They are **twice dead**, since as a consequence of their fruitlessness, the farmer destroys them (Matt. 7:19).

13 / Jude carries on with his vivid word-pictures. **They are wild waves of the sea, foaming up their shame.** Undisciplined, out of control, all they do by their feverish surging is to stir up rubbish and spew it on to the shore—never a pretty sight. Barclay (p. 195) describes how the waters of the Dead Sea are so pregnated with salt that they strip the bark off driftwood. When such wood is thrown ashore, it gleams bleak and white, more like a pile of dried dead bones than a branch from a living tree.

These men are **wandering stars**: navigators cannot safely chart a course by them. The Greek term (*planētai*) suggests that the reference is probably to planets, whose irregular movements were not then understood. Ancient lore associated the planets with disobedient angels (hence Jude's use of the personal pronoun **whom**). The false teachers had wandered off course because of their rebellion against God. Their destiny is settled: **for whom the blackest darkness has been reserved forever**. Their utterly hopeless and fearful doom is underlined by the double expression **blackest darkness**.

In verses 12–13 Jude has splashed a series of vivid pictures of the false teachers. They are as dangerous as reefs, as selfish as greedy shepherds, as deceptive as rainless clouds, as dead as barren trees, as polluted as the foaming sea. They are doomed as surely as the fallen angels.

Additional Notes §7

---

12 / **These men** in the Greek is a single disparaging word, *houtoi*, *these*, and is witheringly reiterated six times (vv. 8, 10, 12, 14, 16, 19). The same caustic curt reference to enemies of the gospel is frequent in apocalyptic writings (e.g., Rev. 7:14; 11:4; 14:4; 1 Enoch 46:3; 2 Enoch 7:3; 18:3).

Blemishes as a translation of *spilades* is in fact rare; only one other example is known, and that is from the 4th century A.D. So, despite Jude's use of the corresponding verb *spiloun* to mean "to stain" in v. 23, "rock" is the more likely translation here. It certainly makes good sense. These men are like treacherous reefs to others sailing the sea of faith.

Shepherds as a metaphor for "ministers" is frequent in both OT and NT (e.g., Num. 27:16–17; Eccles. 12:11; Ezek. 34:1–10; John 21:15–17; 1 Pet. 2:25).

Uprooted: The uprooting of a useless tree is a biblical metaphor for judgment (Deut. 28:63; Ps. 52:5; Wisd. of Sol. 4:4; Matt. 15:13). Such trees were commonly burned (Matt. 3:10; 7:19; John 15:6).

Twice dead: cf. Heb. 10:29; Rev. 20:14.

13 / **Wild** (*agrios*, untamed) is used of waves in Wisd. of Sol. 14:1. **Wild waves . . . foaming up** reflects the Hebrew of Isa. 57:10, "But the wicked are like the tossing sea, which cannot rest, whose waves cast up mire and mud."

Foaming up translates the Greek verb *epaphrizein*, found only here in the NT. The Greek poet Moschus (*Idylls* 5.5) uses it to describe seaweed and other flotsam being carried along on the crest of a wave before being dumped on the shore.

Shame is plural in the Greek and could refer to these men's deeds or to their words (or both). In either case, their effect is to spoil, not to edify; to soil, not to beautify the lives they touch.

Wandering stars (*planētai*): There is a play on words between *planētai*, wanderers off course, and *planē*, error (v. 11). Theophilus of Antioch (late second century) uses similar language. The righteous are law-abiding, like fixed stars. But planets "are types of men who separate themselves from God, abandoning his law and its commands" (*To Autolycus* 2.15.47–49).

14–15 / Jude supports his words by citing a prophecy. This is taken, not from the canonical OT, as is usual with NT writers, but from a popular writing of the day which his readers would appreciate. Jude quotes, nearly verbatim, from the book of Enoch, which reads: "And behold, he cometh with ten thousands of his holy ones to execute judgment upon all, and to destroy all the ungodly; and to convict all flesh of all the works of their ungodliness which they have ungodly committed, and of all the hard things which ungodly sinners have spoken against him" (1 Enoch 1:9). Jude is not treating a favorite tract of the time as inspired Scripture, but doing what every preacher should do: he is employing contemporary language, readily understood by those he addresses.

Irenaeus (*Against Heresies* 4.16.2) points out the appropriateness of the reference here to **Enoch**. Whereas the wicked angels mentioned earlier had forfeited their heavenly home on account of their disobedience, Enoch gained his place in heaven by obeying God. His remarkable spirituality is described as a walk with God (Gen. 5:22, 24).

Jude calls him **the seventh from Adam** (counting inclusively, as was the custom: there are five names between Adam and Enoch in the lists of Gen. 5:3–24 and 1 Chron. 1:1–3). To the Jew, *seven* was the "perfect" number, signifying completion (as in "sabbath," the seventh day, marking the completion of creation; Gen. 2:2). The application of **seventh** to Enoch would be taken as adding weight to the authority of his words.

Jude interprets "he cometh" in the prophecy he quotes from the book of Enoch as applying to the second coming of Christ. When Jesus returns in glory, it will be with **thousands upon thousands** (*myriasin*; RSV, "myriads") **of his holy ones**, that is, angels forming a heavenly army beyond reckoning. Jesus is coming in order **to judge everyone**, by which is meant all the ungodly (v. 4). He has been authorized to pass sentence as judge by God the Father (John 5:27–30). The sonorous repetition **ungodly . . . ungodly . . . ungodly . . . ungodly** drives home the solemnity and certainty of judgment against these evil men, like so many nails in their coffin, on account of both their **acts** and their **words**.

16 / These men are **grumblers** (*gongystai*) and **faultfinders** (*mempsimoiroi*), both Greek terms occurring in the NT only here. The splendidly onomatopoeic *gongystai* is used in the LXX of the Israelites who grumbled against God in the wilderness (Exod. 15:24; 17:3; Num. 14:29). These men, too, Jude is saying, are complaining against God and his directions for living, preferring their own way—but then blaming God for anything that goes wrong for them. The *mempsimoiros* was well known in Greek literature as a discontent, always finding something to moan about in his lot. His attitude is exactly the converse of Paul's "godliness with contentment is great gain" (1 Tim. 6:6).

They follow (lit. "are journeying down the road of") **their own evil desires**, for they reject divine authority. "To them self-discipline and self-control are nothing; to them the moral law is only a burden and a nuisance; honour and duty have no claim upon them; they have no desire to serve and no sense of responsibility. Their one value is pleasure and their one dynamic is desire" (Barclay, p. 198). Furthermore, **they boast about themselves**, engaging in bombastic speech in an effort to impress. They are quite prepared to **flatter others** if they think they can wheedle something out of them **to their own advantage**. The false teachers both bluster and fawn.

Additional Notes   §8

---

14 / **Enoch** is also mentioned in the NT in Luke 3:37 (as an ancestor of Jesus) and in Heb. 11:5 (as a hero of faith).

The seventh from Adam is the usual description of Enoch in Jewish writings (1 Enoch 60:8; 93:3; Philo, *On the Posterity and Exile of Cain* 173; Jubilees 7:39; *Lev. Rabbah* 29.11).

The Lord is coming is lit. "came," (*ēlthen*), the Greek aorist used prophetically (as in 1 Kings 22:17, "I saw all Israel scattered").

With thousands upon thousands of his holy ones: angels, the heavenly army attending the returning Lord of glory (Deut. 33:2; Dan. 7:10; Zech. 14:5; Matt. 16:27; 25:31; Mark 8:38; Luke 9:26; 2 Thess. 1:7).

15 / The evil men's words are described as **harsh** (*sklēros*, hard, rough). In 1 Enoch 27:2, Uriel speaks of the valley in which are confined all those who have spoken hard things against the glory of the Lord.

16 / **Faultfinders** (*mempsimoiroi*): "You are satisfied by nothing that befalls you; you complain about everything. You don't want what you have got; you long for what you haven't got. In winter, you wish it were summer, and in summer that it was winter. You are like some sick people, hard to please and a *mempsimoiros*!" (Lucian, *Cynic* 17).

They boast about themselves (*to stoma autōn lalei hyperonka*): lit. "their mouth talks big." The Greek expression *lalei hyperonka* does not appear elsewhere in the NT, but it is used of Antiochus Epiphanes' blasphemous utterance against God in Theodotian's version of Dan. 11:36.

§9   Peril Foretold by Apostles (Jude 17–19)

17 / Jude now turns from his series of illustrations provided by OT types and prophecies (vv. 5–16) to remind his readers of a much more contemporary voice. They are urged not only to recall what the inspired writers of earlier centuries have foretold, but to **remember** that in their own day **the apostles of our Lord Jesus Christ** have warned of the rise of false teachers. The constantly needed admonition to **remember** is frequently repeated in the Scriptures. Forgetfulness of divine directions inevitably tends to spiritual weakness: one degeneration (of mind) leads to another (of soul).

18 / The reassuring apostolic words that Jude now goes on to mention are not recorded elsewhere in the NT, except in 2 Pet. 3:3; but it is unlikely that Jude is quoting from 2 Peter (see Introduction, pp. 13–14, 18). **They said** (*elegon*) is imperfect, "they used to say," and could indicate that Jude's readers heard first hand at least some members of the apostolic band in days gone by. Be that as it may, they were well aware of the tenor of the warning which the apostles were in the habit of giving.

The NT writers were convinced that they were living **in the last times,** an expression they frequently used to describe the days that would usher in the messianic kingdom and the return of Christ in glory. A sign of their nearness will be attacks on the Christian faith by those Jude calls **scoffers.** In the parallel passage in 2 Peter 3:3–4, the scoffing takes the form of scorning the orthodox belief in the second coming. Jude applies the scoffing to libertines who deride believers that refuse to join them in taking advantage of their Christian liberty to **follow their own ungodly desires.** Jude had made the same point earlier in his letter when he described such men as those "who change the grace of our God into a license for immorality" (v. 4).

19 / **These are the men** (translating the contemptuous single Greek word *houtoi* once more) **who divide** (*apodiorizein*). The Greek verb occurs in the NT only here and rarely elsewhere, and means "to mark out boundaries in order to separate." By the way these men are carrying on, they are in effect drawing a circle around themselves with the purpose of shutting out other people, whereas such a circle should be drawn to include others. Their false teaching is tending to split up the church membership into those who **follow mere natural instincts** and those who are truly spiritual.

Jude's irony is evident. The men who are setting themselves up as the spiritual élite above all the rest are themselves the unspiritual ones. They can properly be described as Pharisees in the popular sense of the term, for that name means "separated ones." Far from being a spiritual aristocracy, these men in fact **do not have the Spirit**. They are not Christians at all (Rom. 8:9) and thus fail to understand the things of God (1 Cor. 2:14). They are not on the right wave-length. But the arrival of such alien intruders was foreseen by the apostles (v. 17), and they gave due warning of what was going to happen (1 Cor. 11:19). In that Jude's readers can take comfort: things are working out exactly as spiritually minded believers have forecast. The doom of the false and the glorifying of the true are alike sure to follow.

Additional Notes §9

---

17 / **But, dear friends**: The emphatic **but** linked with Jude's direct address of his readers as **dear friends** (*agapētoi*, beloved ones, as in v. 3, and later in v. 20) signals a contrasting change of tone.

Remember is a frequent and needful warning to God's people all through both Testaments: see, for example, Exod. 20:8; Num. 15:40; Deut. 7:18; 8:2; Josh. 1:13; Eccles. 12:1; Isa. 46:9; Mal. 4:4; Matt. 16:9; Luke 22:19; 24:6; 2 Tim. 2:8; Rev. 3:3.

18 / **They said**: A similar warning about scoffers is repeated in Acts 20:29; 1 Tim. 4:1; 2 Tim. 3:1–5; Didache 16.3. Jesus himself had alerted disciples to the certain rise of those who could lead others astray (Mark 13:5–6, 21–22).

In the last times (*ep' eschatou tou chronou*): The same notion is rendered in several ways in the LXX and in early Christian literature, often using *hēmerai* (days), but sometimes reading *kairos* (season), as in 1 Tim. 4:1; 1 Pet. 1:5; Didache 16.2); *chronos* (time) occurs in the phrase only here in v. 18 and in 1 Pet. 1:20.

Scoffers (*empaiktai*): The Greek term is found in the NT only here and in 2 Pet. 3:3 and has overtones of "persecution" (see Turner, p. 141; *TDNT*, vol. 5, p. 633). In the OT, the "scoffer" is one who spurns religion and morality (Ps. 1:1; Prov. 1:22).

Desires (*epithymia*) can be a longing for some good, as with Jesus wanting to share the Last Supper (Luke 22:15) and in Paul's desiring to depart this life to be with Christ (Phil. 1:23) or to see the Thessalonians again (1 Thess. 2:17). But usually *epithymia* means an unsavory craving for evil.

19 / **These are the men** translates the contemptuous single Greek word *houtoi* once more, as in v. 16.

The Greek verb *apodiorizein*, **divide**, occurs in the NT only here and rarely elsewhere. It is used by Aristotle (*Politics* 4.3.9) to mean "to define exactly with a view to classifying." A simpler form of the verb appears in Deut. 20:24 LXX, where God says he has set the Israelites apart from other nations. They are special in God's sight. **Men who divide** (there is no **you** in the Greek) means those who are divisive, creating factions and cliques in the church.

§10 Call to Persevere (Jude 20–23)

20 / The contrast Jude draws is highlighted as he again speaks directly to his readers and comes to the heart of his letter. He has already said that he is writing to urge them to "contend for the faith" (v. 3). Now he explains what this means in practical terms. His manner of address sets the foundation. As in verses 3 and 17, his readers are **dear friends**, the NIV translation of the Greek *agapētoi*, "beloved ones," that is, beloved by God, because they share in the same spiritual relationship as do Jude and all true believers.

The infiltrators are doing their utmost to disrupt the Christian fellowship and to break it down. Jude's friends, by contrast, are to concentrate on a spiritual construction program. **Build yourselves up in your most holy faith**, he tells them. This is to be achieved by an ever deepening grasp of what God in Christ has done for them, according to the teaching handed down by the apostles (v. 3). Although Jude does not spell it out, this building up is the consequence of Bible study, meditating upon the word of God as recorded in the Scriptures, as other early Christian writers consistently make clear.

But it has to be borne in mind that Jude's exhortation is addressed to the whole body of believers. He is not suggesting that individuals should concern themselves only with their own spiritual progress. All have a part to play in strengthening the Christian community as a whole. The biblical metaphor of "building up, edifying" is invariably communal, not individual (1 Cor. 14:12, 26; 1 Thess. 5:11; 1 Pet. 2:5).

The Christian faith is described as **most holy** because it comes to us not through human reasoning but by revelation of the holy God about himself. The basic biblical meaning of "holy" is "set apart as different." The **most holy faith** is one that is different from all other religions in being unique in its message and in its moral transforming power.

The readers must also **pray in the Holy Spirit** (John 4:23–24; Gal. 4:6; Eph. 6:18), an expression that includes, but is not confined to, praying in tongues (1 Cor. 14:15–16). God's Spirit alone can teach believers how to pray aright (Rom. 8:26). Without him, prayer can easily become self-centered or at best off-course. Such Spirit-prompted prayer is vital to the Christian life and its development. By contrast, the false teachers, since they do not have the Spirit (v. 19), cannot pray aright—and perhaps they do not even pray at all, as some "advanced" modern-day professing Christians freely admit. But Jude clearly implies that prayer has a major role in building up Christian life.

21 / Jude exhorts his readers, **Keep yourselves in God's love**. That love was responsible for their call to faith in the first place (v. 1). But believers have their part to play. They must continue to respond to God's love (John 15:9–10; Rom. 8:35–39; 1 John 4:16) and thereby maintain and strengthen their relationship with him. The false teachers have demonstrated that it is all too possible to turn away from God's love (Rev. 2:4) and as a consequence to cool in their love for others.

Persistence is called for in this matter, as in so many other aspects of the Christian life. The final outcome for believers is assured, and this certain hope is referred to by the words **as you wait**. Yet this expectant attitude toward the future must be balanced. "If too great attention is paid to the future hope, the Christian tends to become so other-worldly that he is not much use in this world. If, however, as is the greater danger today, the future element is soft-pedalled, Christianity becomes a mere religious adjunct to the social services" (Green, p. 185).

All God's gifts to the believer are due to the divine **mercy**, a note struck in the opening prayer (v. 1). God has committed the final judgment to the **Lord Jesus Christ** (John 5:22), and it is he who will **bring you to eternal life**, for that life is his gift (John 17:2). It begins in this world, and will be known in all its fullness in the next.

22–23 / Having urged his readers to develop their spiritual life, Jude turns to the practical expression of that life in service to others, and in particular toward those who have been infected by false teaching. **Be merciful to those who doubt**: "There are some doubting souls who need your pity" (NEB). These are church members who have fallen under the influence of the false teachers, but have not yet succumbed to their blandishments. So it is not too late for them to be recovered by the efforts of faithful believers.

In some cases, more urgent and vigorous steps need to be taken: **snatch others from the fire and save them**. The verbal imagery is from Zechariah 3:2, "a burning stick snatched from the fire." Rescue from destruction is still possible for those in spiritual peril. **To others show mercy, mixed with fear**. The exercise of Christian mercy in seeking to restore those who have been infected by immoral and corrupting teaching must be qualified by caution. True believers can easily be contaminated themselves, if they are not on their guard. **Hating even the clothing stained by corrupted flesh** is another vivid image from the same passage in Zechariah (3:3–5). As Jude's readers will be well aware, Zechariah goes on to speak of clean clothes replacing the filthy garments, a picture of God's mercy in forgiveness and restoration.

Additional Notes §10

---

20 / The Greek verb in **build yourselves up** is *epoikodomein*, lit. to build upon (*epi*-), and is used in secular Greek of, for example, erecting a wall. In the NT the meaning is always metaphorical. It applies to the spiritual growth of believers and is closely associated with the judgment seat of Christ. It points to what God's grace has achieved in the believer's life (1 Cor. 3:10, 12), whether or not the believer has been truly building in the spiritual sense (1 Cor. 3:14). The church is composed of elect and precious stones (1 Pet. 2:5), built on Jesus Christ as the chief cornerstone and on the apostles and prophets (Eph. 2:20; Col. 2:7). The believer's part in the building-up process is often related to the study of the Scriptures (2 Tim. 2:15; Heb. 5:12; Polycarp, *To the Philippians* 3: "If you study the epistles of the blessed apostle Paul, you can be built up in the faith given to you."

Verses 20 and 21 together foreshadow trinitarian theology with their reference to the **Holy Spirit . . . God . . . Lord Jesus Christ**. The NT evidence on the subject of the Trinity is surveyed by R. T. France, *The Living God* (Leicester: InterVarsity Press, 1970).

Pray in the Holy Spirit: "A reference to charismatic prayer, including glossolalic prayer, may therefore be presumed for Jude 20" (J. D. G. Dunn, *Jesus and the Spirit*. London: SCM Press, 1975, pp. 245–46).

21 / **Eternal life**: in this world: John 3:36; Eph. 2:5; 1 Pet. 1:3; 1 John 5:13; in the next: Matt. 25:46; Rom. 2:7; Gal. 6:8; 1 Tim. 6:19; Titus 3:7; Rev. 22:1–5.

22–23 / The Greek MSS show many differences and give rise to a number of translations. Apart from textual variations of individual words, some MSS refer to *two* classes of people ("on some have compassion; others save with fear"). Other MSS refer to *three* classes (those who doubt; others who are snatched from the fire; and a third group who receive pity). The earliest known MS of Jude (P⁷², third century) has the shortest text of any, and omits v. 22: "Snatch some from the fire, but on those who dispute/doubt have mercy with fear." In view of Jude's predilection for arranging his material in threes (see vv. 2, 4, 5–7, 8, 11), the original text may well have concerned *three* classes of people. This is the view taken by NIV, and follows the recommendation of Bruce M. Metzger, *A Textual Commentary on the Greek New Testament* (New York/London: United Bible Societies, 3rd ed. 1971), pp. 727–29.

22 / **Those who doubt** (*diakrinomenous*): The Greek verb has already been used in v. 9 ("disputing"), but here it is in the middle form, meaning "be doubtful, waver."

23 / **Fire** is reserved for the punishment of the impenitent wicked on the last day (Matt. 18:8, 9; 25:41).

Clothing (*chitōn*): an undergarment worn next to the skin, and by both sexes. The image of "stained clothing" is taken up by the glorified Christ in his verdict on the church at Sardis (Rev. 3:4).

§11   Doxology (Jude 24–25)

24 / Jude ends his letter with a great ascription of praise. Having bidden his readers "to keep (*tērein*) themselves in God's love" (v. 21), Jude balances that thought with the assurance that for his part God **is able to keep** (*phylassein*) **you from falling** into the sins of the false teachers. It is a reminder that in facing temptation the believer must depend not on personal, inner strength but on the power of God. Jude's two different Greek verbs, while synonyms (and both rightly translated "keep"), have a slightly different emphasis: *tērein* means "to have watchful care," while *phylassein* is "to stand guard," implying custody and protection. So the dual thought is that it is the believer's duty to keep him or herself in God's love by maintaining a steady gaze upon God; it is God's responsibility to do the active protecting from evil attack, however open or insidious that onslaught may be.

God is able to keep believers **from falling**. The Greek is more exactly translated "without stumbling." It does not necessarily imply falling flat on one's face. God can keep us from lesser as well as greater temptations. The grace of divine strength and ability is available for those who will draw upon it (1 Cor. 10:13).

On a more positive note, God can make us, frail and liable to sin as we are, fit to stand in his glorious presence **without fault**, *amōmos*. The Greek word is a sacrificial term and applied in the OT to perfect animals suitable to be offered on the altar to God (Exod. 29:38; Lev. 1:3; 3:1). God can do still more. He can bring us into his presence, not with the fear and shame that would be appropriate to our characters, but **with great joy**, his great joy as well as ours. God's supreme object is to make the church of believers fit to be presented to himself (Eph. 5:27) as a sacrificial offering, "through" the actual perfect sacrifice of "Jesus Christ our Lord" (1 Pet. 1:19). The same thought is in Eph. 1:4; Col. 1:22; 1 Thess. 3:13.

25 / He is our **only God**. The expression reflects Israel's creed "Hear, O Israel: the Lord our God, the Lord is one" (Deut. 6:4). While the further descriptive term **our Savior** is one that the NT more usually applies to Jesus Christ, Jude is not alone in speaking of God as Savior (see Luke 1:47; 1 Tim. 1:1; 2:3; 4:10; Titus 1:3; 2:10; 3:4). What follows is not a prayer (which would make nonsense of **before all ages**) but a declaration of praise: **be** [not in the Greek] **glory, majesty, power, and authority**. The four terms describe God's attributes. **Glory** is the essential radiance of divine light; the word for **power** means dominion, the absolute control God has over his world, which ensures his ultimate triumph over all opposition from whatever source; transcendent **majesty** is applied only to the Father (Heb. 1:3; 8:1); **authority** expresses his sovereign ability to do all that is necessary to met human needs (delegated to the risen Christ, Matt. 28:18).

The expression **before all ages, now, and forevermore** is the best words can do to cover the past, the present, and the future (cf. Heb. 13:8), and thus it further emphasizes God's total and complete charge of all. The final **Amen** is the Hebrew affirmation "So be it!" and it has from the earliest days of the church regularly concluded prayers and doxologies.

Additional Notes §11

---

24 / **To him who is able to keep** completes a trio of NT doxologies that begin in this way (see Rom. 16:25; Eph. 3:20; cf. 2 Cor. 9:8). The wording in Jude and Romans is similar enough to suggest that a doxology along these lines was widely used in the liturgy of the early church.

With great joy (*en agalliasei*): God's joy as well as that of the believer. The Greek noun *agalliasis* is rare and found only in the NT (Luke 1:14, 44; Acts 2:46; Heb. 1:9) and in 1 Enoch 5:9; *Martyrdom of Polycarp* 18.3.

God's ability **to keep** is often emphasized in the NT: John 10:28–29, "no one can snatch them out of my hand"; Rom. 14:4, "the Lord is able to make him stand"; 1 Pet. 1:5, "who through faith are shielded (*tērein*) by God's power." See also Eph. 3:20; 2 Tim. 1:12; Heb. 7:25.

From falling translates *aptaistos*, without stumbling, not tripping over, sure-footed, and occurs in the NT only here. But the thought is frequent in Scripture: cf. "He will not let your foot slip" (Ps. 121:3); see also the lovely expression used three times in the OT (KJV): "he makes my feet like hinds' feet" (2 Sam. 22:34; Ps. 18:33; Hab. 3:19). The hind is more sure-footed and can climb higher than any other mountain creature, outdoing even her mate, the hart.

Presence (*katenōpion*) occurs only here and in Eph. 1:4; Col. 1:22; Polycarp, *To the Philippians* 5.2.

Without fault (*amōmos*) also appears in Eph. 1:4; 5:27; Phil. 2:15; Col. 1:22; Rev. 14:5. The sacrificial reference is most explicit in Heb. 9:14 and 1 Pet. 1:19.

Great joy (*agalliasis*) occurs in messianic and eschatological contexts. Luke 1:14 refers to Zechariah's coming joy and delight at the birth of Messiah's forerunner; in Luke 1:44 Zechariah's wife Elizabeth declares that the babe in her womb leapt for joy at Mary's greeting; Acts 2:46 expresses the first believers' joy at their breaking of bread, which was to be "until he comes" (1 Cor. 11:26); Heb. 1:9 applies Ps. 45:7 to the joyful anointing of the Son as messianic king (see Turner, pp. 148–50). Rabbis associated the eschatological theme of ecstatic joy (at the drawing of water in the Feast of Tabernacles) with the future outpouring of the Holy Spirit, in view of Isa. 12:3 (b. *Sukka* 55). See *TDNT*, vol. 1, pp. 19–21; Hillyer, "First Peter and the Feast of Tabernacles," *TynB* 21 (1970), pp. 39–70.

25 / **To the only God**: As in v. 2 (see Additional Note), the concluding doxology finds another parallel in *The Martyrdom of Polycarp* (20): "To him who is able to bring us all in his grace and bounty to his heavenly kingdom through his only-begotten child Jesus Christ, be glory, honor, dominion, and majesty forever."

The term **Savior** is relatively infrequent in the NT (24 times; by contrast the name Christ occurs on nearly 600 occasions). This may well be due to the fact that Savior was a title commonly used both in the Greek mystery religions (of Asclepius, the god of healing) and in emperor worship. See *NIDNTT*, vol. 3, pp. 219–21.

Amen, along with *Hosanna* and *Alleluia*, are the only three words which are transliterated straight into all other languages, whenever translations of the Bible are made.

For Further Reading

Commentaries

Barclay, W. *The Letters of James and Peter*. Rev. ed. DSB. Philadelphia: Westminster, 1975.

_____. *The Letters of John and Jude*. Rev. ed. DSB. Philadelphia: Westminster, 1975.

Bauckham, R. J. *Jude, 2 Peter*. WBC 50. Waco: Word, 1983.

Beare, F. W. *The First Epistle of Peter*. Oxford: Blackwell, 3rd ed., 1970.

Best, E. *1 Peter*. NCB. London: Oliphants, 1971.

Bigg, C. *A Critical and Exegetical Commentary on the Epistles of St Peter and St Jude*. ICC. Edinburgh: T. & T. Clark, 1901.

Calvin, J. *Commentaries on the Catholic Epistles: The Epistle of Jude; The First Epistle of Peter; The Second Epistle of Peter*. Ed. and trans. by J. Owen. Grand Rapids: Eerdmans, 1948.

Cranfield, C. E. B. *1 and 2 Peter and Jude*. TBC. London: SCM Press, 1960.

Green, E. M. B. *The Second Epistle General of Peter and the General Epistle of Jude*. TNTC. Grand Rapids: Eerdmans, 1968.

Grudem, W. *1 Peter*. TNTC. Leicester: InterVarsity Press/Grand Rapids: Eerdmans, 1988.

Kelly, J. N .D. *A Commentary on the Epistles of Peter and Jude*. ThC. Grand Rapids: Baker, 1981.

Leighton, R. (d. 1684). *A Practical Commentary upon the First Epistle of St Peter*, 2 vols. London: SPCK, n.d.; reprint Grand Rapids: Kregel, 1972.

Lenski, R. C. H. *The Interpretation of the Epistles of St Peter, St John and St Jude*. Minneapolis: Augsburg, 1966.

Marshall, I. H. *1 Peter*. Leicester/Downers Grove: InterVarsity, 1991.

Mayor, J. B. *The Epistle of St Jude and the Second Epistle of St Peter*. London: Macmillan, 1907; reprint Grand Rapids: Baker, 1965.

Michaels, J. R. *1 Peter*. WBC 49. Waco: Word, 1988.

Moffatt, J. *The General Epistles: James, Peter and Judas*. MNTC. London: Hodder and Stoughton, 1928.

Mounce, R. H. *A Living Hope: A Commentary on 1 and 2 Peter*. Grand Rapids: Eerdmans, 1982.

Plumptre, E. H. *The General Epistles of St Peter and St Jude*. Cambridge: Cambridge University Press, 1892.

Selwyn, E. G. *The First Epistle of St Peter: The Greek Text with Introduction, Notes, and Essays*. London: Macmillan, 1949.

Stibbs, A. M., and A. F. Walls. *The First Epistle General of Peter*. TNTC. Grand Rapids: Eerdmans, 1960.

Wand, J. W. C. *The General Epistles of St Peter and St Jude*. WC. London: Methuen, 1934.

Studies

Brown, R. E., K. P. Donfried, and J. Reumann (eds.). *Peter in the New Testament*. Minneapolis: Augsburg/New York: Paulist Press, 1973.

Clowney, E. P. *The Message of 1 Peter*. Leicester/Downers Grove: InterVarsity Press, 1988.

Cross, F. L. *1 Peter, A Paschal Liturgy*. London: Mowbray, 1970.

Cullmann, O. *Peter: Disciple, Apostle, Martyr*. London: SCM Press, 1953.

Dalton, W. J. *Christ's Proclamation to the Spirits: A Study of 1 Peter 3:18—4:16*. Analecta Biblica 23. Rome: Pontifical Biblical Institute, 1964.

Daube, D. "Participle and Imperative in 1 Peter." In *The First Epistle of Peter*. Edited by E. G. Selwyn. Pages 467–88. London: Macmillan, 1947.

Detzler, W. *Living Words in 1 Peter*. Welwyn: Evangelical Press, 1982.

Elliott, J. H. *The Elect and the Holy: An Exegetical Examination of 1 Peter 2:4–10*. NovTSup 12. Leiden: Brill, 1966.

Green, E. M. B. *2 Peter Reconsidered*. London: Tyndale Press, 1961.

Green, G. L. "The Use of the Old Testament for Christian Ethics in 1 Peter." *TynB* 41(2, 1990), pp. 276–89.

Gundry, R. H. " 'Verba Christi' in 1 Peter: Their Implications Concerning the Authorship of 1 Peter and the Authenticity of the Gospel Tradition." *NTS* 13 (1966–67), pp. 336–50.

Harland, J. B. "Sodom and Gomorrah." *Biblical Archaeologist* 5 (2, 1942), pp. 17–32; 6 (3, 1943), pp. 41–52.

Hemer, C. J. "The Address of 1 Peter." *ExpT* 89 (1977–78), pp. 239–43.

Hillyer, N. "First Peter and the Feast of Tabernacles." *TynB* 21 (1970), pp. 39–70.

_____. "Rock-Stone Imagery in 1 Peter." *TynB* 22 (1971), pp. 58–81.

Johnson, S. E. "The Preaching to the Dead (1 Peter 3.18–22)." *JBL* 79 (1960), pp. 48–51.

Leaney, A. R. C. "1 Peter and the Passover: An Interpretation." *NTS* 10 (1963–64), pp. 238–51.

Moule, C. F. D. "The Nature and Purpose of 1 Peter." *NTS* 3 (1956–57), pp. 1–11.

_____. "Some Reflections on the Stone-Testimonia in Relation to the Name Peter." *NTS* 2 (1955–56), pp. 56–59.

Nestle, E. "1 Pet. 1.2." *ExpT* 10 (1898–99), pp. 188–89.

Neyrey, J. H. "The Form and Background of the Polemic in 2 Peter." *JBL* 99, (1980), pp. 407–31.

Reicke, Bo. *The Disobedient Spirits and Christian Baptism.* Copenhagen: Munksgaard, 1946.

Selwyn, E. G. "Eschatology in 1 Peter." In *The Background of the New Testament and its Eschatology.* Edited by W. D. Davies and D. Daube. Pages 394–401. Cambridge: Cambridge University Press, 1956.

Thiede, C. P. *Simon Peter: From Galilee to Rome.* Exeter: Paternoster Press, 1986.

Thornton, T. C. G. "1 Peter, a Paschal Liturgy?" *JTS* 12 (1961), pp. 14–26.

van Unnik, W. C. "Christianity According to 1 Peter." *ExpT* 68 (1956–57), pp. 79–83.

_____. "The Critique of Paganism in 1 Peter 1:18." In *Neotestamentica et Semitica.* Edited by E. E. Ellis and M. Wilcox. Pages 129–42. Edinburgh: T. & T. Clark, 1969.

_____. "The Teaching of Good Works in 1 Peter." *NTS* 1 (1954–55), pp. 92–110.

Wuest, K. S. *First Peter in the Greek New Testament for the English Reader.* Grand Rapids: Eerdmans, 1942; reprint 1983.

_____. *In These Last Days: Studies in the Greek Text of II Peter; I, II, III John; and Jude.* Grand Rapids: Eerdmans, 1954.

Other Helpful Books

Bengel, J. A. *Gnomen of the New Testament.* 5 vols. Edinburgh: T. & T. Clark, 1858.

Bishop, E. F. F. *Apostles of Palestine: The Local Background of the New Testament Church.* London: Lutterworth Press, 1958.

Brown, C. (ed.). *The New International Dictionary of New Testament Theology.* 4 vols. Exeter: Paternoster Press/Grand Rapids: Zondervan, 1976–86.

Bruce, F. F. *Biblical Exegesis in the Qumran Texts.* London: Tyndale Press, 1960.

Cullmann, O. *The Early Church.* London: SCM Press, 1956.

Daube, D. *The Exodus Pattern in the Bible.* London: Faber & Faber, 1963.

_____. *The New Testament and Rabbinic Judaism.* New York: Arno Press, 1973.

Davies, W. D. *Paul and Rabbinic Judaism.* London: SPCK, 1955.

Deissmann, G. A. *Bible Studies.* 2d ed. Edinburgh: T. & T. Clark, 1909.

Derrett, J. D. M. *Law in the New Testament.* London: Darton, Longman and Todd, 1970.

Dodd, C. H. *According to the Scriptures.* London: Nisbet, 1952.

Dunn, J. D. G. *Jesus and the Spirit.* London: SCM Press, 1975.

Edersheim, A. *The Life and Times of Jesus the Messiah.* 2 vols. London: Longmans, Green, 1900.

_____. *Sketches of Jewish Social Life in the Time of Christ.* London: Religious Tract Society, 1876.

_____. *The Temple, its Ministry and Services.* London: Religious Tract Society, 1874.

Ellis, E. E. *Paul's Use of the Old Testament.* Edinburgh: T. & T. Clark, 1957.

Guthrie, D. *New Testament Introduction.* 4th ed. Leicester/Downers Grove: InterVarsity Press, 1990.

_____. *New Testament Theology.* Leicester/Downers Grove: InterVarsity Press, 1981.

Hemer, C. J. *The Letters to the Seven Churches of Asia in their Local Setting.* Sheffield: JSOT Press, 1986.

Horsley, G. H. R. *New Documents Illustrating Early Christianity.* 5 vols. Ryde, NSW: Macquarie University, 1981–90.

Jeremias, J. *The Central Message of the New Testament.* London: SCM Press, 1965.

Longenecker, R. N. *The Christology of Early Jewish Christianity.* London: SCM Press, 1970.

Marshall, I. H. (ed.). *New Testament Interpretation.* Exeter: Paternoster Press, 1977.

Metzger, B. M. *A Textual Commentary on the Greek New Testament.* 3d ed. New York/London: United Bible Societies, 1971.

Moore, G. F. *Judaism*, 3 vols. Cambridge, Mass.: Harvard University Press, 1927.

Morris, L. *The Apostolic Preaching of the Cross.* 3d ed. London: Tyndale Press, 1965.

Moule, C. F. D. *The Birth of the New Testament.* London: A. & C. Black, 1966.

_____. *An Idiom-Book of New Testament Greek.* Cambridge/New York: Cambridge University Press, 1953.

_____. *Worship in the New Testament.* London: Lutterworth Press, 1961.

Ramsay, W. M. *The Church in the Roman Empire before A.D. 70.* 5th ed. London: Hodder and Stoughton, 1897.

Robinson, J. A. T. *Redating the New Testament.* London: SCM Press, 1976.

Smith, G. A. *The Historical Geography of the Holy Land.* London: Hodder and Stoughton, 1931

Stibbs, A. M. *The Meaning of the Word "Blood" in Scripture.* London: InterVarsity Press, 1947.

Turner, N. *Christian Words.* Edinburgh: T. & T. Clark, 1980.

Vermes, G. *The Dead Sea Scrolls in English.* 3d ed. Sheffield: JSOT Press, 1987.

Subject Index

Scripture Index

New Testament